A FOOL'S JOURNEY

A FOOL'S JOURNEY

TO THE BEACH BOYS AND BEYOND

A MEMOIR BY
CARLI MUÑOZ

Interlink Books

An imprint of Interlink Publishing Group, Inc.
Northampton, Massachusetts

*This book is dedicated to the memory of my
loving parents, my dear friend Jack Rieley,
and to the memory of Carl and Dennis Wilson.*

First published in 2023 by

Interlink Books
An imprint of Interlink Publishing Group, Inc.
46 Crosby Street, Northampton, MA 01060
www.interlinkbooks.com

Library of Congress Cataloging-in-Publication data available
ISBN-13: 978-1-62371-751-3

Printed and bound in Korea

9 8 7 6 5 4 3 2 1

CONTENTS

PROLOGUE

There was something perplexing about being back in New York City. It was a hot, sticky Friday afternoon in July 1971, throngs of New Yorkers poured into Manhattan's Central Park. In spite of the oppressive humidity, the folks were there to party and enjoy every bit of the summer event. Here I was on stage, in front of an array of percussion instruments—from orchestral to Latin percussion—along with top brass musicians and America's quintessential vocal harmony group.

The crowd was predominantly young and true to their carefree trends carried on from the late '60s—and with my Hendrix afro and colorful hip rags, I was no exception. A blur of still-burgeoning youth, with painted faces, tie-dye shirts, and bandanas, combined with Western and military garb, populated the horizon. What had been an open green area in the park was now a kaleidoscopic bulge ready to explode, and the excitement felt contagious.

Indeed for me, being back in New York City was beyond nostalgic— rather confounding. Perhaps it was that I was now revisiting the streets I had roamed aimlessly not so long ago, when I panhandled for a daily meal. A city where, just a few years before, I was at best invisible, for being invisible I could hide my misery. I had diminished myself to an inconsequential mishap, battling loneliness, depression, hunger, and drug abuse.

Now, in contrast, the enormous and roaring crowd in the park, which extended as far as the eye could see, pandered to us—a handful of musicians. "I'm part of something big and meaningful," I thought. The stage was in the middle of the park, with clusters of skyscrapers flanking the green scenery on all sides. We were the center, the magnet that would attract every New Yorker in sight to the pulse of a single heartbeat—a free Beach Boys concert in Central Park.

Back on the West Coast, having gravitated to the right place, at the right time, I had been hired firsthand to play percussion with the Beach Boys. I had always been a keyboard player before, but playing percussion felt natural to me. It was all part of a musical intelligence that, no matter how far I had gone down the paths of misery, remained intact. Soon enough, I found myself back on the piano and organ bench. I had become part of the engine that was driving a new cultural revolution—a solid base I could evolve from, I thought, or perhaps just another chapter on my fool's journey.

The journey began during an idyllic childhood in San Juan, Puerto Rico, with a profound desire to know the essence of human nature, a relentless search for love, and an ever-increasing compassion for humanity's suffering. Even when I was only nine years old, I walked alone around my neighborhood kicking stones and reflecting on these questions. Back then, I was uncertain about my path forward. Eventually I discovered I could play music, which became a common thread that would remain with me throughout my entire journey.

When I was sixteen years old, the roller coaster began. It went from temporary bliss, with a mix consisting of my co-founding of an up-and-coming rock band, psychedelic drugs, and carefree island life, to descending in free fall into an abyss in the dark soul of the streets of New York. An epiphany in a subway station and tough decisions leading to fortuitous future events helped me get back on my feet and move forward. But it was my passion for music, a thirst for knowledge, and a relentless digging for answers that brought light to my quest. And more than being just a career, music became the center of my life—my vehicle through thick and thin.

My life had a pleasant beginning. Most everything about it was safe and fun, until I succumbed to my inquiring nature. "You are flexible," a stranger told me when I was still in my mid-teens. She was like a sorceress who could "see" there was something meaningful brewing up ahead. I never forgot it. Rather, I embodied the idea of "being flexible," a blessing or curse, and remained that way. Unexpectedly, a fool's journey means a life lived with purpose, risks, uncertainties, and a desperate search for answers: from youth's innocence and the burden of facing the void and all its treachery to the lightness of being. This is that story.

PART 1

THE FOOL.

THE FOOL

While armed with infinite potential and the courage to leave behind his current life and try something new, the Fool is vulnerable and has not yet experienced the ups and downs of life. Still unaware of the magnitude of his strength, his optimism and excitement for adventure will be his driving force.

One ordinary early summer day during the 2020 coronavirus siege, I was in the sunny kitchen of my San Juan home eating pasta and listening to "Don't Talk (Put Your Head on My Shoulder)" from the Beach Boys' classic album *Pet Sounds*. I recalled the 1970s when I had played keyboards with them, especially the excitement of playing the final concert of the Fillmore East in New York City, along with the Allman Brothers and others, or jamming out on "Leaving This Town" in stadiums packed with 100,000 screaming fans. From there it was just a short glissando to the question of which piano to play when I reopened my restaurant, Carli's, after two months of quarantine, and whether to livestream my playing from the restaurant or from my house.

The Steinway piano at Carli's is in better shape than the one at my house, I thought, but the one at home, also a Steinway, is an heirloom and in good shape for its age. The heirloom idea gave me a sense of continuity—belonging. I had another bite of pasta and looked around the room. Then, the heirloom idea took my mind way back before the Beach Boys—to when I was a boy and there was another Steinway piano that would have been the most significant of all—had I not rushed into the unknown on a fool's journey...had I not walked away from all the golden goods of a privileged youth and into the risk and loss of life's roller coaster. "Fools rush in where angels fear to tread," wrote the poet Alexander Pope. I rushed in.

I didn't burn any bridges, but leaving home right after graduating from high school was serious and definite. When I left, I didn't look back. I then hastily renounced not only my new concert grand piano but also a life of comfort and security. Specifically, I left behind my super-cool parents, a comfortable home with delicious and wholesome meals 24/7, the promise of a top education and lucrative career, social status, a fiancée, and lifelong friends—not to mention, an Austin-Healey 3000 Mk III, along with other fortunate boys' toys.

A year or so before I rushed into a fool's journey, my father, based on the notion that his son might have some talent for music, surprised me on one quiet afternoon with a gorgeous ebony Steinway D piano. The D model was the mother of all keyboards—a nine-foot concert grand piano—and here it was being offloaded from a large moving truck parked at the side of our house, destined for our living room. "Hey, kiddo, lucky you," shot Bruni, my one and only older sister, with a half-cocky sneer.

My excitement was hard to contain—I stayed focused on watching the spectacle, not saying a word. Having that piano in my living room was almost too good to be true. Once inside, we all gathered around the piano, and the focus turned on me. My father, especially, was eager to hear the first notes emerge from that behemoth, which now occupied a third of our living room.

At first I explored sounds, along with visual and other sensorial delights. The Steinway's massive presence and smooth curves were like the hourglass figure of an Odyssean siren. The scent of oils on the assortment of woods—even the sounds—evoked fragrances ranging from a perfectly tuned, pristine plink reminiscent of lemon and zesty mandarin orange to a thunderous, honey-sweet nectar and musk tone. It was all insanely exciting!

From then on, the piano became a source of inspiration. There wasn't a day I didn't get up super early (that being a stretch for me) and glide down the stairs to the living room just to play that magnificent and perfect instrument. Quickly, the neighborhood also became aware of the piano.

My dad, being an architect, had designed our house. It was a two-story structure built on a lot that forked to two streets. The piano sat majestically in the living room downstairs, where a set of French doors opened wide to an open area. Beyond the manicured half-moon hibiscus hedge surrounding the front terrace, the panorama expanded to the ample street where the fork was pointing. The scenery evoked the perfect neighborhood concert—at the crack of dawn every morning, and sometimes even into the night.

Pushing back further to my first years, our temporary home before moving to Ocean Park was tiny. It was in one of the first urban housing developments in San Juan and was called Urbanización Roosevelt. The house was in front of a baseball park, which gave the area its center. Other buildings around the park were a church, a grade school, a movie theater where I saw my first movie, and the College of Engineers and Surveyors. It was in that little house where the muses threw their first music sparks at me.

My nine-years-older sister, Bruni, was taking piano lessons, and there was a spinet piano in the living room of the house where she practiced. In addition to a nanny, my sister often looked after me, which I always enjoyed because she was invited to a lot of parties, and sometimes even as a toddler, I had to go along. She was lively and pretty; older guys in the neighborhood used to circle around the house like vultures just to get a small glance at my sister if she was out on the porch or the patio watering the plants.

There my mom taught me my first song. It was a Hispanic lullaby, "Muñequita Linda" ("Pretty Little Doll"). The melody was easy to play because the verse was simple and played only on the black keys. My sister also showed me a few simple riffs on the piano, among them a boogie-woogie bass line, "Chopsticks," and the typical accompaniment to "Blue Moon." Later, when I would hear her practicing the same song from sheet music, year after year, I realized that my sister wasn't gifted musically.

I remember the kid next door, Ian, wanting to put a cigarette out on my face. Maybe it happened or not—I recall the threat, the pain, and the anguish—but there are no visible scars. Another event I remember is trying to impress a girl, Maritza Betancourt, who lived at the corner of my block about five or six houses down from where we lived. I couldn't have been older than four, but I can remember Maritza's big black eyes, chubby cheeks, and braided dark hair. Her dad was a doctor, and their home was modern and beautiful. One time she was on her tricycle on the sidewalk playing in the front of her house. My big move was to impress her by running past her, so she could see how fast I could run, and come back. But as I was going past her, from the excitement, a sudden loud string of wet flatus unexpectedly blared out of my butt. I was so embarrassed that I just kept on running and never saw her again.

Visiting our new house that was being built in Ocean Park with my dad was fun and refreshing. I enjoyed walking in between the wood frames and finding interesting pieces of discarded wood and making my own contraptions. I was also fascinated by the tadpoles inside the sewage holding tank on the ground. While playing around the construction, I ran a massive nail through my foot. Another time I fell on my face, getting the proverbial jaw scar all kids get.

I must have been five when we finally moved to Ocean Park, and it was instant happiness being there. The air was different—the sky always seemed blue, and the sea air, the trees, and the space around became my own.

I soon met my first friend, Raul, who lived across from my house. Makes me think about life as a set of wheels, perhaps like a transmission pairing gears, meeting the right people at the right time—then you shift gears. Raul and I must have been around five when we met on the street where we lived. It seemed to me that Raul was the only kid who existed in the world, my world. Raul and I terrorized the neighborhood. We regularly threw rocks and eggs, and lit firecrackers on a heart patient's window and also at the cash register line of the local supermarket, causing panic—we must have been neighborhood trouble lasting throughout the frightening sevens. Still, we remained buddies until the beginning of high school, when we naturally transitioned to other groups of friends.

Carli with neighbor friend Raul

But I remember a stretch of time when I preferred being alone. I was feeling awkward and different from everyone else and becoming aware and self-conscious of my appearance. I'd taken notice of my big shiny nose, and now it was becoming an issue. Pimples were also part of my demise, and getting an occasional volcano on the side of, or worse, at the tip of my already beaming nose was enough reason for total seclusion. Add curly hair when everyone around seemed to have hair like the 1960s actor Troy Donahue, plus being "too" tall and skinny, and fuck me thrice! Making matters worse, my sister kept telling me to tuck down my upper lip because she thought that it would thin out my nose. She also thought my lips were too thick. Thankfully, I didn't give a rat's ass about the lip thing—too fake, I thought. But my sister got stuck into doing it herself for a lifetime—even at her old age my sister still walked around sucking her upper lip—an ugly habit she would never overcome.

My sister and I got along well when we were kids. I'd sometimes bug her by scaring her, suddenly appearing where I wasn't supposed to be and silly stuff like that, all in a playful spirit. I also remember twisting her nipples (of course, over the bra and the clothing), saying that I was changing the (TV) channel. I think the worst was giving her a victorious sneer if I got something that she wanted—that'd piss her off to no end! She would get back at me, telling me that I was found in a trash can and never belonged in the family. First, I would cry; then, I'd go ahead and prepare a bindle on a broomstick to run off like a tramp. Those were probably my first thoughts of being on a fool's journey. But we also did some cool things together. We used to dance a lot—she showed me the Jitterbug, the Bop, the Bunny Hop, and other fun dances of the times. After she got married, everything changed. Somehow a gap formed that could never be bridged. But still, we got along fine...or so it seemed to me.

Ocean Park was an ideal place to grow up. In the '50s and '60s, it was a tranquil, upper-middle-class coastal residential area in San Juan, resting between the busy touristy areas of Condado and Isla Verde, covering one-half square kilometer. The neighborhood, like most, didn't lack its eccentric characters. There was a man, Don Joejoe, who lived on the opposite side of my block; he tried committing suicide twice and failed. The first time, he shot himself in the chest and survived. Then, he jumped out of a second-story terrace and landed on a boat he had in his driveway. The story goes, he did all of this to get away from his wife and then another stalker woman. Perhaps it is no small wonder that his dogs were always in a humping frenzy when I'd walk by his house. On the other extreme corner lived Olga Iglesias, a world-renowned soprano opera singer whose daily serenade expanded the neighborhood's melodiousness with her vocal exercises.

In those days past the frightful sevens, when not in school, I'd spend most of the day outdoors playing with friends or kicking stones, exploring, or daydreaming and absorbing the area. On my daily walk to school, I had to cross a park, which extended to the beach. A two-lane road and a parking lot with a small cafeteria in the middle divided the park from the beach area. The coast was always there, a stone's throw away from almost anywhere in my neighborhood. The climate was perfect all year round. While the temperature would remain at a pleasant average in the eighties, the seasonal storms and rains were part of the area's subtle and dynamic beauty. Often, you'd feel a gentle sprinkle from a passing cotton cloud with the sun shining, and as the rain hit the ground, it would produce an alluring ozone smell evoking sweet memories. Even the rainwater streaming down the concrete gutter with an assortment of leaves and twigs floating away was exciting to watch.

Somewhere between mid-April and late November, during the most precipitation, the light would transform from moment to moment with a variety of passing clouds, producing rainbows with their elusive beginnings or endings, always evoking a chimerical treasure hunt. Particular sounds, like raindrops, were a part of this magical experience. There was a curious variety of sounds that became part of our sensory landscape. I figured that since the rain ever started falling on the forest canopy, tree branches, water bodies, and the variety of soils that have existed for so many millions of years, there must be a primal memory attached to those certain rain-sound sensations. The sounds of birds, the ocean, and the wind must play a similar role.

Other sounds remain that are also part of that nostalgia we so much crave. Although quotidian, one of those sounds is that of a small airplane. From where I lived, there was a small airport about seven kilometers to the west and a more significant one five kilometers to the east—they are still there, and to this day, the sound of a small airplane going by is also a pleasant reminder of my youth.

Only a faint but precious sensation remains from the memory of the brief window between twilight and dusk. It was a non-time—it is the closest I can remember of just being in a no-time zone. The less I did during that time, the more I enjoyed it. Sometimes, just being alone, absorbing the moment on the porch or the terrace upstairs, perhaps even sharing quality time with my parents or a friend, was exhilarating. I remember during those quiet times when alone having moments of romantic fantasies, which later translated to the way I perceived music.

In Ocean Park, my parents' house was in an area called Park Boulevard. It is the only section in that area with a boulevard between the more spacious homes and the beach, hence Park Boulevard. Past one block and farther inland, the houses were still spacious, each having their own character but less assuming. Trees lined the sidewalks, and a trail of bushes ran through the backyards of houses, where we often would pretend to be explorers.

I remember big rubber trees on the side of our home and the bats they attracted. The bats might have been feasting on the giant flying cockroaches that also lived in those trees. In those days before air conditioners and being in the tropics, the homes were open most of the time. I remember my mom and my sister frantically chasing an occasional flying cockroach that snuck inside the house. The nasty critters were relentless—like kamikazes, their tendency was to fly straight to your face. I have often wondered where they frequent these days, but good riddance!

There were also a few alleys that would connect long blocks of houses to the street behind. Those alleys were fun and useful to us kids; it was a quicker way of getting around in the neighborhood. They were also a sure way to outrun the police (nothing that would require more than a slap on the wrist, if caught) on foot, skates, or a bicycle—and later on a motorcycle.

For me, the simple things we did were the most memorable. Sometimes later in the evenings, I remember sitting on the sidewalk curve with my friends. There we waited for the milk delivery truck to show up at 4 A.M. It would be easier remembering my last psychopomp than what our silly dialogue must have been like, but the time spent was fun. The smell of sweat and wet socks under rubber shoes from a long, humid evening is still pulsing in my hippocampus. But the chocolate milk, which we'd irreverently and concertedly gulp by the quart to the last drop, was worth the wait—sweat smell and all!

Upstairs on the second floor of our house, Bruni and I had adjoining rooms separated only by rubber accordion-like curtains, which were the new thing for dividing living areas, like those still in use in convention halls today. My parents' bedroom was the larger room, then my sister was in the middle, and my bedroom on the north side was the smaller room and didn't have a private bathroom. If I well recall, I think on the second floor, there was only one comfortable bathroom for all of us to share, and it was near my sister's bedroom, past a large closet. Then, there was the open terrace in the front, which had a panoramic view of the southwest and northwest sides of the island, facing Condado and Old San Juan. We weren't on a hill, but there weren't any tall buildings then to block our view—the closest tall buildings were at King's Court, a little over a mile ahead. From the terrace on the right, you could also see part of the long coast dissipating into Condado and Old San Juan.

Bruni often had pajama parties, and they were always exciting. All of my sister's friends were beautiful, and some voluptuous. Best of all, when I might have been nine or ten, they were eighteen or nineteen, same as my sister's age. Being the cute little guy around gave me a license to hang around the girls while they did their girly things. I can't forget one night when I had just tucked myself into bed; one of my sister's friends came into my room in her nightgown to kiss me night-night. Her name was Sylma, and she was the top-heavy, voluptuous one of the bunch. When she bent over to kiss my forehead, there they were. It was a sure boner, one of the first ones that I could remember. But that aside, most of the time was clean fun just being around them. It is fair enough to consider that a preadolescent's closest thing to pornography would have been the lingerie section of the Sears catalog—that was hot for me!

Sex with girls in early puberty wasn't even a remote possibility. The local adults guarded their girls better than the Holy Grail, and some boys sometimes opted for less than accepted alternatives. It was usual for young boys to want to explore in the woods, hang out in the bushes, or climb to the rooftop to play or pretend to have an adventure. It was also a place to hang out and feel you were in your own space. And doing that with a friend made it more special. It was in one of those places where I smoked my first cigarette, exchanged baseball cards, and experienced other rites of passage.

One time while chilling on a rooftop, a kid who was a neighbor, whom I had never hung out with before, asked to see my genitals. "Let me see yours—I'll show you mine," he said. My what—your what? At first it was confusing, but soon I got the gist. I had two options, I thought: to show my dick or to be one. The episode lasted three to four seconds. In the urban Catholic milieu we were in, you might call it pure adolescent curiosity, innocence, or homosexual tendencies, but all I see in it is just labels for something not yet understood, or that even mattered then.

This could shock and be too weird for some. But on two occasions that I remember, word ran out in the neighborhood that some kids we knew had friends over for sex. Both times it occurred in the middle of the day at their parents' house. To make the event weirder, on both occasions, the participants were two brothers, a few years apart—oh brother! In neither case were either effeminate or the awkward type. And the curiosity among all who were there was compelling. My friend and I visited the unusual event and found that many of our neighborhood friends were there. Some were spectators and some were participants.

The scene was surreal. One of the two brothers would lie down on the floor, while the participant kids would line up to take turns getting on top, "analyzing" the guy on the floor. The other brother would then take a turn, also on the receiving end, and the perma-humpers would line up again for another piece of the action. I can't imagine a weirder scene than that among my school buddies!

These were the same kids I'd see the next day in school or in the neighborhood. The kids I'd be playing with the day before or the day after—as if nothing had happened. But admittedly, it was exciting to watch—it was sex, after all—the closest that us kids could be to any kind of sexual activity outside of masturbating to some impossible fantasy during our sorry puberty.

In hindsight (no pun intended), was that an isolated freak thing that just happened to kids in our neighborhood? And only then? I've heard no one talk about anything like this or even read about it anywhere. Perhaps you may hear of something similar in the news, happening among the Catholic Church's clergy (OK, maybe not like this). Still, it would be unlikely that this would have been an isolated event. It could be rather embarrassing for most people to admit it. I suspect that this kind of activity has always happened. And most everywhere, in times, places, and societies where guarding females' virtue is top priority. It beats sheep, I'd imagine...

As cliché as it may sound, there was a time when, in the evening, we'd build bonfires on the sand and gather around roasting hot dogs and marshmallows, telling stories, playing guitar, and singing—a normal thing to do in a beach community. Our way of life wasn't any different from Malibu Beach or anywhere along the coast in Los Angeles, California.

This reminds me of an impertinent question I get from American visitors at my restaurant: "How is it that as a Puerto Rican you got to play with the Beach Boys?" I say to them that Puerto Rico has bonfires, surfers, surfer bunnies, hot rods, Woodies, Corvettes, beach parties, and anything that Los Angeles has along its coast—not to mention great musicians—only with better weather.

For some reason, the wall piano we had in the house in Roosevelt didn't make it to our new home in Ocean Park. From when I was four until eleven, 1952 to 1959, I was just a kid going about a kid's life. My dad and I sometimes went fishing on the bridge that joined Cangrejos Yacht Club with Piñones, a pristine reserve with mangrove canals and deserted beaches, stretching from the eastern tip of Isla Verde to the town of Loíza. He kept a small wooden cabin cruiser at the club, where he'd play dominos and drink Cuba Libres with his friends when we weren't on the water. The smell of the salty air at the marina combined with the smell of fish and gasoline from the boats still reminds me of timeless mornings and afternoons spent roaming about the docks at the old yacht club!

Often, while alone in my room, reading comic books and wishful shopping in the Sears catalog kept me busy. Water obsessed me. On many a lazy afternoon while in bed with a fever or just daydreaming, I would imagine the ceiling over me and beyond, flooded with water. It was my upside down water world, and my mind would roam around the different pools divided by the room partitions in the ceiling. Back on the ground, my bed would become a raft with the mosquito net acting as sails tied to the pillars. Even our house, with a design that resembled a boat's shape, would float around the neighborhood. A recurring fantasy while floating around the area was rescuing the girl in my dreams.

It was in the water during a bath where I had my first sexual experience. Yet I don't think I even knew it! It was the first time I had an ejaculation. I was in the bathtub taking my time, daydreaming as usual. Mostly, I remember suddenly noticing a whitish viscous liquid coming from my penis and not quite blending with the water. I got scared, for I didn't know what it was—I thought I had gotten sick or something like that and wanted to reach out to my mother—but didn't dare to. I'm not sure what happened after, but that was the beginning, I suppose, of my puberty.

It had been nearly a decade since my mother and my sister gave me my first piano experience, when I was a baby. When I turned ten, my dad bought me a portable electric organ, and my interest in music sparked again. The organ had an electromechanical bellow that would blow air into a set of reeds on the keyboard, producing the sounds. It was the same principle as an accordion but was instead a wooden console with legs and used electricity. It came with a booklet of western folk classics with songs like "Oh Susannah," "Oh My Darling, Clementine," and "Home on the Range." I quickly learned them all by ear and would play them when family and friends gathered at our home.

The musical experiences that followed were sporadic, like venturing on a piano during a visit to a relative or friend's house. One of my uncles had a white baby grand piano at his home, and one time I surprised everyone by playing it. I can't remember what I played, but it must have been coherent. At another time, while having dinner with my parents at a nearby restaurant in Isla Verde, Cecilia's Place, I bravely stood up from the table and walked right to a piano sitting in the middle of the room and played a song. I must have been around thirteen because the piece I played was "Al Di Là," which was first released in March 1961. It became famous again in 1962 with the movie *Rome Adventure*.

Other instruments caught my attention, but patience was never my virtue, at least with music. I remember when my dad allowed me to rent a tenor sax to learn to play it. I couldn't get a tone out of the reed on the first attempt, so I threw the sax on the couch and never picked one up again in frustration. The same happened with a violin and a trumpet. I just couldn't get a decent sound.

I wanted to play the drums, but fate (my father) had other plans. On my birthday in October that same year, 1961, my father gave me a spinet piano as a present. I suppose that the "Al Di Là" deal yielded windfall gains. But there must be some truth in the old cliché, "Youth is wasted on the young." It wasn't what I'd expected for my thirteenth birthday, and it took several months before I started paying attention to having a piano. Once I did, all became very clear to me. The keyboard became my drawing board and lab, and demystifying music became my passion. Everything flowed from then on.

A memory I treasure is getting my first double strap leather school bag—the smell of the leather was indelible. I mostly remember the tropical morning's chilly air. It gave the morning a certain sprightliness that, along with the solitude on the street, made the world anew. On the way to school, while crossing the park, I often had to outrun some of the bully kids from the public school nearby. It became a routine.

Once in the classroom, I would continue my sleep, and if I couldn't get away with sleeping, I'd spend the morning daydreaming about girls and motorcycles.

The school had open windows, and the constant and gentle ocean breeze flowing into the quiet classroom was perfect for my indulgences. Sometimes I'd put my head down sideways over the top of my school desk, pretending to be sleeping, but really listening to catch any minute sound I'd make on the wood or the metal with the tips of my fingers. The sounding board was a thin metal plate in the bottom front where I would tap, experimenting with different rhythms. No one could hear them except me.

In the early years of high school, the short walk from home across the park became more fun with my new classroom friend, Vinnie. There was a down-to-earth quality about Vinnie that was pleasant; I can only describe Vinnie as classy, humble, observant, and witty. One thing for certain is that Vinnie and I clicked right away. Somehow, we both soon discovered each other's interest and ability for music, which created a special bond. Also, we lived within walking distance, and our parents knew each other.

Vinnie's family had a chauffeur, Mariano, who would sometimes take us out for burgers and sodas and "manly" advice. We also got into occasional trouble, like wrecking rented motorcycles and other stupid things kids do. One time, we ventured into a brothel, and Vinnie came back home with gonorrhea, which got him into big trouble with his parents. I had better luck!

On our way to school, we'd often detour in the opposite direction to a nearby barroom called El Coquí, in Punta Las Marias, walking distance from both our homes. We would go in the morning while the bar was closed for cleaning. I'll never forget the smell of stale beer and smoke lingering from the night before. The person in charge of cleaning would always let us into the empty club to play a Hammond B3 organ they had on a small stage. If we knew where to find an instrument, we'd skip school as often as possible. We would also play hooky for pinball or a swim in the ocean, but playing the Hammond organ was the ultimate thrill for us.

Vinnie had older siblings who played piano, so there was always a lovely grand piano in the living room at his home. There were even two grand pianos in their living room for a time, waiting for a long-overdue pickup from the music store—so convenient for us! We were both into the music, and it flowed. Neither one of us was interested in taking music lessons; perhaps we were being foolish, but we just wanted to play. Later on, we'd form our first music combo. I find it fascinating how kids are drawn together like magnets when they have common interests—Vinnie and I had enough in common to forge a lifetime friendship.

My first band ever was a loosely formed garage combo that Vinnie and I formed, Los Colegiales ("the collegians," even though we were just beginning high school). The band was integrated with some of my closest friends from school and the neighborhood. I was the catalyst—the almost dictator-like one to tell my friends what to play and how to do it. Besides me, only Vinnie, who played guitar, bass, and piano, had a natural knack for music. Vinnie's cousin, Toñi, who was studying accordion and was also a neighbor, joined in. The drummer I picked as if assigning duties: "Okay, Jorge, you are going to be the drummer, so tell your parents to buy you a set of drums." Then I taught Jorge how to play the drums, which I had never really played before—at least in this lifetime.

We sounded terrific. We opted to play popular local dance music, which was in demand, and before we knew it we were making a decent amount of money playing at social clubs and fraternities. We kept on adding musicians and singers. The band sprinted to a different level with alto sax and trumpet; both players were older and professional musicians. When we brought in singers, we also started doing torch songs from the American songbook.

It was around the year 1962, and rock 'n' roll was becoming more popular. From Los Colegiales, we made a reduction, forming a rock trio where I played bass on an electric guitar that was missing two strings and sang lead. Jorge remained on drums, and Vinnie was on lead guitar and also lead vocals. We played popular recent hits like "Twist and Shout," "What'd I Say," "The Twist," "Rock Around the Clock," and "La Bamba."

I remember being surprised when being interviewed before our first gig. Someone had suggested we wear the same cheesy red vinyl short-sleeve shirts, which we did, and when the promoter asked the name of the band, we realized that we didn't have one—we hadn't even thought about it! So I looked down at my shirt and the other guys and said, "We are the Red Fever."

We were short-lived.

The only significant date we did was in mid-1962 when we played at a girls' orphanage. The bandstand was in the middle of an open courtyard, surrounded by the building, which had balconies on the second floor. The structure itself was rustic and old (nowadays it is the main building housing the San Juan's Conservatory of Music). The girls went so wild that they were hanging from the balcony and windows, two stories high, some of them cheering while lifting their skirts for us. Very impressive!

The nuns in high school were brutal, I thought, but they'd let me sleep during class. I can't remember having a more lethargic experience than in religion class. Having to memorize the names of all the angels, the archangels, and their distant cousins was merciless! They were strict and often somber American IHM (Servants of the Immaculate Heart of Mary) nuns and wore white habits. They meant well, maybe. My grades were so low that my dad offered to give me ten dollars if I'd get a D!

The only class I remember doing anything for me was English class. The grammar taught in our high school was decent—for me, it was one of the more useful subjects and worth keeping. That all the classes were in English, except for Spanish, was gainful. I can't blame the nuns for my lack of interest. But I perceived no effort on anyone's part in going a little deeper and seeing me outside the cookie cutter. My dad believed I was more; he thought that maybe I was just in the wrong environment. I credit my father for having the guts to push forward and act on it.

Going into my sophomore year, the school summoned my parents for a meeting. The nuns told my dad I was stupid, that I couldn't learn. My father got concerned and took me to a prominent psychologist for a professional evaluation. I still remember taking the proverbial IQ test. I danced around it. And the score was "considerably high"—the doctor explained. The psychologists' recommendation was to transfer me to a secular school, which my dad did without hesitation. The new school was further away from my neighborhood, which turned out to be a good thing, for that meant I "needed" a vehicle.

At first, I was taking a bus, or my dad or my sister would take me. There was a car lot across from the school that specialized in British sports classics. One day on my way home after school, I stopped by for a closer look. A brown hardtop Jaguar XK-E and a light blue Austin-Healey 3000 MK III convertible caught my stripling attention. There I was, standing next to the very fabric of my dreams—in full color and something I could smell and touch! When I got home that afternoon, I told my dad about the cars with great excitement. I could usually tell when my dad was listening, and better yet, when he shared my excitement. I now believe that we connected that way. Whenever I'd share something exciting with my dad, he would also get to live that excitement. The next day, a man was delivering the Austin-Healey to my house. My dad could have said, "There it is—you better bring home some good grades now." But he didn't. I did, anyway. All A's and B's!

Getting A's and B's at the new school was effortless. English was a piece of cake, and I became interested in school and did well in biology, chemistry, and algebra. Best of all, the biggest music store in town, Casa Margarida, was right next door! I'd park my Healey with the top down on the sidewalk at the school's front and gravitate to the music store. What a pompous kook I must have appeared to be for some! But I was just operating out of pure adrenaline and wildly active dopamine receptors. I don't remember being pretentious or conceited even for a moment. I didn't have time for that. I may have been subconsciously, but as far as I can remember I was just too busy being a carefree kid enjoying the moment.

There was a piano in the front display at the music store next to the school, and I spent long hours playing. My new self-confidence flung me to the top echelon academically, allowing me equal time between school and the music store. I had been basing my self-esteem on other people's limitations and inadequacies—the nuns'. The IQ test changed me—changed my life. It changed how I felt about myself and how people would perceive me from that point on.

In my daydreaming, and in my night dreams, my fantasy world remained full of adventure. I was also inquisitive. The other part of my inquisitive nature was a curious world of what-ifs. It was the what-if part that got me in the most trouble, and also the part that brought the greater rewards later in my life. Also, a "why" component raised many questions about my existence and social disparity early in my youth. If I find myself bogged down in the present time pondering social injustices, it is who I am and have always been. As far as I can remember, I've never stopped being observant and concerning myself with racial, poverty-related, and other social issues. Perhaps I could see this because the neighborhood where I grew up was near an area of poverty and disenfranchised people living in public housing. Being almost side by side, it wasn't hard to see both worlds. There was plenty of racism and justifications for "us" having the lion's share, as it is still today. All of this was a well-ingrained component of our parents' generation, but perhaps I was able to break through those barriers and reject them from an early age because of my querying nature.

An innate existentialist nature, which kept expanding as I matured, drove me. Daydreaming contributed to the mix and led to romantic and playful notions, merging into a music world. At first, it was just listening to music—toggling between romantic, intellectual, classical, and avant-garde. The romantic side was idealistic. Romantic fantasies gave meaning to music and vice versa: A song like Paul Anka's "Put Your Head on My Shoulder," paired with new teen romance, would be sure to turn one into an ephemeron! Old rock 'n' roll and boogie-woogie were insanely exciting, and jazz and classical stimulated my intellect.

It was avant-garde music, such as the music of French composer Edgard Varèse, that swept me deep into myself and made me even more inquisitive and introspective. This music created a deep, multidimensional space of daydreaming where I could get lost in reverie. Later, Yusef Lateef, whose music was also avant-garde but more tied to jazz, influenced me.

There was another genre of music known as semi-classical. It was mainly piano, orchestra, and vocal, which also influenced me. Semi-classical music sometimes bordered with jazz, with artists such as pianists Peter Nero and Andre Previn and singers like Johnny Mathis, Mel Tormé, and Frank Sinatra. I suppose that part of what attracted me to the crooners was the lush orchestra arrangements. Arrangers like Nelson Riddle, Johnny Mandel, and Henry Mancini were sure to grace the airwaves. Themes from movies and TV shows were also part of that genre. Semi-classical music caught my attention, despite being so common and ubiquitous (even in elevators and offices—also known as Muzak). Still, it was beautiful; it is the reason I know so many songs from the American songbook.

I was also an avid comic book reader. On the back pages of most comic books I had was a full-page ad by Columbia Record Club, a Columbia Records subsidiary. They filled the page with little colorful squares showing the cover art of some of their hottest LPs, like thumbnails, as we would later call them. I remember Columbia Record Club offering something like eight or more free albums if you joined the club with a future promise to purchase more at full price. So, I did, but I was just a kid and didn't know I had to pay for them, which later got me in trouble.

Not being familiar with any of the artists, I chose mostly albums with large grand pianos on their covers—they were just so impressive—and started receiving records from the club. The first one was Peter Nero, a classical and virtuoso jazz pianist—he was my real primary influence as a pianist. His sound was precise and deliberate. André Previn, Henry Mancini, Tony Bennett, and Barbra Streisand were also part of the package. Every one of them influenced my playing and sensibilities. Songs like "People," "The Second Time Around," "Two Coins in a Fountain," and "If I Ruled the World" captivated me. Later, as I matured, my choices of artists and repertoire expanded in depth and scope.

It wasn't until my dad gave me some long-playing vinyl records (LPs) he had brought from a business trip to New York that my influences shifted significantly. One of them was Roaring Twenties and honky-tonk music, another was an all-polka album, and the third one was Art Blakey and the Jazz Messengers plus Sabú. The honky-tonk I appreciated, the polka one I tossed away, but Art Blakey and the Jazz Messengers plus Sabú became a significant influence—it turned around my view of music, especially on jazz. Of all things, it was Art Blakey's album that triggered a series of events that would define my music career forever, especially the Sabú part.

THE MAGICIAN.

THE MAGICIAN

 The Magician represents your innate power to create the inner world, in which your outer world will follow. These skills set you apart from the crowd and can help you begin new projects overcoming adversity. You will fulfill your desire to do anything you set your mind to.

Mornings at home were rarely dull, the norm being a good and fresh vibe. When my dad was still at home before leaving for his office, spirits were high. Then, alone with my mom, it was just a peaceful but an enabling kind of calm. Sometimes in the kitchen at breakfast, my mom and dad would have brief bouts of verbal sparring and jabbing. It was more like entertainment to me, and sometimes outright funny. The kitchen itself was very comfortable. By the time I was in my early teens, my dad had remodeled it with all the latest modern cabinetry and equipment. My mom surely had a hand in the plan and appeared to be happy with the outcome. The kitchen became the center of our home.

As I walked into the kitchen one ordinary morning, my mom made breakfast and my dad was reading the newspaper on the kitchenette table. Out of the corner of my eye I noticed the name Sabú Martinez, printed on a square of one of the paper's pages. It caught my attention, and as I inspected closer I noticed that it was an advertisement for the Holiday Inn in the nearby town of Isla Verde. The ad highlighted the names of performers featured at the Holiday Inn lobby cabaret. During the late '50s and the early '60s, all the major hotels in San Juan had big shows, orchestras, dancers, and big-name stars booked from the mainland, and the Holiday Inn was no exception. I had become impressed with that name from that first hardcore jazz LP ever in my possession,

Art Blakey and the Jazz Messengers plus Sabú, which my dad had given me. So there it was, "the legendary percussionist Sabú Martinez," live in my town. I couldn't miss that for anything!

I asked my dad to let me use the car for that evening (there weren't too many cars on the island at the time, and my dad used to let me drive from age fourteen without a license). Then I asked my dad for a little spending money and put on a suit (my father had insisted that I have at least seven suits to wear—each one a different color for each day of the week). I shaved the three stumps off my face and I was on my way to a new, exciting adventure—one that would forever influence my music playing.

Being taller than most kids my age, I appeared older than I was. The attendants and security would greet me as an adult as I walked into a nightclub, cabaret, or even a casino. I also always dressed nicely for the occasion, wearing a suit and tie, a relaxed attitude, and a cigarette hanging from my mouth. The cabaret at the Holiday Inn was one of the hottest clubs around. (I wish I could remember the name.) It had the right size for a relatively small hotel and had a full stage, proper lighting, professional sound, and a dance floor in the middle of the room at the front of the stage. Their nightly show began with the Monchito Muñoz quartet, featuring my new idol, Sabú Martinez, a bigger-than-life, well-built dark figure with sharp facial features, front and center, majestically standing with his three conga drums, each on an individual stand. After the band played a few hot jazz tunes, the featured singer, Myrna Pagán, an accomplished jazz singer and a real diva, appeared on stage. She always wore an elegant, long sequined dress with the spotlight following her every move. Pagán sang challenging jazz pieces, such as "In the Heat of the Night," "Love for Sale," and other songs from the standard jazz repertoire. At the set's closing, a troupe of about six dancers picked from New York City's famous Peppermint Lounge arrived to deliver a big bang ending.

The show at the Holiday Inn was more hardcore music-wise, as opposed to the more Las Vegas-type revues you'd find at other, more prominent hotels. At some of them, the orchestra was inconsequential, with more of a focus on the entertainer. But this was, at least to me, the real deal, a real jazz club. The aura inside the club was posh and exciting. I can't remember a time when the dance floor wasn't packed. In every sense, it was a typical nightclub cabaret with small two- and four-top tables and a string of booths along the sides, as I vaguely recall. The stage was large enough to accommodate a grand piano and the quartet, plus Sabú with his three congas standing in the front. The featured singer took center stage in front of the band on the dance floor, as the half dozen dancers did when they came out. It was a time of crossroads between jazz and rock, and the conga drums added the flair of Latin jazz, but the band was faithful to the straight-ahead jazz tradition. The musicians at the time were the best and most seasoned on the island. Among them was Juancito Torres on trumpet and Freddie Thomas on contrabass, both highly experienced jazz players. There was a pianist in a wheelchair, Dale Wales, who doubled on trumpet.

Monchito, the quartet drummer and the leader, was the son of a legendary orchestra leader and arranger, Rafael Muñoz. Being around his father at an early age during the New York 1940s Big Band era gave him the grit to move up the ranks and eventually join some notable names in big Latin orchestras, including Tito Puente. Initially, he played minor percussion, and later in his career he moved to the trap set, where he excelled. Monchito was a brilliant musician and also well connected in the international music scene. Other world-renowned musicians, such as Joe Morello, the drummer from the Dave Brubeck Quartet, would frequent the club to listen and jam with Monchito's quartet; I remember blazing jams after the show lasting past sunrise.

There we were at the mecca of jazz with all its possibilities, and anything could happen. Once I was there and tasted the real deal live in front of me, I continued going to the club nightly. I have to assume that it was during the summer or winter after school season; otherwise, my parents wouldn't have allowed me to hang out late every night, all the while going to school the next morning. Eventually, I knew every note played in the show and was hoping for a break, any break, to jump on the stage and save the day by replacing a no-show musician—that was my fantasy.

One night, as I was sitting coolly by myself at a table having a cocktail and a cigarette and eagerly waiting for the show to begin, I noticed a bit of commotion on the stage. I noticed that the bass player wasn't around, and Monchito, the leader, seemed worried and was making gestures of concern to one of the other musicians. Without giving it too much thought, but smoothly enough trying to hide my cocky excitement, I crossed the dance floor and headed toward the stage. Once there, I reached out to the leader, Monchito, and said, "Hey, if the bass player doesn't show up, I can do it—I can cover." Oh boy, I think they had been around enough to realize how young I was. I continued, "At least you'll have someone up there, and you can do the show—I've been here every night, so I'm familiar with it," I boldly declared.

I was going through the motions; I had never even touched a contrabass before—ever! But I couldn't resist the opportunity. After some hesitation, Monchito gave in.

I'd give anything to bottle what I felt at that moment! I'm just glad that it wasn't the trumpet player who didn't show up that evening—that scenario would have been impossible, if not profoundly embarrassing.

But there I was, and I played through the entire show without missing a beat—I might have missed some notes, but not the rhythm. First, the band played some jazz instrumentals featuring Sabú, then we backed the singer's performance, and finally, we played for the dancers. Fortunately, we didn't amplify the contrabass in those days, which allowed me to fake the most challenging parts. As long as I had the rhythm, missing a few notes didn't make a huge difference.

After the set, the band members thanked me for covering for Freddy Thomas, their missing bass player. I let them know that I wasn't a bassist but that I played some piano. Dale, their pianist, who was also doubling on trumpet, had some health issues and needed to break from the keyboard. I recall one of the other musicians wanting to hear me play some piano, and I immediately obliged. I don't remember the details of what happened, but the club owner, Tony Martin, who was also a pianist, seemed interested. He came to me and showed me how to comp (jazz jargon for accompanying) with my left hand on an open spread. It was the advice that made all the difference in my left-hand comping. That opened up the entire world for me. What followed was that the leader, Monchito, asked me if I wanted to stay and play piano in the band permanently. They hired me. It is almost unreal to think I had become the pianist of the hottest performing jazz quintet in San Juan!

Amazing days followed. The experience of playing nightly with the band was beyond exciting. Also, we would occasionally get together during the day at the club to rehearse new material. Tragedy also followed. At some point, Monchito hired a second percussion player, named Monsantito, and he had a Japanese girlfriend. One afternoon while we were rehearsing at the club, his girlfriend came in and yelled, "Monsantito!" Right there, on the dance floor in front of all of us, she committed hara-kiri: She stuck a large kitchen knife into her stomach. We were all in shock. She was immediately taken the nearest hospital, but sadly she didn't survive. I can't imagine what happened, but she seemed desperate, as if her self-worth was severely wounded.

It was still the early '60s, and everything seemed to be moving quicker, and I was fortunate to be engaged at a young age in doing what I loved at such a high level of professionalism. Being self-taught in most everything I did, I lived the ingenuous crudeness of the raw artist—even later as I discovered new art forms. As for the music, I still can't believe that I was accepted at the age of fifteen as a pianist for the hottest jazz quartet around. I didn't know my ass from a hole in the ground—to quote a phrase that seemed popular at that time. When someone would say it, I'd look downward for evidence. Everything I've learned has been out of pure joy and curiosity. I've never sat through studies that I didn't enjoy, not even in high school. I preferred sleeping and daydreaming, possibly, and contrary to common wisdom, making better use of the time and space I occupied then.

"I'm so young, and you're so old, oh Diana, I've been told..." The Paul Anka song "Diana" had been a radio hit in 1957—it became a reality for me six years later.

As fun as the band was to watch, at first, on my early visits to the club, I couldn't help but also notice the dancers; they called themselves the Paper Dolls. They were go-go dancers, clad in skimpy attire and the just-above-the-ankle white boots known as go-go boots. The seasoned dancers came straight from the famous New York City club in the '60s, the Peppermint Lounge. One girl was Diana Costello. There was a unique vibe about her; she was attractive and caught my attention. Also, she turned out to be a singer—of a sort. Her claim to fame was with a one-hit band called the Royal Teens, who had a No. 3 novelty hit in 1958 called "Short Shorts." Diana did the answering chorus on their recording: "We wear short shorts."

It was common for performers at the Holiday Inn to spend time together during rehearsals, and soon enough Diana and I were dating. One time the entire crew was returning from a beach excursion away from San Juan. We were on a bus, and Diana and I were sitting next to each other. She fell asleep, her head gently resting on my shoulder—and that was it.

Curiously, our relationship played out properly. We'd kiss and smooch and one time or another we'd get close, but we agreed to follow the so-called rules of engagement until we got married. Eventually, we got engaged and planned a wedding, with the date and all.

Our age difference must have seemed monumental. When we met, I was fifteen and she was twenty-four. But I was mature—maybe—and she must have thought so, too. She was playful and youthful, so we met somewhere in the middle, and that made it all right, I thought. We made a wonderful couple—it felt good, and we were having fun. I always admired that she could tell when I had missed a day of practice on the piano. She just knew by hearing me play, and she would call me out on it. "You didn't practice piano yesterday," she would say. That is something that always impressed me about her.

The wedding date was all set, and my parents loved her. I flew to New York, where Diana was from, to meet and stay with her parents for about a week. Her parents were lovely, and they also seemed to approve of me—they treated me well, and everything seemed perfect. Preparations for the wedding were underway, and Diana was planning on sending her personal belongings on a ship from New York to San Juan. I could never really understand why my parents were so happy that I was getting married, but they were. I also felt OK with the relationship and the idea of the engagement and getting married—the whole thing. So I played along and went with the flow—after all, we were always happy together, and there weren't any signs that anything would go wrong.

Diana also seemed to be the right fit for what came next. One fateful evening at the Holiday Inn cabaret, several months after I became a member of the Monchito Muñoz quartet, a faint acquaintance, Jorge Calderon, approached me after we played a hot set. I recognized Jorge from a local band called the Vultures, who emulated the Ventures, the American instrumental surf group from the late '50s that made the song "Wipe Out" famous. He asked me if I'd be interested in forming a rock band. Having caught my full attention, Jorge continued with the details, and after his proposal, I agreed without hesitating. Curiously, that conversation is a memory I've been able to retain throughout the years.

The days that followed were exciting. It was undoubtedly the beginning of something different. Calderon was a talented electric guitar player, bass player, and singer. He seemed to have a clear vision for the new group, and his ideas were fresh and progressive. Jorge already had a drummer in mind, Amaury, who was perfect for the newly formed rock band with his wit, raw energy, and good looks.

The first electric bass player who joined the group was good enough, but his commitment wasn't there. Later on, the right musicians would show up and fill the gap. I bought a Farfisa organ, which at the time was the hip keyboard to have in a rock band. Soon after, Diana joined the group as lead singer, which worked perfectly with the material we were doing at first.

We were prospering and widening our audience with each performance, and soon enough the Living End was at the forefront of the rock scene—there wasn't a music event that we didn't fill over its capacity. It was a booming time for rock bands. We also got booked at the main showrooms of major hotels. On one occasion, a large house orchestra backed us at the Vanderbilt Hotel in Condado. But it was at the El San Juan Hotel where we often attracted a big audience. We were as popular as a local band could be.

A top executive from El San Juan Hotel, Mike Segarra, noticed our potential as a mainstream rock group and suggested that to get further ahead we should have proper band management. He recommended someone he knew, Jack Rieley, a brilliant reporter and TV news anchor in San Juan for NBC News. Mike introduced us, and Jack was receptive. He had been a radio DJ in his hometown of Milwaukee, Wisconsin, and with great enthusiasm he became the band's manager.

Jack Rieley was a tall and large-framed man whose presence was unequivocal—he carried his body well and exuded knowledge, power, and transparency. His blond, fluffy shag over his tired, baggy, but knowledgeable blue-green eyes, crooked nose, and full lips all mixed into a perfect picture of power and reliance. Jack blended well with the group because in addition to being as capable as he was, he was also anti-establishment, expressing care for our basic civil liberties and for a better society. He also shared our love of music.

As much success as we were having as a rock band, Diana and I were always together but often away from the rest of the group. It wasn't until Diana went on a trip home to New York to coordinate the shipment of her belongings that I began spending more time with the guys in the band and started smoking pot regularly, getting stupid and just hanging out. Meanwhile, I started to understand why my parents were happy to see me getting married—Diana was much older than I was, and therefore mature. She was also conservative and disapproved of drug use of any kind. It made sense.

The first chemical drug I experienced was amphetamines. I think this was in the early days of the Living End, when we were staying up late at night rehearsing and playing gigs. We thought it was the greatest discovery and didn't have to pay for its effect later. I had also started smoking weed, and mixing the two was euphoric enough to give me a sense of spiritual elation. From that experience, I composed my first song:

> Days of wondering fading away.
> New directions, strange vibrations clearing up my way,
> Mystic thoughts that turn my mind, floating gay—
> I'll never go in the wrong direction; I've just made the
> reincarnation of my soul.
> In the calm of meditation building up inspiration, I'm the Sun—
> Mighty endless golden light, never late, he won't deny he knows
> he's there.

Perhaps these lyrics suggest I had gone through a revelatory psychedelic turn-on. In all fairness, this could have happened after I first took LSD, but I think it was earlier. I also remember a short period of carrying an acoustic guitar and singing the song everywhere I went—I was very young.

The "little song" (no title) was soon discarded. The words eventually felt too cheesy and embarrassing, and after that I never even gave it a second thought. It wasn't until now, in retrospect and for reference value, that it came back to me—I'm surprised I even remembered all the words!

Although we were all still living with our parents, while Diana was absent on her trip to New York, the group rented a house in nearby Punta Las Marias. There we'd have our water pipe as the centerpiece. We were smoking grass and hashish in massive amounts, day in, day out, and listening to any new emerging music, from the Animals and the Four Tops to the Beach Boys and everything in between.

One night we were playing at a popular nightclub, the Scene Au Go Go, in Old San Juan while Diana was away, when we heard on the loudspeaker seemingly out of nowhere a beautiful female voice singing along with our music. While we were doing one of our sets, we had shifted from rock into doing into an instrumental version of a newly released song, "The Girl from Ipanema." It turned out the singer was on a microphone at a DJ booth across the room. Her name was Tessie

Coen, and that night we seriously considered replacing Diana with Tessie as the fifth member of the group. She also played conga drums, which was a big plus, and she was Black and beautiful.

Because Diana was away, we asked Tessie to fill the gap, at least temporarily. Tessie adapted quickly with the group, and almost immediately she and Jorge were in an intimate relationship. While we were all local white teenagers from San Juan, Tessie had been born and raised in New York, from a Black Puerto Rican mother and a Jewish father. She was savvy and had been around. Now, with Tessie as lead singer and playing the congas, the group had a spicier sound. We were ripe for the changing times. Rock music was spreading like wildfire along with its glaring culture, and we were ready to seize the moment. We always had plenty of bookings and were on our way to becoming the most notable rock band in the history of Puerto Rico. At this point, things were moving quickly for the band, and Diana had missed the boat.

Meanwhile, at my parents' house in Ocean Park, we had two unused garage spaces that my dad converted into one-bedroom apartments for seasonal rentals. Two guys from New York, Rick and John, rented one unit, which thrilled my dad—he would often comment on "how nice and clean-cut those kids are." Soon enough, Rick, John, and I became friends, but little did my father know that they were drug dealers. They were bringing hashish and LSD to San Juan, I suppose for distribution. I saw nothing wrong with it and benefited from them being so close. I remember spending countless hours smoking massive amounts of hashish with them and creating an enormous cloud of smoke at the little apartment, and my parents upstairs not having a clue. All they knew was that they were two nice and clean-cut American boys. To up the ante, they had two beautiful light blue chopped motorcycles, a Triumph and a BSA, which they left in my care with the keys whenever they'd travel back and forth to New York. I have terrific memories of riding those bikes—in an altered state of mind!

The house in Punta Las Marias that we had rented as a group didn't last very long, and I was happy living at home with Rick and John feeding my fancies, living just underneath my bedroom—there seemed to be an endless supply of hashish and kief for free. The other band members rented a penthouse in a residence hotel in Old San Juan, a ten-story building at the top of a hill, across from the Castillo San Cristobal fortress overlooking the ocean, which became the group's hangout.

On one occasion as we were entering the hotel's lobby, we spotted a tall and thin mysterious woman checking in. She was wearing an all-black, layered, long dress, with partially braided strands in her long jet-black hair, contrasting her pale white skin and delicate features. The jewelry she wore differed from anything we'd seen, including an upside down cross on her long, pale neck. There was undoubtedly something very different about this woman. We were all mesmerized by her looks and her demeanor and didn't hesitate in approaching her. Her name was Jody Lynn, and she was a die-hard hippie sorceress from New York's East Village, an enigma. There was something obscure but fascinating about her.

Jody, the rest of the band, and I started hanging out together. She had brought plenty of substances from New York, some we had never heard of. I remember spending the day with Jody and the guys in the band and getting high in a wooded area of Piñones. There we had a rhythm jam using some enormous tree trunks that lay in the sand. It was tribal and exciting—something I had never experienced before. While I was doing my best at respecting the absence of Diana, I was feeling drawn to Jody. My bandmates were assuring me how different and happy I seemed now that Jody was around. At some point, not just my bandmates but other friends were commenting about my new demeanor. It seemed that Jody had also taken particular notice to me. One time she took me aside just to tell me, "You are flexible." The way she said it resonated with me still many years after.

Jody and I became lovers—the intensity and passion being insurmountable. Jody seemed to have a full medicine chest, including opium and amyl nitrite, among other unimaginable sensory-enhancing drugs she had brought from New York. All I remember is finding both of us completely turned around on the bed, feet on the headboard, during sex. I only realized after that we must have rotated unconsciously during the heat of getting it on.

Weeks had passed since Diana had gone to arrange moving to San Juan—to me, a lifetime had passed. The group's manager and now friend Jack Rieley took me aside and warned me profusely about the mistake I would make by marrying Diana, or anyone then. I listened to Jack, and it made sense. I also realized that I wasn't ready to commit to marriage, and also my affection had shifted with her absence and everything else that was going on. Before Diana's return, I wrote her a letter cancelling the wedding. For her it meant a breakup, as I reasonably expected. She was devastated, my dad was angry with me, and honestly, I was relieved. Jack was right, there was no turning back; I had gone too far from Diana, the idea of getting married, and beyond. I wasn't just replacing a bride or a girlfriend—it was much more than that. I had awakened to a new world.

This awakening was a double-edged sword. On one side, an exciting new world of possibilities opened up. On the other side, I also became aware of the vast landscape of uncertainty ahead—a broken and fragmented world of winners and losers. I felt bad about the whole breakup issue with Diana, but beyond that, I also felt committed to a higher purpose, some kind of mission.

THE HIGH PRIESTESS

THE HIGH PRIESTESS

 The High Priestess is your call to reflect on yourself and unlock your subconscious. Listen to your inner voice and follow your instincts—the treasures you hold inside are far more than you think. A new awareness will lead you to expansion and inner knowledge never imagined before.

"The man who comes back through the Door in the Wall will never be quite the same as the man who went out. He will be wiser but less sure, happier but less self-satisfied, humbler in acknowledging his ignorance yet better equipped to understand the relationship of words to things, of systematic reasoning to the unfathomable mystery which it tries, forever vainly, to comprehend."
—Aldous Huxley, *The Doors of Perception*

Somehow, a book found its way to me—it was the English writer and philosopher Aldous Huxley's *The Doors of Perception*. I spent hours immersed in deep concentration for days, grasping its profound meaning. I was at the end of my last year of high school, and nothing was more captivating than what I was reading, and my father noticed. One day my dad came close to me and asked about the book, and I was happy to discuss it with him. He mentioned that it contented him that I had such a passion for philosophy. The book was like a primer for facing my subconscious. It provided a gate into so many unknown areas of insurmountable depth, which somehow I resonated with.

Perhaps, while embarking on the psychedelic experience, I would find an answer to my moments of reflection on the meaning of my existence. Little did I know that the inner adventure was soon to come. A few days later, as was usual for me, I slept late, nearly into the

Calle Tranquilidad in Old San Juan, the small structure above is where Carli did his first LSD trip

following day's twilight. When I woke up, I knew I had a strange feeling that something special and earthshaking would happen that evening. The sensation was almost eerie. That night I had my first LSD experience.

Our new singer Tessie, and Living End's guitarist and co-founder Jorge, rented a small penthouse apartment in an old building on Calle Tranquilidad in Old San Juan. The building was on a corner where two narrow cobblestone streets met and cars could barely make the turn. The edifice was only a three- or four-story structure, and nobody seemed to live on the floors below the penthouse. The only way up was by stairs entrenched in a dark, steep corridor on the building's side. Once upstairs, the living quarters were small, more like a one-room efficiency with large open windows. The ceiling had dark, thick wooden beams crossing it, with a light-beige fiber mesh in between, often used in the old city. It was a "tiny square house," surrounded by a small terrace with a veranda and an incredible panoramic view extending from the Atlantic shore to the rainforest.

That night when I visited, it would have been an ordinary evening until Tessie said, "Do you want to take an acid trip?" Tessie had brought a batch of one hundred tabs of white pure Owsley LSD from New York's Columbia University, an experience that none of us had ever had before. Owsley Stanley was an audio engineer and the preeminent drug chemist of the hippie era, famous for making the purest product and his association with the Grateful Dead. (He was later immortalized in the Steely Dan song "Kid Charlamagne.") Everyone there, including two more guys—Hans, who was a visitor, the band's drummer Amaury, and

Jorge and Tessie—ended up tripping. But I can only describe my own experience. I took a full dose, a tab of ten milligrams, and it took longer than I expected to take effect. The wait was only a few minutes, but a little unnerving. Then, suddenly, what seemed to be a reality was no longer. It is almost silly to explain an LSD trip—there are no words. Seriously, the experience itself is untouchable in ordinary language.

I discovered very soon that I had to be willing to lose my mind. I found that resisting insanity or holding on to my rational mind during the LSD trip would be self-defeating, if not impossible—and dangerous. Losing one's mind has to be one of the scariest predicaments for the rational mind—it is the last thing you want to give up. Any time I tried hanging on to my sanity while on an LSD trip felt like I was fighting the flow—like fighting my innermost nature wanting to explode with expression. A high level of self-trust was necessary to let go of every notion, every belief, and my certainty of who I thought I was. And once the compartment doors were open, the subconscious flowed, revealing an otherwise inconceivable myriad of ideas, sensations, images, colors, and sounds. I'd imagine that getting past the point of sanity is not for everyone, and that's why so many people fear psychedelics. There's no way out, only through. But there must be a seed, a yearning somewhere in every sentient being to touch or release that inner essence that seems to be inaccessible but ever-present somewhere within.

As the journey began, I was sitting on the floor in front of Tessie. Images now were going through my mind like a strip of film rolling through my head. The speed of the images and elasticity of the sounds mesmerized me. Soon after, I must have been beyond sanity. Tessie later told me I had grabbed a fried fish she was eating out of her hand. The Beach Boys' album *Pet Sounds* was always playing in the background; it filled every part of me with a tingling sensation throughout my body while partitioning everything in my vision into separate multidimensional layers. The baritone sax, the woodwinds, and the percussion on "I Just Wasn't Made for These Times" radiated a sound dimension different from anything I've ever heard or even dreamt. There was an aspect of a deep red color somehow related to the music of *Pet Sounds*, and there was plasticity and round edges everywhere I looked.

The slow pace, the organ, and the whole vibe of "Don't Talk (Put Your Head on My Shoulder)" pierced through my being as if a cosmic spear had penetrated through all of my past and future lives, connecting every experience all at once; I felt a strange and unfamiliar kind of heat in my body—a quieting sensation of love unfolding. Even the air had a specific density with moving translucent paisley patterns. All of these led to a yet more profound transformation—indubitable wisdom abounded without pride, without self-importance, and everything was new and surreal.

After the initial mélange of images, sounds, and sensations, I felt a lucidity that I had never imagined possible. I remember walking out to the deck, and everything in the world was now new, but not just outside. It was a palpable sensation that vibrated every atom in my body. One of the first things I did in my new super-conscious state was climb and walk on the veranda. I recall as if it were today that, in my mind, I was challenging the myth that taking LSD would make you jump from buildings. The view was beyond amazing. You could see Condado, right beyond the Dos Hermanos Bridge, and it looked in the distance like an amusement park made of twinkling diamonds. In contrast, a made-up transvestite junkie passed by on the street below, and the image was impressively weird—there was a sense of displaced urgency, and her face looked off-axis, like the ones you'd see in some of Fellini's movies.

Someone else had been tripping with me; it was Hans, the other new guy I had met at the apartment in Old San Juan. He wasn't someone I knew well, but his company was pleasant. However, I could detect some sadness in him. Hans remained quietly alongside me as much as he could, and I never saw him before or after again. In hindsight, he was like a silent guardian or companion while the trip lasted—I didn't have any idea of where Hans came from...When I was doing acid a few years later in New York, I also had a tripping buddy, Frenchy, whom I never saw before or after. I feel fortunate for both occasions.

After sunrise and still tripping, I went home to share my LSD experience with my parents. They were both attentive and didn't give me even the most minimal vibe of disapproval or negativity. On the contrary, they seemed to share my excitement. My sister was around with her first newborn child. I held the baby in my arms in awe and numinous tenderness. Everything had new meaning, and I was experiencing new sensations.

My dad's tenants and now my friends, Rick and John, were out of town, and their two blue chopper bikes were parked at the house. I grabbed one of them and had the psychedelic joyride of my life. An acquaintance later described me as "the maniac on the iron horse." I was riding the chopper all over Ocean Park. I remember speeding along on McLeary Street, shirtless, just wearing bathing trunks and cowboy boots. My hair, she mentioned, was all sticking up as if I had been electrified. Everything meaningful I had done before taking LSD I had to do all over. Now I had to get a new experience out of playing in the water, boating, hiking in the rainforest, playing music, and basically re-experiencing my life anew—even the simplest things were new.

I became obsessed with LSD. Everything was vibrant, and I was able to see the world from a completely different perspective. I tripped again the next day and then again the day after. But I started noticing that the more I did it, one trip after another, the intensity seemed to diminish—I suppose a natural occurrence, as in most anything, but it was still a transcendental experience each time.

Thrill-seeking was the norm. Sometimes my friends and I would sneak in through the back of the international airport, where after crashing a cyclone-fence gate we would be surrounded by a dirt road overgrown with foliage that would lead us to the start of the runway. It was particularly thrilling to lie down on the runway on acid as the big airliners would fly right over our bodies when landing. Another time we somehow ended up with four or five boxes full of all kinds of fireworks, including large rockets and cherry bombs. A bunch of us went out tripping during the night to a wooded area near the beach next to a cluster of buildings called Pine Grove, where some of our friends lived. After one of the guys went over to tell our friends to look out their windows, we spread out the boxes of fireworks all over the woods and lit them all at the same time. The chaos of rockets shooting randomly all over the place was a spectacle like no other. We were all running all over the place in the middle of the pandemonium. I kept getting images of how it would be being in the war in Vietnam!

Tripping became almost a regular routine for us throughout the mid-'60s. One day, all of us in the band were tripping on LSD and driving around when the Beatles song "Strawberry Fields Forever" played on the car radio for the first time. It sounded so indescribably amazing, I had to stop the car on the side of the road. Everything, including the steering wheel, became elastic with the song, and it wouldn't have been wise to keep on driving while it played. It was the only time ever that I didn't think I could drive while on acid. I was always the designated driver in that state because it was easy and even fun for me. I just never

The meeting place on the beach

had a problem with it; on the contrary, I felt even more aware of my surroundings. Sometimes I felt even safer because I would project my vision as if I was hovering over the car, so I could see everything 360, all around. It's totally insane, now that I think about it, but it seemed to work. To me, it was all very real—perhaps it was.

Eventually more kids in the Condado area were turning on. There was a meeting point on the beach where all of us who had been tripping throughout the night would meet at sunrise. The beach spot was at the north end where Santa Ana Street ended in Ocean Park. There we'd all connect to watch the sunrise and tell our stories.

Aldous Huxley's quote, "The man who comes back through the Door in the Wall will never be quite the same as the man who went out," couldn't be a more accurate statement, and it will always resonate with me. But its true meaning was completely incomprehensible without the actual experience. When I first read *The Doors of Perception*, I could have just as well been reading about any magical adventure—it could have been *Peter Pan* or *Alice in Wonderland*. But it was an experience, all rather inward, and the beauty for me was that it was all doable.

After the lysergic acid diethylamide 25 became an experience, and all my senses got to perceive all they did, and I felt what I felt, life could never be the same. I had come back through the Door in the Wall not "quite the same." I could easily speculate that it would have taken me several lifetimes to evolve on certain matters of importance the way I did during and after the psychedelic experience. I feel I owe much to that experience.

It is true that at some point things got out of hand. As deep and significant as the events were, there was nothing methodic or specifically controlled about it to call it a real experiment, in any sense of the word. There weren't men and women in white robes or doctors taking notes. It was all intuitive and random. I was just another curious kid wanting to know more about myself and willing to stretch at any length to reach my full potential and place in the universe. But it is notable that I rarely did drugs for kicks or just to get stoned (except with grass and hashish sometimes). There was always a purpose. I truly cared about what lay underneath, or maybe I just enjoyed so much having a super vision, seeing colors that I'd never seen, connecting with people beyond surface barriers, or hearing music like I'd never heard it before—even "seeing" music and just experiencing the wonder of it all. In essence, whatever I did would be experienced from a completely different perspective never, ever experienced before—like suddenly living in another dimension, a completely foreign world.

I remember one time showing up at my parents' house somewhere between 3 and 4 A.M. tripping, with a bunch of my friends, and waking up my dad and asking him to let me use his car. I poked him while he was still sleeping, and I said, "Dad, my friends and I took some LSD, and we want to go to the rainforest. Can I borrow the car?" Half asleep, he answered, "OK, my son, the keys are over there. Be careful." Pointing to one of the night tables, he said, "I'll take a taxi to work," then went back to sleep. My mother then generously offered to make us sandwiches, and off we went tripping to the rainforest in my dad's car.

The experience of being in the forest at night and then at sunrise while tripping was overwhelming. The aliveness of the whole surroundings, the earthy smell with the infinite varieties of floral fragrances, mixed with the sounds of mating calls from all kinds of forest creatures, was dumbfounding. One of the most dazzling things is realizing that the colors we usually see are subjective to how we perceive them. The green of the forest I saw that morning is a green I never even dreamed existed—the same goes for all the other colors and sensations. Anything we perceive with our senses is relative to our state of mind; the fragrances we smell, the textures we touch, the sounds we hear, what we taste, everything!

After leaving the rainforest, we spent the rest of the morning at a beautiful, secluded spot we found near Luquillo Beach, a state beach minutes from the rainforest featuring a stretch of pristine ocean shore. The state of mind was just transparency, playful, and enjoying the moment. It was only when acid was chased with weed or hash that it became denser. I personally preferred not mixing, but the idea sometimes was to smoke some weed toward the end of the trip to come down and to be able to get some sleep, but it didn't always work that way—the clarity of mind would then be compromised, becoming mucky.

Many of my friends then and still now wonder how come my parents were so relaxed about my use of LSD. I let them know how different things were then. Besides LSD not being illegal, there was no evidence of adverse effects or reactions related to its use, at least that they knew of. Besides, my parents trusted me. Their bet was on the kid they raised, and they knew my character. Possibly they didn't anticipate the depth and the danger of what I would be exposed to later on by my continuous experimentation with drugs. Perhaps they suffered silently, but apparently their faith and confidence in who I was would be enough to sustain them throughout the painful process of my perilous journey. I must say that their trust in me ultimately sustained me as well.

I've seen how some of my friends sadly lost their way permanently by taking LSD, even by taking it only once. There are two occasions that I remember early on as a teen when it happened to two of my friends, Henry and Tony. They were both from families who lived near our neighborhood—nice, clean-cut, educated kids. But in both cases, their families seemed to be broken. Henry lived with his mom. Maybe he had a dad or siblings, but I never saw them, and his mom was always hysterical. One time Henry went home on acid to get something from his house, and his mom formed a big scene while we waited outside. She ended up taking Henry to a hospital where he was given another drug to bring him down—they brought him down permanently. From then on, you could see Henry on the streets talking to himself and being in a completely different reality—we lost him.

Something similar happened to my other friend Tony. Apparently, he also had a fallout with his family and ended up roaming the streets emotionally and neurologically damaged—gone. I wouldn't attribute any of these events to luck or randomness. I have always believed that at least the first batches of reputable brands of LSD were pure, and the experience you'd have solely depended on your own mental and emotional stability. Your relationship with your parents also may have played a role, as well as the environment.

The trust I had all along from my parents was essential for me getting through the '60s—it was, along with other attributes, less weight to carry on my back. Life is hard enough with the little cart we begin carrying from the pitfalls of our youth, which we keep on filling up throughout our lives with unresolved issues—big or small. Before we know it, unless we are fortunate enough to purge along the way, we find ourselves carrying a heavy load, sometimes a crippling load. I can't begin to imagine someone carrying a heavy load on their back and suddenly having to face their lifelong issues all at once. Sadly, I witnessed young folks who already carried a substantial load, and when they had an LSD experience they couldn't cope. For this reason, I am infinitely thankful that my parents were relaxed about my experimentation with psychoactive substances. They saw it for what it was, instead of demonizing an experience they couldn't possibly understand or know anything about.

The new colorful world now became part of our daily experience, and the other band members and I stuck together like glue. When we weren't rehearsing or playing, we would be listening to music or just doing nothing or anything, but together. At first, playing with the band on LSD was beyond exciting and gave us a tremendous edge as a group. The first thing we did was to weed out the songs that weren't relevant or that didn't say much or express the real voice of the band. After that, everything we'd play was awesome—every bit of it.

When the band first formed, we played faithful covers of hits like "Good Lovin'" by the Rascals and the Beatles' "We Can Work It Out." But then we added our own arrangements of lesser-known hits like Ray Charles' "Sticks and Stones" and Charlie Chaplin's "Smile" and then drifted heavily into the Motown direction where Tessie's voice was perfect. Also, we started doing originals. Part of the group's strength was the vocal harmonies, which were mostly arranged by Jorge, but the collective arrangements and overall sound of the group were transcendental. While a great number of our fan base were acidheads, everyone who heard the group perform was thrilled and moved by it. At some point we were only playing our original music and special arrangements we made true to our own style. The band had a definite identity.

Back in the early '60s, new rock bands began to sprout in San Juan and some in other parts of the island, but the Living End remained at the top. In those days "battles of the bands" were common, and we participated in all of them. An old acquaintance who played in one of the other bands later reminded me of the first time when we entered a rock band competition. We were the underdogs then because we were ill-equipped—our amplifiers were small and underpowered, and we were going to compete against a new band that had the latest equipment from the start. There was a third band that we had just beaten that also had better equipment, and they offered us the use of their amps. We won, beating the next band silly. There were subsequent battles of the bands, and we won them all. The final battle was held at the newly built 18,000-seat Hiram Bithorn Stadium, sealing the legacy of the Living End as the best rock band in Puerto Rico.

After the battles of the bands, we entertained the idea of leaving the island, but some of us were still in high school, and dropping out with so little left before graduating wouldn't have been a smart option. But the rock explosion was spreading massively. In San Juan, playing music high on acid was uncommon but new and extremely exciting. For us, if the music wasn't the hub, it was the messenger of the '60s counterculture movement. The Beat culture of the '50s opened the tastebuds for intellectual inquiry with literature, which was alluring for some of us, and conflicts like the Korean War and then Vietnam were questionable and became a subject of mistrust and protest. But it was through the spread of music and consciousness expansion that we kids would connect worldwide through a common language. A new era had begun—an era of fulfillment derived from inner and outer experiences propelled by music, mind-altering drugs, and idealism.

Rock soon became a way of life and quickly changed the social structure in the metro areas. Surfers became groupies, and the gap between classes narrowed because of the flow of drugs between the upper-class suburbs and the impoverished housing projects. Old San Juan became more colorful and a hub for artists, art galleries, nightclubs, and hippies. To my knowledge, our group, the Living End, was the first local band to publicly use LSD—it was still legal then. It wasn't until 1966 that it became illegal in Nevada and California. But word soon got around, making us the focus of a front-page newspaper article about local musicians using drugs and disrupting society. We knew it was time to leave.

After we left San Juan, we played and lounged in St. Thomas for about a year, and it was over-the-top fun. We were turning on, creating havoc with the local youth, and just being a rock band in a carefree paradise on LSD. One time the band's lead guitar player, Billy Soto, and I flew back from St. Thomas to San Juan to pick up some supplies. On our way back to the international airport to catch a plane from San Juan back to St. Thomas, in addition to having smoked some pot, we each took a tab of "Orange Sunshine" acid. It was nighttime, and once we reached the airport we got lost on the tarmac and couldn't find the small plane. We were so high that we kept going from plane to plane, guessing which was the right one. By then we were a bit anxious and broke into a laughing fit, but somehow we finally found the right airplane.

The vessel was an eight- to twelve-seater, but there was only one passenger riding along with us, a middle-aged man wearing a gray suit. As the plane took off and picked up speed and altitude, the fuselage felt like what I would imagine being inside a vacuum cleaner is like, which was impressive, to say the least. The man in the suit was sitting in the middle of the plane facing the rear, and Billy and I were aft, at the extreme rear of the plane, facing him. Apparently, the man in the suit was having a miserable time; he gave the appearance of being drunk or at least intoxicated and occasionally heaving. Our laughing fit subsided for a moment while the plane took off and leveled, but the sight of the intoxicated man's face having a hard time during the flight and the occasional gagging became too much to bear. We couldn't stop staring at him, and with a burst that I wouldn't wish on anyone, the laughing fit returned and lasted throughout the flight to the point where tears were flowing and our jaws were hurting. It must have been obvious that we were laughing at the poor man, but it was impossible to control.

Once we landed in St. Thomas and got off the plane, the variety of bright colors of the houses on the hills surrounding Charlotte Amalie and the charcoal blackness of the locals were spellbinding. Now we were suddenly in awe. On that same evening, after joining the rest of the band, we went back to town to get a bite to eat. In those days there were US sailors all over the town, a lot of them Black, who stuck together in small groups. The sight of Jorge, who was white, and the Black and beautiful Tessie being a couple and holding hands, plus us having long hair, created tension among the Black American sailors. On some occasions, the sailors would say something to them to pick a fight. Of course, being on acid, it seemed more than absurd, and we would often laugh about it, which only made the sailors angrier. On that night it was just a close call, but on another occasion the same thing happened near a club where we were about to go onstage.

We were all in an alley close to the stage door when some sailors started a fight, but this time one of them broke a glass bottle and charged Jorge. Jorge was on acid—we all were—so their actions appeared to be in slow motion, and Jorge was able to protect Tessie by fending off the sailor with his leg. But then the rest of the sailors began charging toward us, and a fan who was following the band and happened to be carrying a gun shot a bullet in the air. The sailors backed off and left us alone.

Most memorable was a time spent on Jost Van Dyke, a small island about twenty kilometers northeast of St. Thomas. The island, with its forty native inhabitants, only measured eight square kilometers. There we turned its governor, Foxy, on to LSD. In awe, he soon left his habitat to go and "see the world." Upon his return, he created history in his native Jost Van Dyke—the birth of Foxy's annual Wooden Boat Regatta on Labor Day weekend and the also world-famous "Old Year's Night," one of the top three places in the world for a New Year's Eve celebration. We were there for three days having the time of our lives until we got "rescued" by an American Coast Guard cutter. There had been a storm in the area, and the fisherman who had taken us in their little boats in the first place didn't return for us.

Back in St. Thomas, with the band having gone missing for a few days from getting stuck in the storm in Jost Van Dyke, and worse, wilder than ever, we eventually caught the local police's attention. We knew then that we had to move on again. I remember walking shoulder to shoulder with the police chief begging me, "Please, at least don't smoke pot openly on the street." But even that was too much to ask. Some guys ended up in jail at different times, which was fun. The jail cell was part of an old fort with an ocean view—we all wanted to be in it!

But the headlines again, as had happened in San Juan, demonized our presence in St. Thomas. We had to take the giant leap across the Atlantic to the mainland as if following the rainbow's end going for the pot of gold (hmm, unintended pun). It took all the money we had to transport the band out of St. Thomas. We arrived in New York with only a few personal items, our musical instruments, a BSA motorcycle, and just eleven dollars left in my pocket.

WHEEL OF FORTUNE.

WHEEL OF FORTUNE

The Wheel of Fortune reminds you that nothing is permanent; you must cherish the lessons that this moment is bringing you. When you receive this tarot card, you have a fair amount of good and bad times. Same as when you're riding a roller coaster—sometimes you're up in the sky, and sometimes you're at the bottom. The lessons learned from these experiences will be life changing.

We arrived at John F. Kennedy International Airport without a plan, or even a clue as to what to do, where to stay, or where to play. We were just sitting around with our luggage and instruments at the terminal staring at each other, trying to figure out our next move. I looked in my wallet to find that I still had eleven dollars, which I offered to share with the rest of the band. Also from my wallet I pulled out a crumpled piece of paper with the phone number of two TWA flight attendants, Mary Ann and Sandy, whom I had met briefly in San Juan just a few months earlier. I called the number they had given me from a payphone at the terminal, and Mary Ann picked up. I felt a little awkward, but I explained our situation.

"You can spend a few nights with us," Mary Ann kindly said. The two young flight attendants let us stay with them at their apartment in Woodside, Queens, which was conveniently not too far from the 59th Street Bridge to Manhattan. The stay with my new roommates was genuinely fortunate, not to mention fun. The other band members were unruly and were kicked out in a matter of days, basically for name-tagging food in the refrigerator—bad, bad! However, Mary Ann and Sandy extended their welcome to me, and I ended up staying with them for almost a year as the band made progress. The rest of the group members stayed with Tessie's relatives in the Bronx and with other friends in different parts of New York City.

Mary Ann looked a little older than Sandy, but perhaps it seemed that way because Mary Ann was more the intellectual type; she was taciturn and occasionally wore reading glasses. Her dark, reddish hair, falling a few inches below shoulder length, framed her noble, classic European-sculpted face. Her subtle smile and the spark in her black, round, crystalline eyes colluded with her risorius muscle, forming affective dimples—a perfect triangle with her aquiline nose at the apex and broad lips at the base.

Both Mary Ann and Sandy were slender, but Mary Ann was taller and had a larger frame. As much as Mary Ann had a noble and sturdy demeanor, Sandy's looks were of the typical but desirable blonde girl next door. Her short, silky hair and thin, wispy bangs over her little round face and full lips gave her a cute appearance.

Sandy was high-spirited and youthful; her blue eyes were sometimes silly, other times seductive. She was engaged to a guy who was a mortician, which seemed to conflict with her personality. One time her fiancé invited me to a party at his apartment with his other mortician friends. Their idea of fun was to drink as much beer as possible and recount nefarious jokes about the dead. An eventual passing of a joint would be their peak mischievous act. Then they'd turn the light off, leaving just a blacklight on. Of course, they all wore white short-sleeve shirts to get a bang out of the blacklight. I thought it was hilarious, and my exit cue.

Halfway through my stay with Mary Ann and Sandy, another flight attendant came to live with us at the Woodside apartment. Her name was Joanne. She was shy at the beginning but adjusted soon enough to having a male roommate. Sometimes I felt like I was their pet hippie boy—I didn't mind. I refrained from having amorous relationships with any of them. I was more concerned about having a stable roof over my head, conserving their friendship, and focusing on the success of my band.

The apartment was a spacious three-bedroom, and I always slept on a comfortable couch in the living room. The living room was my domain. There I had my crated collection of LPs and a few books—besides clothing, that was the extent of my possessions. It was OK for me to smoke pot and do acid anytime I wanted to. On occasion, Mary Ann and Sandy would join me for a smoke and a record-playing soiree.

I usually slept late, but one morning Mary Ann and Joanne came into the living room and woke me up. They said they needed a favor. I was still half asleep when they almost dragged me to the last room in the hallway where Sandy slept. Sandy and her fiancé were getting married that week. Her roommates had planned a special gift for her— me. Looking beautiful, almost translucent, Sandy was lying on the bed naked; her slim body seemed relaxed but alert. Mary Ann instructed me to remove my pajama pants and lie with Sandy; she said it was her last chance to get laid before getting married.

I noticed Sandy's eyes were half-open. I just wanted to be sure she was awake and consented to what was about to happen. Along with the anticipation, the event excited me to no end. I was stiff and eager, but I still felt a bit self-conscious with the other girls being in the room. But soon the passion of the moment overruled my shyness. I removed my pajamas, and I lay in bed with Sandy. I turned myself, supporting mine over her light body, and she didn't hesitate to accommodate my lower body's contour, looking to interlock into the right fit. At this point the presence of the other girls didn't bother me; on the contrary, I could tell they were enjoying it almost as much, as they seemed to be exploring from all angles.

I didn't rush. Still supporting my body over Sandy, point-in-line, I teased her senses by barely touching her already wet labia minora with the extreme of my extremity—no parry. I could sense her pulses calling in for a closer encounter of an ardent penetration and slow retraction. Each stroke glided to and fro, slowly reporting steadily to all of the senses. Sandy's grip became stronger, almost pompoir. Each of my hands and fingers were independent and well-appointed as I became well aware that the anus contracted and the blooming nipples hardened. With expanding girth, each stroke filled the warm and moist embracing cavity with a cocktail of life's ambrosial elixir of warm milk and honey—touché. The inexhaustible delectation leaped to a new level of boundless pleasure when our lips met and we succumbed to our little death—clenched toes, goofy face to a prolonged sigh, then we rested.

The Living End's first gig came from an audition just two weeks after our arrival in New York, at Scott Muni's Rolling Stone, a happening club on 48th Street near Second Avenue. Our confidence that we were a high-performing band landed us gigs almost immediately at the top city clubs. We got the house band gig—not bad at all for starters. Our unique combination of psychedelic and R&B was hot—we were at our peak of creativity and would often incorporate hypnotic jungle jams, revving up the crowds into euphoria.

The group attracted a large, hip following, top management, and mainstream record labels—all the great opportunities were there for the taking. In less than a year, the band got signed to Capitol Records on a label we created—Hand Records—a precedent in those days. By that time, our manager, Jack Rieley, was back with us and negotiated the deal with Capitol.

Capitol assigned us the enigmatic producer George "Shadow" Morton[1] for our first studio recording. Morton got his nickname because he had a knack for suddenly disappearing from the job—some say this was because he had become Phil Spector's "shadow." Either way, the name suited him well. The recording studio[2] was in Hempstead, Long Island, a one-hour train ride from Manhattan, so we ended up renting an apartment in Long Beach to be closer to the studio.

The recordings turned out to be a fiasco because Shadow missed all but one or two of the sessions and we had to carry on without him, without our producer. The few times he did show up he was drunk and pretended to direct the music with occasional meaningless hand waves from the booth.

We were a great-sounding live band, but recording was a whole different discipline. We ended up jamming and experimenting with very little direction. The result was neither a representation of the great live group we were nor a polished studio album—so much potential down the drain! The album had its moments, but overall it fell in a gray area of mixed genres and a hotchpotch of original and cover material. That's all we had—all we had to deliver to Capitol. The

---

1   George Francis "Shadow" Morton had formerly been with the Marquees and is credited with writing the songs "Remember," "Walking in the Sand," and "Leader of the Pack," putting the Shangri-Las at the top of the heap.

2   The recording studio was Ultra Sonic Studios located in Long Island, New York. Fortunately, John Linde, who was producing alongside with Shadow Morton, stepped in with quality engineers Bill Stahl and John Bradley to help with the project. But the sessions took quite a while. When the LP finally came out on the market in 1969, there was no promotion.

album, called *Space*, made it to a first pressing, but eventually Capitol Records decided to shelve it.

We continued doing local tours around the city and the upstate New York area, all the way up to Buffalo. The drives to Buffalo during the winter were brutal. I remember driving a van with the band and the instruments in the back, on the icy snow, slipping and sliding throughout the night with little to no visibility in the mountainous regions. During the summer we really enjoyed performing at a beach bar called the Castaways, in the Hamptons. It was right on the beach, and we packed the place every night we played. We got booked at the Castaways for several weeks at a time. Another favorite club we packed every night was the Wagon Wheel[3] in Manhattan, alternating with another group called the Elephant's Memory, which later enjoyed brief fame for performing with John Lennon and Yoko Ono as the Plastic Ono Elephant's Memory Band. Both our bands signed with the same management.

One time, Billy Soto, our lead guitar player, and I were invited by our friends Rick and John to go water skiing on a lake in New Rochelle, just outside of the city. Rick and John were two Americans who used to stay at the apartment at my parents' house in Ocean Park. They had just purchased a brand-new high-powered speedboat. As soon as we got on the boat, we all dropped acid. I'll always remember the sensation of water skiing on acid. It was like cutting through hard ice, and it felt so exhilarating! I was screaming like a maniac the whole time I was up on the skis. Consistent with the reputation of Rick and John's dealers, the acid was clean and super powerful.

It was getting late, and the Living End had a performance that evening at the Wagon Wheel. At that time there was some friction within the band. Jorge and Tessie had turned vegetarians and gotten into Transcendental Meditation. They emulated John Lennon and Yoko Ono with the white garb, beads, and all. Along with the image they became the disciplinarians of the group. It felt like they had a spell on the rest of us. Most of the time I felt controlled and run by their presumptuousness. All that did was create more resistance and resentment. It was Jack who brought me out of their

---

3   The Wagon Wheel was run by mafia mobster Johnny Biello. Located at 128 West 45th Street, this place was formerly the Peppermint Lounge. Biello was gunned down in a 1967 shooting that was never solved.

spell and assured me of my self-worth and potential. No one knew it then, but it was the beginning of the end for the band.

The drive back from the lake took longer than anticipated, and Billy and I arrived at the club late. The club and the dance floor were full, and we had to hustle our way through the thick crowd. The band was on stage already playing. As we climbed the stage, Billy and I were still peaking on the acid trip, and everything looked like a Van Gogh painting in motion. With the band still playing, Billy and I got up to our posts with our instruments. From that point on, the organ and I had an intimate relationship.

Hammond organs are also called church organs. That is because they are. A vital part of the equipment and what acts as the amplifier and speaker is the Leslie or tone cabinet, or Leslie tone cabinet—a large wood cabinet with speakers inside that turns with rotors that spin and throws the sound out into the room. There is a peculiar way to turn on a Hammond organ and its Leslie speaker, which is connected by a long, thick power cable to the organ. The start, or on-off module, is built into the organ cabinet, and the process involves holding a start switch for eight to ten seconds until you hear the tone generator inside the organ come up to speed. Then you have to turn the run switch on while still holding the start switch for a few more seconds and then releasing it. Then the instrument is ready to play. It is all a very mechanical contraption: Not only is the tone generator now up to speed, but the large bottom speaker and the upper dual horns inside the Leslie cabinet are now spinning.

So, there we were, tramping our way through the dense dance floor and crowd and then climbing up to the stage where the rest of our band was already playing. They were pissed at us. Having just turned the organ, I fixated on the lower speaker inside the Leslie cabinet spinning and becoming my little world. I got hung up on the whooshing sound it made while spinning. With my senses intensified by the acid, it was like a combination of watching and listening to an amplified washing machine and the gurgling of a bad digestion—I was mesmerized by the sight and sounds.

After a while of clinging to that little but intriguing and brand-new bizarre world of watching the speaker spinning, I leaped up to the organ bench. Even if I had played the organ tripping a zillion times before, every experience remained new. More dramatic, acid-induced scenery followed where the organ keyboard seemed curved and longer than usual. I just sat there in wide-eyed bewilderment with dilated pupils. I could imagine the look on the other band members' faces, but my new world was much more interesting. I remember as if it just happened: When I hit the first note, just a single high note in staccato, I jumped back. It was so powerful—like the cry of a banshee! From there on I got into the music and had the time of my life playing.

After we finished the gig, I didn't want to stop playing. I remained at the organ, and a guy from the audience with a set of Indian tabla drums offered to play along. I excitedly agreed, and the two of us played. The tabla player was good—the real deal—and the jam was out-of-this-world magnificent. I can hardly think of a more exciting experience. The energy was so vibrant that we had the whole crowd around us in awe. That night I left the club in excellent female company. I had earned it.

Her name was Gina, and she was a young Italian goddess. Her slightly curly dark hair rested loosely on her perfect teardrop D's. She carried herself with poise—it seemed to me as if a narrow ray of light spotlighted her, making her an unintended focal point. Her ravishing unassuming beauty pierced through the crowd and got my attention—her big, black, beaming almond-shaped eyes beckoned me. The attraction seemed mutual.

Gina filled a gap in my complex puzzle, as I did in hers. We managed to spend as much time together as possible. The streets of New York looked different, and the air was breathable for once. In the city we spent most of our time in Central Park and in Midtown window shopping. I remember on our first walk I bought Gina a pair of jeans, and I couldn't believe how happy she was.

Gina lived in Queens, not too far away from Woodside, where I was still living with Mary Ann, Sandy, and by now Joanne. One time Gina invited me to the apartment where she lived with her mom. She explained that her mom was away traveling with her boyfriend, Xavier Cugat, a famous musician and orchestra leader with a long career from the 1930s to the '60s, also known as the Rumba King. The apartment was plush and meticulously decorated. There was a thick puffy white rug at the center of the living room surrounded by French Provincial, elegantly placed furniture. Gina had mentioned earlier that she had read or heard about LSD and was curious about tripping, so I brought two acid tabs with me, and we took them soon after we arrived at the apartment.

Sex was literally in the air, and foreplay was a mere gesture of abstract relevance. Instead there was a sense of urgency in stripping to skin and bone and entangling our bodies into one. Our sweat and her wetness were a cocktail of fragrances releasing their own feral scents, from salty to sweet—especially to the acute nose with its heightened senses. The ambrosial scent even had colors: at first a dark, reddish mist, turning into a light, powdery blue mizzle that sparkled in the air. Once engaged in the reciprocal combustion of flesh and fluids, we became one, and the colorful palette of hallucinations intensified. Climaxes abounded one right after the other, a roaring waterfall of fresh gametes competing for ascendancy, flowing through a dark and dense forest into a welcoming plunge pool. We carved a home for ourselves in each other, in those moments, in the sensation of timeless, perpetual pleasure that begged for permanent residency.

The intensity was such that for a moment I panicked—I stopped! I felt something big and hairy tickling my throat that was seriously lumpy and filled my mouth. I was afraid to look at Gina, for I was sure that, in extreme, otherworldly euphoria, I had unconsciously bitten part of her flesh with hair and it was still in my mouth. Gina also panicked, mainly because I did. If I had bitten off a body part during all the excitement, most likely she wouldn't have felt the pain, which might have been mixed in with pleasure. To my dismay I finally realized what I had done. During the euphoria, I had unconsciously bitten off a piece of the rug, a large piece—her mother's beautiful, shaggy white rug now had a black hole the size of my fist, which was now filling my mouth!

The first reaction was of big relief because there was no harm done to Gina. But soon enough we realized that we still had a problem, a big one. How was Gina going to explain the piece of missing rug to her mom? I suggested through my mouthful that we move the furniture around some so that the hole would be under a piece of furniture. Then, I spit out the hairy lump from my mouth. Another option was to let it dry and glue it back to the once flawless and beautiful, shaggy rug it had been. Or blame it on mice.

The next day, back at the apartment with my roommates, I broke the news that I had a girlfriend. Mary Ann seemed unexpectedly taken aback by the news. That evening we hung out longer than usual in the living room where I slept. Mary Ann insisted on taking LSD, which she had never done before and had never shown interest in doing. I gave her a tab and took one myself for company. Somehow and regretfully, we ended up having sex. I can't say it was eventful, not because of Mary Ann, but because my heart wasn't in it. Mary Ann was just a friend, a roommate, and I now had someone I was getting to know and appreciate, possibly for a long-term relationship. If someone ever said that I was honest to a fault, you better believe it—to a fault. I told Gina what had happened between Mary Ann and me, and it was a big mistake. Gina couldn't handle it and rightfully shut me from her life, but worst of all I blamed Mary Ann. I packed up my few things and left the apartment.

There is an analogy I use to illustrate when someone is going through an unexpected relationship heartbreak. I gather two thin and long objects—it could be two pencils or something similar—and place them crossing each other, shifting them at different angles. Each line represents a path for each person, the intersection of the two lines being the relationship. Any variation on the angle from its axis represents the length of the crossing—the wider the angle the shorter the relationship—to near-parallel lines representing a long or lifetime relationship. I see it as a simple but powerful representation because one is able to see a path from an ample point of view. Different people have different paths, and sometimes we converge from a variety of angles. I've found that, however brief or long a relationship may be, there's always a purpose, something to learn. As bad as it may seem, there's always something to be gained in a lesson well learned, and better sooner than later.

I felt a huge loss, losing Gina, but more so parting from Mary Ann and the girls. Their kindness and friendship were everything to me. Blaming Mary Ann for losing Gina was selfish, cruel, and unconscionable on my part—a reaction I should have kept to myself and worked out on my own. Soon I was full of regret but too ashamed to look back. I will always regret parting like that from my friends.

THE MOON.

THE MOON

This card represents the thoughts, feelings, doubts, and fears that you carry internally. You are lost and in the dark, where you're unsure, allowing these fears to override the memories of your past and your faith in the future. The moon's light will bring you clarity to see through these tough times and guide you where you will find peace and understanding.

Leaving the apartment in Woodside was the beginning of a downward spiral. Tessie offered me a free room in the basement of a building in the Bronx, near 189th Street and Southern Boulevard, where her uncle was the superintendent. Outside of friends I had visited in Washington Heights, I'd never been to the Bronx, and it was like being in another country. I was further removed from the world I once knew. I made a new life in the little room inside that basement. It was just a rectangular four-hundred-square-foot room with a small utility bathroom just outside the door. To compensate for the bleak nature of my new dwelling, I had to transform it. I needed a bed, so I gathered some wood and made a frame in the shape of a grand piano. Then I cut a piece of foam the same shape and had a bed. The wall on the side had a ledge where I put all kinds of candles, letting them melt and making a colorful wax sculpture from the drippings along the entire wall. There were pipes all over the ceiling, which I painted fluorescent colors. Then I made all kinds of contraptions with tiny battery-operated motors hung from springs to make them vibrate—about six of them. Those I also painted Day-Glo and hung from the pipes on the ceiling.

I made my little colorful world in the middle of a concrete jungle in a tiny room that I seldom left. I don't recall having a fridge—maybe I did—but there was a White Castle nearby. I had a record player and still

65

kept my records in a crate. They were now mostly jazz records, mostly Coltrane and other Impulse label artists, along with some rock favorites like Simon & Garfunkel, Procol Harum, Gene Clark, the Byrds, and *Pet Sounds*—and that seemed to be enough. There I did a good share of tripping by myself, and with some of the other guys in the band who came to visit occasionally.

At this point, 1967 or so, we were still doing gigs as a group, although not as much as before. With me now living in the Bronx and the other guys in the band scattered around the state of New York, it was more difficult to remain together and rehearse regularly. So we gathered what little we had and rented a loft in the city, where we could have our instruments and stay there as well, at least on occasion.

Our new dwelling was a cheap loft on East 14th Street, above a cuchifrito stand, where the food was mostly fried with lard. The smell was intolerable, and eventually it was all over the loft, where we housed our band's equipment and claimed spaces on the floor for basic sleeping arrangements. We constructed a makeshift bathroom and there was not much more. It was at the East 14th Street loft that I wrote my first song that eventually got published, "It's Not Too Late." It was released forty years later, in 2008, on the posthumous Dennis Wilson album *Bambu*, and also in 2017 on my *In My Soul* album.

My recent relationship with Gina was brief but intense, but it didn't get much traction in my emotions. At the time I was still regretting the loss of Jody Lynn. Jody had gone back to New York a few weeks after we met, and we lost contact. As soon as I had arrived in the city with the Living End, I made a few attempts to find her in the East Village, where she lived, but to no avail. I wrote the song in despair thinking of her. I was alone on the Hammond organ at the loft, on mescaline and blindfolded when I wrote it. "It's Not Too Late" was among a few of my compositions where everything, the music and lyrics and even the arrangements in my mind, came about all at once during just the duration of the song. "All Alone," also released on *Bambu*, happened the same spontaneous way. The two songs were rerecorded and arranged many decades later just as I had imagined and released on my album *In My Soul*.

The differences among the group members were widening, and soon enough the drugs, power struggles, and being together so much gave way to petty bickering. Ego trips took over, escalating to irreconcilable distancing and ultimately a band breakup. After the band's separation, it was our manager, Jack Rieley, who was most supportive of me, but eventually we all went our separate ways. Jack went to Delaware to work for the local Democratic Party headquarters, and I remained in New York.

Blurry events took place following the band's breakup and Jack leaving. I remember a wild circle of friends, percussionist Gerardo "Jerry" Velez, who later performed with Jimi Hendrix at Woodstock, and singer-songwriter Kenny Rankin among them. We all would hang out at a large apartment on the west side of midtown Manhattan, where two beautiful identical twin girls, Sheila and Joyce, lived. It was a never-ending party with continuous jam sessions and party favors, including acid-laced punch and cookies. Everyone had something to contribute. I wasn't much of a cook, but I remember making beef Stroganoff for nearly fifty people at one of the parties. It was an easy meal that Jack and I had often cooked to keep from starving.

At around the same time, I got initiated into Transcendental Meditation. Jorge and Tessie had become meditators and insisted I join. The meditation felt incredibly good, and it gave me tremendous energy, but I was feeling alienated from everyone else. I felt that everyone else was below me—a feeling far from what I was searching for. I went back to the organization and demanded a refund, which became a tense issue because they claimed that returning the initiation fee was against their policy. But I was determined to walk out of there with it. They returned the $175, and with it I bought an old white Chevy.

With that contraption and a meth spew, I drove to Delaware to pick up Jack. I remember barging into the Democratic Party's office and telling him he had to get the hell out of there. The current state of politics was everything we despised, and there he was taking residence inside the wolf's mouth. We got in the car and headed back to New York. Memories of our time back in the city are even blurrier, and I'd be lucky to squeeze out a single event. I just vaguely remember that Jack and I dissipated into different crowds back in the city—into different worlds.

As for me, even since before I left home, I had been on a fool's journey. But I was now away from my peers—the other band members. They were still my brothers despite our differences. The wicked Apple even sucked my friend Jack into one of its wormholes. Life in the big city became unbearable—I had become a tumbleweed in the poignant and dark soul of New York City. There I was, an idealist island boy with a nearly forgotten past, at the mercy of any random event that the sleepless city would bring.

THE DEVIL .

THE DEVIL

The Devil has convinced you that you are trapped and have no options, but this couldn't be further from the truth. You're being held in your own prison by your own limitations or your unwillingness to move forward. But it's up to you to open the lock. Once you realize this, you can start making positive changes to free yourself from the shackles you have placed upon yourself.

I had been tripping too much—we all had been—and LSD wasn't the same anymore. It was no longer the crystal-clear passage to deeper layers of consciousness where I could draw a sense of clarity and self-awareness. More often, the acid became more and more mixed with speed and other substances, which started making the trips edgy, dark, and uncomfortable, if not outright scary and dangerous. That led me to speed in the form of methedrine to bring myself up or just to ignore the feel of the cold weather on my skinny, worn-out body, but it just made matters worse—I was going deeper and deeper into an abyss. I ended up spending so much of that time submerged in the quagmire of my self-inflicted misery—so much scarcity that soon I had completely forgotten that I had a past—and knew even less of a future. Ocean Park was now but a faded dream without even a glimpse of its once abounding hearthstone.

Not long after we had left the loft we had rented on 14th Street, die-hard hippies moved in, and the loft became a meth parlor. Eventually the loft caught fire as a result of the lard burning continuously and recklessly downstairs. As far as I knew, no one was hurt. Fortunately for me, I had already left the loft, preferring life on the street.

I found myself homeless, a hobo. When lucky, I spent a night or two at the home of a stranger who was kind enough to shelter me, but other times I slept on the sidewalk or under a bridge with other hobos. This is where I learned the true meaning of sharing what little you have with the fellow next to you. In that predicament, however wretched, everyone mattered. In winter, I didn't have a winter coat, and when sleeping on the sidewalk, the only heat at night would come from the subway vents on the ground. I had no money, and I was hungry.

I remember once standing on the sidewalk in front of a bakery, sleepless before sunrise, silently begging for a piece of bread. The man working there just kept on doing his job—and I don't blame him. I felt an unspeakable sense of self-abandon and despair, which led to a spiral of naked self-preservation—almost a state of consciousness blindness. I drifted back and forth between the streets of the East and West Village, at first hoping to meet someone in kind, hoping for a lucky break. On a good day of panhandling, I'd be able to buy a square pizza slice and an egg cream on the corner of MacDougal and West 3rd Street.

Eventually roaming the streets of the East and West Village of the wicked Apple, my conscience became barely a whir. I was spent, and hope wasn't even on the table, for how can hope exist within a consciousness trapped in a conundrum of feral madness? There was nothing but chaos in the inner and outer surroundings. Eighth Street became a highway of fleeing vignettes and impossible dreams interconnecting two worlds of eventful non-events. The dynamics of color and sound paired with whimsical debauchery—a bacchanal of uncertainty and neurasthenia, all the while the partakers seemingly unfazed by the surroundings.

I needed hope. A part of me remained—a tiny part. Perhaps my spiritually sound Catholic upbringing, the hardline morals that my parents had fed me, or a combination of both brought me some sense at this crucial moment—but most likely it was the fourth and most intangible reason: my mom's fervent nightly prayers. As I drifted along the way to nowhere, I witnessed a totally unhinged human having a less than human experience. It was a young Asian boy, and the image stuck in my mind. He wasn't doing anything weird; it was the hopelessly urgent level of paranoia, fear, and a grueling disengagement in his eyes that stood out. I could have sworn that there was a fierce, windy storm just around him. The moment reminded me that I had a tab of STP in my wallet that someone had given me. STP is many times more potent than LSD, and it had a reputation for creating a prolonged psychosis of unfathomable intensity lasting several days. The young Asian man embodied in my mind what an STP trip would be like; I threw my tab away.

Discarding the STP tab was a small but possibly life-saving triumph. The act didn't make me a fully functional person, but it might have prevented me from annihilating what little I had left of the gray matter in my brain and from further siphoning my spirit into a bottomless spiral to nowhere. It was just that—a small triumph.

In hindsight, my parents would have ended my misery in a heartbeat, if I had only asked, but that wasn't my path. I was so far removed from the idea of being supported by my parents that I didn't even consider that possibility. I had to make it on my own—do or die.

I instead tried getting a job doing manual labor, which meant having the luck to get picked out of dozens of unemployed workers on some street corner. From that, I did my share of loading freight trains. I had loaded trucks before, but train wagons seemed to have endless space for loading, and the task was hellacious and backbreaking. After that, I managed to get a job at a silk-screening press in the West Village. Only the Lord knows why I was fired after a few days of work. Each day that went by, I'd hit a new low. I begged for money on the street and slept anywhere the night would find me. I didn't steal or hustle anyone, but one time I saw a candy bar in the front seat of a car that wasn't locked. I was hungry and I took it. I must have felt so much self-doubt and fear that I fell in the void and hit bottom.

I was at the bottom of the abyss when a seemingly insignificant but life-changing event took place. While I was meandering in a subway station, I locked stares with a young man about my age. He was the Wall Street type, well dressed and neat, wearing a gray trench coat. We must have been at least four to five meters apart in the crowd. There was a profoundly eventful moment where both our eyes met and fully engaged. As clear today as they were then, my thoughts reflected a sense of total disgust with myself. He was a mirror into my soul. The young man may have been judging me or not. But right there, with that gaze, at that precise moment, I realized how far down the pit I had gone—the wretched creature I had become.

What followed is blurry. I remember being very ill, but with no clue of what was happening with my whole being. I was shaken by the subway station encounter, and somehow I purchased a flight to San Juan.

On the plane, I was seated next to a pregnant young woman. Throughout the trip, I felt uncomfortable and ashamed. I felt dirty and not worthy of sitting next to someone carrying a new and sacred life.

After the flight, I can only recall showing up at my parents' house. I remember it was already evening, and just walking in and seeing my mom and dad standing in the middle of the room. I heard one of them say, "Oh, my god," and I collapsed to the floor, unconscious. The next thing I remember is waking up in a hospital bed, hooked to an IV.

PART 2

THE CHARIOT.

THE CHARIOT

 The Chariot reminds you that your greatest successes won't come through self-imposed limitations. It's when you combine the knowledge of your mind with that of your heart and spirit that you become an unstoppable force. You're about to overcome some significant challenges in your life by maintaining your focus, confidence, courage, and determination.

As if higher forces were being manifested by the young man's presence, the brief, fateful encounter at the subway station turned my life around. It was a pivotal moment, a mirror into my soul. God works in mysterious ways, some would say. So, there I was, convalescing from dire physical illness and emotional darkness—and counting my graces. I had just gone through hell and back, and at least now, while in my sickbed, I knew I had to make better choices, and I made a vow to that effect. I was grateful for still being alive and half sane.

Higher forces must have been at work. I had a strong and spiritual upbringing, and although I often questioned it, I never lost my faith. A new life, a new world, was just about to unfold. Perhaps, in the end, I had gained an adventure, a bittersweet one, and one that left me some deep scars but also a period of roller coaster events and emotions that shaped who I am. I have no regrets.

Like the equestrian who fell, broke some bones, and climbed back up on the horse again, I returned to New York soon after being released from the hospital. There was still much to conquer. As fate would have it, Jack Rieley was still in the city, and he had called my parents to know of my whereabouts. We reconnected and became roommates again. My plan was to get a job, any job, and stabilize enough to move my music career forward. The Living End existed in a quasi-dormant state; we resumed doing sporadic gigs in the city, but not enough to make a living. I was eager and ready to get on with a new life.

While I was still convalescing in San Juan, I also decided to turn fully vegetarian. My aim was to clean my body from all toxic chemicals, including the toxicity of cheap White Castle burgers and other junk food I had consumed during my recent self-abandonment. My new state of mind demanded holistic health, and I was determined to attain it. I became interested in spiritualism and theosophy and began reading books related to all matters of health—physical, mental, and spiritual. Being back in New York City was different now. I had to get back on my feet by any means necessary and climb the rope again. But I needed to start from somewhere, and spirituality seemed like a good place to begin if I was to rebuild myself from the inside out.

Spirituality was always present in me in one form or another. Even when I was very young, I would argue about spiritual matters with some of my friends, sometimes to tears. When I was around eight or nine, I had an older friend who was an atheist who kept trying to shove his beliefs down my throat. I had second thoughts about my friend's integrity anyway because when his dad died in the shower from a heart attack, I heard him say that he was happy his dad was dead because now he was free to do whatever he wanted to do. He was highly intelligent, but his heart wasn't in the right place. Besides, his way of thinking never made sense to me.

Even then, I saw life and my all-natural surroundings as so amazing that I could only attribute them to a higher intelligence. The only difference in perspective regarding that higher intelligence after my LSD experiences was not seeing God's nature as something out there, but rather close—as if we were swimming in that potential at all times.

Religion interested me, beginning with my own Judeo-Christian faith. But for the sake of knowledge, I took interest in all religions. The first thing I learned is that no religion owns a patent on God. While most classic religions aim for civil moral conduct and inspiration, the typical claim of being the "only way to salvation" has always troubled me. I also realized how many religions lose their way, becoming a force of control and dominance over the masses for some self-serving agenda. It's been that way throughout history, and as long as religions are run by us humans, they will remain flawed. I figure the best one can do is find its essence and apply it to one's heart's content. For some, including atheists, applying the Golden Rule, "Do unto others as you would have done unto you," is a sufficient basis for civility, but there is a whole world of inner workings within the world of religions and mysticism.

Being also curious about astrology, I met by chance in San Juan a bright young astrologer from New York. He got my attention with his knowledge on the subject and mentioned a teacher he had back in New York, Ellen Resch. He raved about Ellen, and I was sure he meant she was an astrology teacher. I asked him for her contact info. Later in New York I got in touch with Ellen, and she invited me to come to a session at the Carnegie Hall building on West 57th Street.

After taking the elevator a few floors up and walking down a long hallway, I found her suite. The door was slightly open and I entered. All the lights were off except for a candle in the middle of the floor, surrounded by about a dozen people, some sitting on chairs and some on the floor. With the flickering of the candle's light, I could vaguely see an elegant, middle-aged fair lady sitting on a chair facing the small crowd. While remaining in the back, I joined the group.

Ellen seemed to be giving someone a message from a "guide," as she called it. Afterward, Ellen acknowledged me and, still seated, began giving me what seemed to be otherworldly messages. Some messages were about my family, and everything seemed to fit in. Then she gave me an Aztec-sounding name that she referred to as my spiritual guide. She also said things about my sister and where I was from that only I had knowledge of.

Ellen basically gave me a psychic reading, which is what I realized she did in the group sessions, in addition to doing a form of candle meditation. After the session I introduced myself (not that I needed to) and asked her if I could see her privately. She said yes, and I started seeing her privately at least once every week. She didn't charge me anything—small donations were OK if you had the money.

During the private session, Ellen usually began by interpreting my aura by just looking at it. She also had her own method of portraying the state of the aura, which she would then also interpret. Ellen called it "soul patterns." She made pastel drawings on a piece of paper of the different shapes and colors she would see by just looking at my aura. She made several drawings for me, which of course kept changing over time.

Ellen made me aware of my state of being at the time and forewarned me about my shortcomings by interpreting the drawings. She also made me aware of my spiritual guide, and I don't think I would have been able to survive my quandary without that inner connection, real or not. Later on, Jack went to see Ellen a few times, and she revealed the name of his spiritual guide to him. Jack and I would eventually write a song called "Soul Patterns," which was eventually released on the *In My Soul* album.

Initially it might have been a mistake for me to think that Ellen was an astrology teacher. She was a psychic—a clairvoyant and spiritual advisor. It wasn't what I had originally signed up for, but it actually turned out for the better. I found Ellen at a time when I most needed it. I was at a low point; the sessions were empowering, and her advice saved me a lot of heartache—it brought me a certain degree of peace and clarity.

Besides the drawings of my "soul patterns," our sessions were mostly conversational, often focusing on the meaning of my relationship with my parents. I realized then that it is widely accepted within esoteric spiritual teachings that the soul to be born chooses its parents from the spirit realm. At least within our construct of time, this to me made sense as a mechanism for continued karmic evolution, of course parallel to a biological evolution-ary path that we carry in our DNA. It also made me think about how relative happiness is when there is so much economic and social disparity among us humans. While it is evident that everyone is searching for something, perhaps it's not so evident that the potential for happiness is equally spread among all people, and that, at deeper level, a choice was made.

Take a very poor family—they struggle to survive, or simply strive for something better. Then there is a very rich family. They also struggle for something else, maybe for more riches, or for keeping what they have, or for a higher social status or acceptance—it never ends. But regardless of status or level of social position, a specific path and also a sense of reward and some form of elation is always available to everyone, even the person living on the street—even for a simple reward such as having a hot meal, or even a smile.

If we could truly measure dopamine levels among people of different social and financial status and conditions, this may sound a little naive to some, but I'd bet that we wouldn't find much difference in the levels of gratification and the joy of living. Call it relative happiness. This idea gave me a partial sense of relief and of fairness in life. The only variant to happiness, I suppose, would then be having a clear conscience, or not. Ellen became an essential part of my fool's journey, opening an infinite number of possibilities that I had not even considered before.

Sharing an apartment with Jack back in New York City was much dif-ferent this time around. We were both now focused on being productive and healthy. At least I was. I remained close to Ellen and became friends with some of the other people who were also going to her weekly sessions, most of whom were my age and open to spirituality. Meanwhile, Jack somehow became involved with the original cast of *Hair* on Broadway, and the partying now escalated to a whole new level. Attending the musical frequently for free was fun, but I remained dedicated to the direction I wanted to go and kept a distance, especially when there were drugs involved. Not to say that the cast was involved with hard drugs, but there was a "doctor" who was close to the cast and perhaps with "the best intentions," or not, kept the cast high and energized—a detail that as far as I know has been kept behind the scenes and never publicized.

There had been a continuous onslaught of brutal nor'easter storms going in the winter of 1968, but still, being back in New York City, there seemed to be hope. I had become clear about my path ahead and was willing to do anything to attain it. I was meeting new people, and everything was beginning to flow. The Living End was still partially active, but I now felt less dependent on the band and was considering the idea of also performing with other groups.

Sometime around mid-April of that same year, Jack asked me if I would accompany him on a weekend trip to Los Angeles. Being focused on making my new life in New York, I didn't want to go. I had met another girl when we were playing at the Wagon Wheel. This time I was enthralled, and I was certain she was the one. We immediately clicked like we belonged to each other. It felt magical. But the affair didn't last a week—Jack insisted I go, saying that he had already purchased a ticket for me and kept on pressing. I finally conceded, and off we went for a weekend in LA.

I had never been to the West Coast before. Jack had been there two weeks prior and raved about it. Once we arrived, it wasn't hard to figure out why Jack wanted to go back to Los Angeles so soon. By contrast, Manhattan was dirty and seemed disorganized and in some kind of limbo. I foolishly wrote a letter sharing my excitement to my new "girlfriend," but she didn't seem interested in joining me—I just moved forward and didn't look back. Moving away from New York City marked the end of an era.

THE SUN .

THE SUN

The Sun with its radiance, brings you strength and happiness. It is a powerfully uplifting card, representing happiness, joy, vitality, and optimism—a positive sign that things are working well for you and that you're moving in the right direction. This card points positively toward your feelings of fulfillment.

After living in New York City, being in Los Angeles was like suddenly stepping into a combination of Elysian Fields with a touch of Xanadu. Staying in Westwood Village heightened the experience. Glorious weather, palm trees, attractive and friendly people with smiling faces—everything seemed pristine and beautiful. Even the architecture reminded me of being back home in San Juan. It was a pleasant kind of familiar—the sun was always shining, and New York City became but a distant memory.

In a short time, all went in crescendo, each experience exceeding the previous one. By that time, Jack and I had done our share of tripping, starting in San Juan, continuing in New York, and again in LA during the first few months we were there. In a matter of days, Jack and I moved to a house off Laurel Canyon, then shortly after to Lookout Mountain up the canyon. The entire area was a magical place. Many famous artists and upcoming musicians lived, literally or at least figuratively, in that area of the canyon. Some of our neighbors were Frank Zappa, Joni Mitchell, Carole King, James Taylor, Linda Ronstadt, Jim Morrison, the Eagles, the Byrds, the Mamas and the Papas, David Crosby, Stephen Stills, Graham Nash, Neil Young, and the list goes on. Music and creativity filled the air, and the neighbors' doors were always open. ("The hills are alive with the sound of music..." Just kidding!)

81

The Laurel Canyon area was a village, mostly surrounded by a creative community. The Country Store was the gathering place on the canyon down the hill from Lookout. And the intersection of Laurel and Sunset Boulevard was a hub where you could casually run into a neighbor you may have seen in a movie or heard on a record. It could happen at places like Schwab's Pharmacy, where I had a casual conversation in the parking lot with Donald Sutherland about his vintage VW van, or at the local bank, where I met Stevie Wonder while waiting in line to make a deposit. A Hunan Chinese restaurant stood on the corner of Laurel and Sunset. There I bumped into my old friend Al Jarreau, whom I met at a previous gig, twice. One of those times, he excitedly said, "Carli, I just signed a management contract!" and introduced me to his new manager, Pat Rains. The Source, a great indoor and outdoor vegetarian eatery run by kundalini yogis, was always filled with beautiful people. One of the most popular hangouts west of the strip was Tower Records. It was perfect living in that area—away from the hustle of Hollywood and lacking the huffish appearance of Beverly Hills—just a casual, relaxed, and creative vibe.

Jack and I eventually went our separate ways. I moved to a bungalow on Sunset Boulevard behind the iconic Chateau Marmont hotel. One of the first people I met was Chuck Wein, a close collaborator with Andy Warhol since 1964. He had just gravitated to LA, same as me, in 1969, and had recently finished directing the Jimi Hendrix concert film, *Rainbow Bridge*. We became close friends. Wein introduced me to his circle of friends who met at the old Houdini mansion in Laurel Canyon, an iconic property farther up across from the Country Store. Beautiful twin girls, the "Gemini Twins," lived at the mansion and hosted an ongoing underground wild party. Chuck also introduced me to Clara Schuff, also known as Clara Clairvoyant. She had been Jimi Hendrix's seer and had a cameo appearance in *Rainbow Bridge*. At Wein's insistence, I went to visit Clara in San Diego and got some meaningful and insightful readings from her.

Coincidentally, among the new people I met were a group of actors from the Los Angeles cast of *Hair*—the West Coast version. As if drawn by a magic magnet, I met my new friends at a "tie-dye" party I was invited to in the Mount Washington area where some of them lived. Mount Washington is a hilly, secluded area east of Hollywood Hills, but only minutes away from the metro area. It turned out to be another community of creative people, but lesser known. So I found myself once again attending performances of *Hair* for free and hanging out with

some of the cast. This time, the vibe was more down to earth without
"Dr. Syringe."

Eventually, Jack had to move from Lookout Mountain and we ended up rooming together again. We got busy writing songs. Jack, a journalist by trade, was well informed. He came from a wealthy family in Wisconsin, and it was evident he had had a relatively privileged education. Wherever Jack was, he owned one hundred percent of the space. In addition to his brilliance, he was also a master of drama and manipulation. Jack exuded a depth and complexity of character and executed every task with zest and an enormous, endless flow of creativity.

Both of us were born idealists who wanted to see social transformation. Jack sincerely cared for the underdog, as did I. We would spend hours discussing possibilities, from inciting a revolution to personal awakening. It wasn't unusual to be sitting somewhere, usually in the kitchen, planning a revolution until dawn. The final dilemma was who we'd have to kill—that's where we'd stop because it would be someone we knew—that was always a dead end (no pun intended). Instead, we opted to write songs that had meaning. Typically, I would write the music, and together we'd brainstorm the message we wanted the lyrics to convey. Jack would often come up with the prose, and I'd tweak it for the phrasing. Other times we collaborated on the verses, and I'd write the choruses, as in "No One Is There" and "Follow Me."

As much fun as we were having, we both needed to work and were now looking for "real" jobs. Jack got hired almost right away by a local underground FM radio station, KPFK. After checking in at the Musicians Union Local 47 in Hollywood, I soon started gigging with local bands and became in high demand. Eventually I found myself doing three gigs every night, seven days a week. The first gig was from 8 PM to 1 AM, then from 2 AM to 6 AM and the third one from 7 AM to 11 AM. They were mostly strip joints, and the pace took its toll on me. Playing became too much of a job—not what I wanted, not to speak of the level of sleaze I had to often put up with. The butt naked girls were nice and a welcome sight, but the patrons and the shady bosses were a piece of work. One time after the last gig, at 11 AM, I had to go back, pissed to no end with a huge kitchen knife in hand, to reclaim my pay in real money. They had given me fake hundred-dollar bills, which I got busted for while doing my grocery shopping at the farmers' market. It was a dog-eat-dog world, and I'd had enough.

At some point I decided to call Jorge, who was still in New York with the rest of the Living End, and asked him to come to LA and give the group another shot on the West Coast. In a matter of weeks they were in LA. They drove a truck to LA with all our instruments and belongings. We auditioned at a club in Hollywood called P.J.'s, which was LA's first disco. (It reopened in 1973 as the Starwood and became a premier industry showcase.) We got the gig, but soon realized how different the vibe in Los Angeles was from New York. The club insisted we wear uniforms and play cover music—both of which were deal-breakers, so we turned down the gig. Soon enough we realized that was the way of Hollywood, and we decided to break up the band and go our separate ways.

Back in New York, before I left, our drummer's girlfriend, Sally, gave me a piece of paper with the telephone number of Ed Carter, an ex-boyfriend who played with the Beach Boys. I put it away and forgot about it until I found it one day as I was going through my wallet and called Ed. He agreed to meet me at Mike Kowalski's house in Topanga Canyon, which was relatively close, only about ten miles from West LA, but was in the mountains and away from everything. Going to Mike's house up in the canyon was a beautiful ride. As I remember, the house was at the edge of a cliff overlooking a creek at about a quarter mile down at the bottom of the hill. According to Mike, across the creek at the foot of the mountain was a little cabin where a family had been living since the 1930s. At Mike's house there was a relatively large music studio full of instruments with a view of the mountains. Like Ed, Mike had been touring with the Beach Boys for some time. We jammed and hit it off really well. Mike later told me a story that when Dennis Wilson was visiting, he offered to wash the outside of the windows. Obviously, he was joking because the windows overlooked the edge of the cliff.

Meanwhile, Jack leaped up the ranks at his job at KPFK and became the station's program director. Being a journalist by trade, Jack had the brilliant idea to set up a two-part interview series with the Beach Boys. He thought it would be great for the station and the Beach Boys, and he would be the interviewer. Later on, Jack told me that during the interview the Beach Boys asked him to be their manager. After the second interview, Jack returned to our apartment driving a 1940s Bentley in perfect condition. He said the car was a token from the Beach Boys to consider their offer. But there was a catch: Taking over the Beach Boys' management wasn't all peaches and cream. Part of the deal was that Jack, as their new manager, would have to fire their current business manager, Nick Grillo, who allegedly had mafia ties and was presumed to be skimming money from the group. I remember Jack being a little leery about it, but he took the job and fired Mr. Grillo.

In a media interview much later, Jack denied accepting the Beach Boys' manager's role. Perhaps it was semantics, or he may have just despised the position. But undoubtedly, even if he later denied it, Jack had accepted that role. Ironically, I was once mistaken for the Beach Boys' manager. I found out about the error when my cousin Karen Biddle, in Philadelphia, sent me a copy of an article from a local newspaper with a candid picture of the promoter Bill Graham and me having a conversation backstage at the Fillmore West, photographed in the early '70s by renowned photojournalist Robert Altman. The caption refers to me as the Beach Boys' manager. The photograph circulated through museums on the East Coast with the wrong information as

Backstage at the Fillmore West, with promoter Bill Graham—the Beach Boys were late; photo taken by (iconic 60s photographer) Robert Altman

part of an exposition on Jewish achievers in America. Of course, Bill Graham was the Jewish achiever.

Back in Topanga Canyon after an afternoon jam session, Mike Kowalski asked me if I played percussion. I said I did. He then asked me if I was interested in going on tour with the Beach Boys playing percussion. I said I was. I had never been a percussionist. I just knew how to slap the conga drums the right way and knew a few "tumbaos," particular Latin rhythms that Sabú Martínez had shown me back when we were playing at the Holiday Inn. Not to mention all the practice I had gotten when I was young on my school desk while pretending to be asleep. But I *was* entirely familiar with *Pet Sounds*, which required a fairly sophisticated level of orchestral percussion. Thus, I was confident I could do it. A decade earlier, taking the contrabassist position with a top jazz quintet proved to be a much more significant challenge. Playing percussion with the Beach Boys was a piece of cake for me.

I was thrilled to have such an exciting job. All I had to do was be there and play. Everything else was taken care of. Even a few months back, who would have thought my roommate Jack Rieley and I would meet on the road, hired by the same employer—the Beach Boys?

We all wanna be. The tragedy is how long we remain in that silly state of longing. The 1970s were a fresh start for me, and the prospect of California and the Beach Boys wasn't a shabby way to go, especially when I thought the new decade didn't have much to offer, at least in music and ideas, and especially after the cultural surge of the '60s. Disco and cocaine epitomized the '70s, along with ephemeral socializing around celebrities, fusion jazz, and ugly cars. I wasn't into any of it, but I could see it coming. I felt I had done it all, even more profoundly. Also, I resented the coming of disco music because it killed live music at the clubs, and the new flashy cocaine culture was going nowhere fast and didn't offer any substance or personal growth. As Mr. McGuire said to Benjamin Braddock in *The Graduate*, "There's a great future in plastics."

During my first four years with the Beach Boys, my participation was mostly local and scattered. In 1969 and 1970, the Beach Boys were mostly touring Australia and Europe, and by late 1970 I had moved to Mount Washington, built a recording studio, and was doing some touring with Wilson Pickett. In 1971, with the Beach Boys' return to North America, I was back on tour. We played mostly on the East Coast and some cities in the Midwest. In Montreal, we performed at the gorgeous Place des Arts concert hall. Later, returning to Montreal and Toronto was always a lot of fun. In Toronto, I befriended a group of theater actors, including Dan Aykroyd's brother, Peter, an avid vintage tie collector. When I got back to LA, I sent him my small collection of vintage ties.

In New York, performing at the Fillmore East and jamming with the Grateful Dead was amusing because a few years before, I would hang around those places and was too broke to get in. On that same tour, we also performed at the Schaefer Music Festival in New York's Central Park. On the same bill were Boz Scaggs, who opened the show, Kate Taylor (James Taylor's sister) billed as "Sister Kate," Carly Simon in her first national television appearance, and Ike and Tina Turner. At the end of the concert, the Beach Boys ripped it apart.

Playing the Beach Boys concert in Central Park was cathartic. The excitement of the magnitude of the event brought memories from a too-soon forgotten past roaming the streets of New York. Images of being homeless, hungry, and struggling raced through my mind while I watched the colorful spectacle of die-hard fans filling the park area. I found myself shifting between crippling painful past emotions to a liberating sense of joy. In all, I felt fortunate, a survivor.

In 1972, at a rehearsal in New York while I was still a percussionist with the Beach Boys, the horn section—composed of avid jazz players— had decided to stay and jam during a lunch break. The Beach Boys' pianist, Daryl Dragon, didn't play jazz, so the piano seat was vacant, and I took over the piano. When Carl Wilson and the other Beach Boys returned from lunch to the rehearsal hall, they heard me playing my ass off with the horn players—they had no clue I played piano, let alone jazz. I had met the Beach Boys socially with Jack Rieley back in 1969, when I recorded some of my songs at Brian's house in Bel Air. But that was an isolated event. At the time, I wasn't even thinking of touring with them.

After the jam Carl asked me to audition for the group. His words were: "If you can play that sophisticated music, I'd like to know what you can do with us. Have you played a Hammond organ before?" he asked. My reply was that I had been playing a Hammond D3 for the last eight years with my rock group the Living End. In addition, Carl was a fan of Wilson Pickett, and he was also impressed I had toured with him. In 1973, with certainty that Daryl Dragon was leaving the band to form Captain & Tennille, Carl called me to join the Beach Boys on Hammond organ and piano.

Being officially hired by the Beach Boys was for me a kind of shelter from the post-hippie era. And more so when the Beach Boys were in their metamorphosis to hipdom—the performances at Fillmore East and in Central Park in New York crystallized it. It is undeniable that a new era had started for the Beach Boys, which Jack Rieley had much to do with. There seems to be some misinformation about Jack's involvement concerning the Beach Boys' resurgence. Since Jack was my close friend and roommate in New York and now in LA, I know how it went; I was there. Jack rattled and swayed the Beach Boys out of *Let's Go Snarfing* to *Surf's Up*. The transformation was real but also brought conflict within the group—there was resistance on Mike Love's part for sophistication. Jack was brilliant but also manipulative. I would also give Jack credit for most of the significant emotional upheavals within the Beach Boys during his participation with the group—Jack had a knack for inducing unsolicited growing pains. But you can't take away that Jack Rieley revamped the Beach Boys' image to match the times—a hipper and more sophisticated image, which was at the time a much-needed endeavor for their survival. There was still a bit of an old tug-of-war at the time between the Beatles and the Beach Boys, competing for pop rock supremacy. Jack was well aware of that, plus there was a surge of newer players in the arena, both from the UK and the US, gaining tremendous popularity.

Going on the road was exciting. Suddenly having a limousine waiting to pick me up at the end of my driveway gave me a sense of freedom—leaving everything behind and going off on a new adventure. The Beach Boys planned every minute of our tour and executed it perfectly. The blueprint was the itinerary. It listed the venues by date, city, arrival time, name of the hotel, wake-up-call time, pickup time, soundcheck, showtime, and time of arrival back at the hotel, and even offered tips on restaurants open late and other useful and not-so-useful footnotes. The luggage would magically be waiting for us in our room.

Once at the venue, we'd find all the musical instruments set up and ready to go. When walking onto the stage, the crowd's roar was exhilarating—so much excitement, and from such a massive number of people! To me, the effect on the audience was the essence of it all. The rest was just having fun playing with both, the audience and the group having the time of their life.

The set always started with "California Girls." It began with the full band hitting the first four fanfare-type eleventh sustained chords preceding the song. Then, I established the beat on the Hammond B3, with a mid-tempo shuffle pattern on a B major chord for the first four bars. The vocals would then follow with the rest of the band. It was common to hear the roar of the crowd continuously throughout the first third of the show. We used the middle of the set to slow down the pace or experiment with new songs. Then we picked up the tempo again to a climax, playing the old hits and finishing off with "Fun, Fun, Fun." There'd be one, two, or three encores to appease a still insatiable, roaring crowd.

An emotional void always followed the big shows—a kind of melancholy that sometimes was challenging to manage. Taking part with your buddies in giving ten, fifty, or one hundred thousand people or more the time of their lives, but then it's suddenly over and you find yourself alone, created anxiety. It must have something to do with energy and the body's internal process. I assume it could happen with rock, jazz, or any music genre to a degree, and I also imagine it could happen in sports and after any other high-performance moments with a high yield of adrenaline.

After expending that kind of energy, going straight to bed is not an option. After the show, I always had a compelling urge for an afterglow, ideally with girls, for some kind of soiree, where there would be at least a fighting chance to end up in comforting company or find a place to eat or drink.

While on tour in Texas, one night after the concert, one of the other musicians and I were waiting for a taxi outside the hotel lobby to get a bite to eat. We heard a familiar whisper: "Hey, guys." We turned to see Brian Wilson wearing a robe and barefoot. Brian went on, "Are you guys getting some food...Can I come?" We consented. Somehow, he had escaped from the two male nurses traveling with him.

When Brian was persuaded to travel again in the mid-'70s with the Beach Boys, male nurses were hired to keep him on track. Brian had a history and tendencies of gluttony and excessive consumption of whatever came to him. He had some serious mental health issues, and the Beach Boys' management hired nurses, or more aptly bodyguards, who were supposed to be with him at all times.

The three of us took a cab and went to the only available option, a nearby Denny's. After I explained to the manager that Brian Wilson was with us (otherwise, they wouldn't have served him barefoot and just wearing a robe) the three of us sat in a booth and ordered.

My plate, steak and eggs, arrived at the table first. When I noticed Brian looking anxious and staring at my steak, I cut a piece of lean meat next to a large and solid blob of grease and offered it to him. Instead, he reached over my plate, grabbed the hunk of fat, and gulped it down in one shot. At least I got to eat the lean part of the steak.

Earlier that same evening, while in one of the hotel's elevators, a server got in, balancing a large tray filled with large green cocktails. It got my attention, and I counted ten of them. I asked the waiter what those drinks were and where the party was. He said they were Grasshoppers and that they were all ordered by Mr. Brian Wilson.

Where were the nurses?

To deviate from the sameness of concert touring the way we had been doing it, someone had a brilliant idea: to pick a region, in this case the East Coast, and use motor homes to get to the venues. We would divide the RVs between two, four, or more people. In our camper was Blondie Chaplin, I think Ricky Fataar, my girlfriend Jan, and me. Stocked with a copious amount of hashish, we took turns driving.

Jan and I had met at the first gig I ever did in Los Angeles with a rock group at a small club in Orange County. I didn't have a car then, and I don't even remember how I got to the club. But it was far, and I needed a ride back. The stage was small, but high. I met Jan during the break after the first set, and soon we were in her car making out in the parking lot. She mentioned that she had been watching my crotch while I was playing up on the stage. I realized then that California girls don't waste any time—or words. Jan gave me a ride home to Mount Washington and stayed with me that evening. At some point she revealed that she was married. I was never sure what kind of marriage she had, but we remained living together for four years.

Driving through the lush countryside of the eastern states in the motor homes was beautiful and relaxing. Jan was a lot of fun to be with, and I brought her along frequently on tours. We had an inflatable boat we had purchased on the way at a Walmart, and we would stop to spend the night at beautiful lakes, which there were plenty of. We used a map to pick the most scenic routes. A cool thing about it was that we traveled independently from the other band members and were able to choose our own route, smoke a lot of hashish, and get lost along the way. Also, we didn't know much about motor homes. One night after a college concert, on our way back to the RV, we noticed a group of fans surrounding the camper and standing on urine- and fecal-contaminated water that overflowed from under the camper. We scrambled out of there with great embarrassment—leaving behind our digestion from the trip. No one had had a clue that septic tanks need to be drained. Lesson learned.

Appreciating the full spectrum of being with the Beach Boys while performing with them is like looking at the forest from the trees. It was a job, and my focus was clear—it had to be done right. Most of the time I had tremen-

With girlfriend Jan and dog

dous fun playing their music, but I wasn't really enjoying the experience. The single best Beach Boys appreciation moment for me was the time they gathered backstage (Brian, Carl, Al, Mike, and Bruce) to sing "Their Hearts Were Full of Spring," a cappella. The version of the song by the Four Freshmen was a favorite of Brian's, and the group's innovative vocal style was a formative influence on him. They sang it just for the fun of it, and it stopped me in my tracks. Suddenly I found myself being a spectator—they were doing something I couldn't do or participate in. It was the Beach Boys at their purest, and I felt extremely fortunate at that moment. All I did was enjoy it!

Being on the road was fun and exciting, but spending time back home between touring became more meaningful. Fortunately, the Beach Boys had a steady pace of two to three weeks off before hitting the road, and that was perfect. I had other friends, musicians who were also touring with other groups. We would often play at the studio I had built at my house in Mount Washington. It was magical living there; sometimes you'd hear the echo of some hot jazz or other music coming from somewhere in the canyon or from one of the many dirt side roads. One time I heard an incredibly exciting African drum ensemble echoing throughout the canyon. It took me about a week, but by following the sounds of the drums I finally found them. There were about a half dozen

African musicians living in a secluded house off the beaten path. There they had all kinds of African drums and percussion, including an impressive ten-foot-long drum carved out of a tree trunk lying on the floor. In my conversation with them I remember a metronome constantly ticking. They mentioned that they always kept the metronome ticking, even while they slept.

Eventually, the jamming at my studio morphed into a group called Your Own Space. It started as a jazz trio with bassist Putter Smith and drummer Sam Provenzano, mostly playing at a winery called The Winery, on San Fernando Road by the railroad tracks, down the hill from the southwest side of Mount Washington. But as other musicians kept joining, it became more eclectic. I wouldn't use the word "fusion" because we turned out funkier and more unique than the term "fusion" would imply. The repertoire was mostly my compositions, which I often wrote specifically for the ensemble.

While the tours continued at a steady pace, often with three-week breaks in between, Jan and I eventually had a falling out and we split apart. We had both ended up being unfaithful to each other, and the breakup played hard on my emotions. I was still living in Mount Washington, and I recall myself on the piano drowning in regrets. That was the moment I wrote one of my most gut-wrenching ballads, "All Alone." It was a unique experience. The words and the music all came together within the duration of the song—in other words, it took me the three-and-a-half-minute length of the song to compose it. It was the real deal—the outpouring of my soul.

In 1978 I produced "All Alone," along with "Constant Companion," "It's Not Too Late," and "Under the Moonlight," for the *Bambu* project with Dennis Wilson singing the lead.[4] Unfortunately, I had to withdraw from the project when Dennis's drug abuse—a major contributor to his death five years later—got out of hand.

The original four songs I produced got rereleased multiple times, but it wasn't until 2018, with my own *In My Soul* album, that I finally rerecorded and completed the songs the way I had always thought they should be.

---

4 "All Alone" was released later in 1998 on the Beach Boys' *Endless Harmony* soundtrack album.

"All Alone" Lyrics
By Carli Muñoz

If I could live my life again
I'd never do you wrong
You better know, oh

If I just had a chance again
To spend my life with you
You know, it's in my soul, oh

I'd be standin' by your side
Not to ever let you go

If I only had a chance to live a life that we belong
Would I be strong?
If I didn't take the time and never tried to understand
Ooh, my love, where it's gone

In the sadness that our love has left behind
I'm standing all alone

If I could stand to love again
Plant another seed, you know,
Well, would it grow, oh
If I must share my life again
With all the love I have for you, my love
Well, would it grow? Where would it go?

Ooh, my love
Well, it's gone
In the sadness that I love is left behind
I'm standing all alone

All alone

I met my first wife, Brenda, in Vancouver, British Columbia, in late
1975, at the end of a Pacific Northwest tour. I know this won't sound

"politically correct," but beginning in San Francisco, I always noticed and welcomed the progressive change in young women's demeanors and looks—at least compared to LA. The further north we went—Oregon, Washington state, and British Columbia—the less stylized, more natural, and healthy they looked. People in general farther north just seemed more down to earth and less concerned about their looks. I did meet interesting women on that tour, but when I met Brenda in Vancouver, I knew somehow that she was going to be the mother of my children.

On the evening after the first of two concerts programmed for Vancouver, one of the guys from the band, Elmo Peeler, and I went to a downtown Vancouver nightclub called Pharaoh's. Brenda was there at the club with some friends, and as soon as we walked in past the front door, she came up to us and said, "Can I help you? Let me find you a table." The funny thing is that, as it turns out, she used to work there, but she wasn't working that night. She commented right away: "You guys aren't from here—let me help you out."

My bandmate asked Brenda to dance. I stayed back watching her. When they came back to the table, I asked my friend if he didn't mind me having a dance with her. That was it! Later I found out from Brenda that the gentlemanly gesture of me politely asking my friend is what truly turned her on toward me.

I knew she wasn't a groupie because she hadn't gone to the concert and didn't even know that the Beach Boys were in town—the less she associated me with the Beach Boys, for me, the better. Everything about her looks attracted me to no end. She was radiant and fresh, and looked super healthy. Her eyes were green, and her hair was long, thick, and golden-brown, and naturally straight with a slight natural wave. Everything about her body, from the milky tone of her white skin to her Venusian body type, denoted fertility, good health, and self-care. She also displayed intelligence and kindness along with a solid maternal demeanor—I'd found the one, I thought.

The next evening I brought her along to a second concert, where she met all the guys in the group. Later after the concert, Carl said to me in the limo, "Carli, you are going to marry that woman."

Within a few weeks, the tour ended and I was back home in Mount Washington. Brenda then flew to LA to spend a couple of weeks with me. From the studio on my cliffhanger house, which had large picture windows overlooking Los Angeles, we could see a beautiful lone tree down the steep hill. It was there under that tree where our first child was conceived—somehow we later knew it. After the two weeks together, Brenda went back home. It was then only a few more weeks until I got the news that Brenda was pregnant. My reaction was excitement—I asked her to move in with me in Los Angeles.

Soon after we were living together, we decided to get married. I still was living in the hills of Mount Washington in my idyllic hippie house with the recording studio with a view. But, in the spirit of settling down, we bought a beautiful five-bedroom 1916 Greene & Greene bungalow style house in an affluent neighborhood with large front and backyards, in Pasadena. Close to nine months after we met, our first child, Marcel, was born. We really wanted a second child, perhaps a girl. Instead, about a year later, we had a set of identical twin boys. As much as we adored and welcomed their arrival, we still wanted a girl. Three and a half years later, Melanie was born.

Before Melanie was born, Your Own Space, the group I had formed to play in between tours back home in LA, regularly played a small circuit of underground clubs to a faithful crowd around the LA area. The Blah Blah Cafe in Studio City and the Come Back In in Venice Beach were some. We'd often alternate with Al Jarreau and Rickie Lee Jones before they were "discovered." Sometimes we would join each other on stage. After the sets, we all got paid by passing the hat. In those days the small clubs didn't and couldn't pay for entertainment, so all we could do was pass a hat around after the set. We would then divide the spoils equally among ourselves. I remember a time splitting $16 of a total night's income among six musicians. It was the same for Al Jarreau and for Rickie Lee Jones. The playing was always one hundred percent passion.

This reminds me of a call I once got from my dear friend Duke McVinnie at 2 AM. I was with my family at home in Pasadena sleeping when Duke called to ask me if I would record a demo for Rickie Lee Jones—at my house. Duke knew about the recording studio I had put together in the maid's room. I said something like, "Sure, now I'm awake—let's just do it." Rickie and I knew each other from the same club circuit we were playing, and Duke, who had taken an interest in helping Rickie, was the bass player in my group.

When they showed up at my house not long after the call, I had the studio already prepared. I had turned the bathroom of the maid's quarters-now studio into an isolation booth, where I had set up two mikes for acoustic guitar and one for vocals, a room mike, and the headphones for monitoring. I sat Rickie with her acoustic guitar on the toilet, rolled tape, and off we went. We recorded "The Last Chance Texaco," "Easy Money," "Young Blood," and "After Hours"—the songs that would get Rickie Lee Jones an unusually hefty $6 million album deal with Warner Brothers that same year. No new single artist had gotten an amount that large as a primary budget before. No, she didn't thank me, and I didn't charge. I just handed her the ten-inch reel of the direct-to-two-track recording, and she just asked on the way out, "Do you know where I can score some smack?"

Al Jarreau and I had met much earlier, at a gig we were both doing at a club in Hollywood called the Bitter End West. My group performance was back in the principal room, and Al and his small group—just electric piano and a drummer—were in the front. During a break, I peeked into where he was, and that was it—it was the best jazz vocalizing and performing I had ever seen and heard. I also loved his writing. From that moment on, we became friends. He always showed an interest in my songwriting and asked me to join his touring band twice. One of those times was outside of Donte's Club in Studio City, while I was on break from a performance with Your Own Space. We had played to a loaded audience—it was a magical evening. That night, along with Al Jarreau, in the audience were all the guys from the Jazz Crusaders and most of the group Chicago. Also, jazz trumpeter Freddie Hubbard, who that evening asked me to join his quartet. Sadly, I had to decline both offers because I had just renewed a contract with the Beach Boys.

During the break at that performance, I got a note from one of the waitresses saying, "Jimmy Smith wants to see you." At the time, I was still engaged in conversation with Jarreau and Hubbard, and I quickly dismissed the note. I figured it had come from no one I knew, or from a guitar player who used to hang around the group a lot whose name was also Jimmy Smith.

The break was over, and we played another set. As we were leaving the stage, the waitress returned with another note: "JIMMY SMITH WANTS TO SEE YOU!" This time the waitress pointed across the low-lit room. The first thing I saw was a mouthful of teeth floating about six feet and then some inches in the air that looked pretty darn familiar.

In a split second, memories of some of the most transcendental and gravity-defying keyboard playing I've ever heard filled my mind! As if in one quantum leap, I found myself being grabbed by this towering figure and lifted off the ground. My sense of joy was overwhelming. Still holding me, he said, "Who do you like, man...Herbie or McCoy?" I was a little thrown off by the question because I liked them both. In fact, Herbie Hancock and McCoy Tyner were among my favorite contemporary keyboard stylists.

"Well, uh...I like them both, but...McCoy."

"Ohhhh, noooo, man..." he said. Then, after a sudden ambiguous pause, he looked me straight in the eye and said intensely, "Yeahhh... That's the one, man. That's the one!"

I suppose he had been listening and noticed some of my influences.

Once we got through that unusual and exhilarating first encounter, we hung out all night talking about music and playing piano. This man *only* talked about music; this man *was* music. That same evening, he invited me to go with him to his supper club in San Fernando Valley. I remember his club as cozy and dark. If there was a bar or tables, I would never know because my focus and attention as I walked in went straight to a little stage straight ahead and slightly above the ground, which cradled the Hammond organ that has brought so much joy to a whole generation of jazz lovers. There was probably a set of drums next to the organ, but I don't distinctly remember seeing it.

Jimmy took me straight to the back of the stage, where he had an old spinet piano facing the back of the stage. He sat and played the piano, and there we just carried on for the rest of the evening having fun and sharing musical ideas.

As if it wasn't enough to have been touched by Jimmy Smith's music throughout my formative jazz years, this most special event sealed the man in my soul. I wrote this epitaph when Smith passed away:

Jimmy Smith, 1928-2005
King of the B3 Hammond Organ
Long live the King's memory!

A few years after Al Jarreau and I met, we'd occasionally bump into each other. By then he was playing larger venues, and he invited me and my girlfriend Jan to a concert at the Civic Auditorium in Santa Monica where he was opening for the funky horn-driven group Tower of Power. Jan had a brand-new gold Corvette that her husband had recently bought for her. On the day of the concert, as we drove down a steep hill on our way to our house in Mount Washington, Jan was having a jealous fit about something I had said, and we got into an argument. I was behind the wheel when she shoved her foot over my foot on the accelerator pedal, and like a raging missile, we crashed into our little wooden house on the side of the hill. Thankfully, no one was hurt. I remember my concern was the cats. I had ten of them, but they were unharmed. The Corvette looked like a crumpled piece of paper. We still had a show to go to that evening in Santa Monica, about twenty miles from Mount Washington. I called a tow truck to get the car, and Jan and I caught a ride to the auditorium in the front seat with the driver. We arrived in time for Al Jarreau's performance.

Our social life back home in LA was still sometimes Beach Boys related. Brian's wife then, Marylin, asked me to give piano lessons to their daughters, Carnie and Wendy, and I did. Maybe that bit of insight I gave came in handy later on when they formed the Grammy-nominated, million-selling act Wilson Phillips. On occasion, I used Brian's home studio to experiment with some of my songs, and other times I took part in close family activities.

I don't remember the occasion, but I remember going to meet Marilyn's parents, Irving and Mae, at their home. If I well recall, they lived near Fairfax in West Hollywood and were super kind and hospitable. I might have even had matzo ball soup. It's hard to forget the enormous Jewish medallion Irving wore around his neck—I can still picture Irving with his medal, hair combed back, and with his confident and kind leaning-forward demeanor. Another time, Billy Hinsche kindly invited me for dinner with Carl Wilson and his wife, and Billy's sister Annie, at their parents' home in Beverly Hills. Simple family events among friends were always heartwarming and pleasantly remembered.

My preference was always to enjoy time with my new family between tours, but Dennis Wilson and I would sometimes end up together for one thing or another. I was later his partner in crime for the renowned surprise party serenade that Dennis gave Fleetwood Mac's Christine McVie on the lawn at her house in Beverly Hills on her birthday. Part of the plan was to play "You Are So Beautiful" backed up by a piano and chamber orchestra. I was to play a grand piano set on the grass, along with the woodwinds and the strings section, and Dennis would sing to Christine. That was the plan. We rehearsed it, and it sounded great with Jimmy Haskell's excellent arranging and conducting. But after all the extravagance, pomp, and anticipation, Dennis got distracted, throwing people in the pool and doing other stupid stuff, and forgot to sing.

I had just bought a Camcorder. It was an early JVC unit with a separate camera. That same week, Dennis and Christine McVie leased John Wayne's private yacht, the *Wild Goose*, a 136-foot minesweeper converted into a luxury vessel, to spend the weekend sailing around Catalina Island. After a smooth sail from Marina Del Rey, we anchored near the island with Avalon always in sight. Stevie Nicks and other celebrities were seen also spending the weekend boating in the same area. Christine and Dennis invited me to come along with Brenda and a handful of close friends, of whom I only remember Ed Roach, Chris Kable, and Bill Oster being there. Ed Roach later reminded me of a scene I shot: "[Dennis] came out of some girl's cabin at sunrise. He was wearing John Wayne's peacoat, his admiral's cap, and his jockey shorts! He did a whole bit into your camera, saying how everything fits so well. Then he opened his coat and said, 'All except his jockeys. They're too tight in the crotch!' He then proceeded to do a toot, fumbled with a bottle, and almost lost it overboard!"

It was a quirky but memorable weekend. And there are many more silly moments, some precious and some infamous, from that weekend recorded on video, collecting dust in some old box in a closet somewhere in my house.

XVII

THE STAR.

THE STAR

The Star reminds you that the universe is working in your favor and encourages you to have confidence in where you are being taken. It brings a message of renewal, optimism, and inspiration. It reminds you to have faith and belief in yourself as you go through any challenge in life.

An impactful back-at-home event was when the Wilsons' mom, Audree, and Carl's wife, Annie, came up to me excitedly about a seminar training they had just done. Carl, Dennis, and Ricky Fataar had also taken the training. It was EST, a transformational seminar that had originated in San Francisco and earned tremendous popularity by the mid-'70s. Audree and Annie were convincing, and it tickled my curiosity. The first two weeks of basic training took place in a convention hall and were attended by 150 people from all walks of life. Then I went head-on and did what they called the advanced training, with a smaller group, which was much more intense than the basic.

Although they were completely different, I would dare say that there was a transcendental quality to the EST experience that was similar to LSD. And like the LSD experience, EST was also an experiential process that is impossible to describe in terms of its essence. While LSD is basically a psychoactive chemical substance that triggers profound changes in perception—but in a Russian roulette fashion, depending on the mental and emotional state of the individual who takes it—EST was brilliantly designed for a transformational purpose, and it was guided throughout. In my experience with EST, the level of intensity and depth at a given moment and the permanent transformational effect are not to be underestimated. Although at different times, and in much different

101

ways, both the LSD and the EST experiences produced tremendous value in my life.

After EST I did another powerful but smaller-scale seminar called The Game. The Game was also transformational. It originated from an actors' workshop in the epicenter of Hollywood. While it had a similar aim as the EST seminar, The Game took a much different approach. The Game used video cameras throughout the intense two-week workshop. The trainers were actors, and many of the participants were actors as well. Even if EST was a major shift in the contextual mind, The Game took it a few steps further, "showing you" as you are seen by others. We were assigned challenging individual exercises, which were filmed throughout the whole process and then played back to the whole group. There, escape through subterfuge was impossible.

But EST certainly got my full attention. There was a substantial amount of purging of the past on my part that otherwise would have continued running my life, especially coming from the outcome of my past relationships. One of the big issues I was carrying was an episodic relationship I had had from the beginning of my teens, which had turned burdensome. It was all about a girl named Carol Banderas (the name has been changed). She was a beautiful girl who also lived in Ocean Park. Everyone admired her natural beauty. I would see her around sometimes at local parties and proms, but her sinister mom, whom Carol lived with, jealously guarded her.

Carol was not the Barbie-doll type; instead she had a unique and sophisticated beauty. Her geometrical, angular features defined her square face, framed by her straight black hair and blunt bangs—or pulled back, exposing her noble forehead. Her skin was a light olive shade, her eyes were a piercing forest green, and her body was perfectly carved. Carol was a little older than me by a few months, which at the time was significant, but I remember having some light conversation with her. For the green larva I was then, that alone was a triumph. We had a brief discussion about cars and I remember her saying she liked the Jaguar XK120—good taste! It was a warning that she might be high maintenance. That only excited me more, and the conquest became more challenging. She was on my mind continuously.

Her mother restricted Carol's movement, making it impossible to visit her, let alone take her on a date. Carol, who was still underage, managed to get a job as a flight attendant with Eastern Airlines to get away from her mother. She rented an apartment in Queens, where she would stay during layovers. One time at a party back home in Ocean Park, I arranged with Carol to fly to New York to visit her during one of her layovers. I must have been mature looking, as I was still in my early teens, and my parents didn't mind. I would stay with a guy named Jerry, an older graphic designer friend who lived in the city, and from Jerry's loft I would go to see Carol at her apartment in Queens. It was on a winter night, it was snowing, and it took me a while to find her apartment from an address she had scribbled and handed me during our earlier encounter in Ocean Park.

A tingling sensation suffused my body as I knocked on the door of her apartment. Many self-sabotaging thoughts were going through my head: Am I doing the right thing? Will she be there? Will she receive me? Is this a foolish idea? Every negative thought went through my mind until she opened the door and welcomed me.

The apartment was cozy and had character. We sat on a couch in the small living room, and she might have offered me something to drink. It was already late, and I felt lucky being sheltered from the snowstorm I could glimpse through the front windows. Our conversation about her job, being away, and my stay in the city was timid but pleasant. Still, my feelings of awkwardness remained throughout our small talk.

The air felt dry from the heater, and there was a slight but familiar smell of burnt dust, possibly from the furnace. Carol sat close to me on the couch, close enough where I thought I could smell her hair—I almost tried. My heart was racing. I felt there was a mutual attraction, and the moments were flowing. As the small talk shifted to a more personal whisper of how glad we were to see each other, it only took the slightest movement forward and our lips met. We melted into a long, soft, and awakened exploration of unexpected pleasure—our tongues would gently meet, playing hide and seek. Then, I knew there was a heaven.

At some point, gravity took over, doing its work by turning the axis we lay on, stretching our entangled bodies into a horizontal position on the couch. We were in the heat of further exploration when Carol suddenly, in a blunt quantum leap, was now sitting on the sofa with a half-smile on her upper lip. She coldly offered to call a taxi.

I was in shock, confused, and internally devastated—someone had poured a tank of ice water over my head. I declined the cab, but I got up, restored my composure, put my winter coat on, nodded a disheartened but polite farewell, and disappeared into the storm.

Hours later, after I got back to Jerry's downtown loft, I shared the full scope of my bitter disappointment with him. I then realized how young and naive I was. For a moment, I wanted to be my mature and unscathed friend. I could agree with being prudent, taking it slow, and choosing not to go any further—but was there a need for cruelty? I would have never gone further than allowed, that night or any other. It's a matter of respect—for the other person, but also for yourself. We could have stopped and gone on being friendly, but perhaps wrongly, I sensed in the way it ended misplaced power and the desire to humiliate me.

About a year later, having gotten over the incident, I bumped into Carol at a friend's house party in Ocean Park. She approached me, and we started hanging out some. She seemed curious about tripping. We talked about it, and Carol suggested that we take LSD together. By then I might have dropped a respectable amount of acid and had been to the other side of sanity, faced my ego, and come back, but I was still green and wasn't ready to deal with someone else's trip, which didn't even cross my mind—it should have.

We took the acid at a friend's apartment in Isla Verde on Inga Street, half a block from the beach. We were on the second floor on a large balcony, in the front where there was a hammock. The friend who lived in that apartment didn't interfere. I had tripped there before with other people, and it was a pleasant vibe. We each took a tab. I was lying in the hammock with Carol sitting or standing nearby—I recall a gentle ocean breeze, and it was already nighttime.

At first, Carol and I were facing each other—quiet but wide-eyed with the anticipation that comes before facing the unknown. As the acid started taking effect, all I remember is that Carol began acting overtly "sexy." In my hyperconscious state, I perceived her actions as utterly grotesque and not sexy at all—she was making facial gestures and body movements that seemed grossly warped and incongruent with her. Carol reacted to my reaction of being appalled, which made her paranoid; worse, it must have crushed her inflated but fragile ego. It became a destructive loop of reaction after reaction—it must have been devastating to her. I still remember how her face became unhinged, and her seeing my response to what I was seeing made it even worse—it seemed like an infinite noxious loop. None of it was intentional. We were both caught in a horrible spiral that neither one of us could have expected or controlled.

It all got to a point where Carol could not deal with it any longer. Then I noticed she wasn't there. I started looking for her frantically, asking other people if they had seen her. We had driven to my friend's apartment together, and I felt responsible for her well-being. By then, I wished I would have had better control of my reactions to her, but given the circumstances it had been impossible; we were both in altered states of consciousness, transparent and out of control. We didn't speak a word while the loop of reactions was happening—it must have all occurred within three to four seconds, maybe less.

I never found Carol that evening. Two days later, I heard from someone that she got home that night and had a terrible exchange with her mother. I can't even imagine what it was like, and I remained concerned, knowing how a traumatic discussion with her Cimmerian mother could cause further damage. A few weeks later, I saw Carol driving by in her car, and I flagged her down. She stopped the car, and I tried talking with her, but she never looked me in the eyes. Her gaze was distant. I wondered then if the effect on her had been permanent or passing. I hoped for the best, but knowing of her and her mother's situation, I feared the worst.

One evening, a few weeks after the nocuous acid trip with Carol, my parents and I were in our family room when an older fubsy lady dressed in black stormed into our house accompanied by a tall gentleman wearing a suit. She was screaming at us while pointing at me. "He ruined her life! He ruined my daughter's life!" My dad got alarmed and asked her to calm down and to explain what it was all about. She went on, charging, "Your son drugged my daughter and messed her up!" At that point, my dad suggested that she hold her horses.

The tall, thin gentleman with her was a psychiatrist and gently asked to speak with me in private. We went to the living room and I dominated the conversation, letting him know that I deeply regretted Carol's condition. I was remorseful. I hadn't had the wisdom to foresee or avoid the event. Then I mentioned that it was *Carol* who suggested taking LSD—and that she was an adult (LSD wasn't illegal). Besides, it was her experience. I explained to the psychiatrist that LSD is a neutral agent, that what she had experienced played to the fears, the notions, and the crap her mother had put into her head. He agreed, and that was the end of the visit. I did get the third degree from my dad afterward. But my dad trusted me, and after a few words of caution he left it alone.

Still, I always felt responsible. It felt as if I had murdered someone. I felt so bad! I wish I had had more wisdom handling a situation like that, but I was a neophyte and dealing with my own inexperience. After that, I didn't see or hear from Carol for many years. I always wanted to see her, and if she was open to it, let her know that no one had control over the effect of the LSD and that she didn't have to worry about anything. I wanted that opportunity so much and never lost hope. Meanwhile, I carried a sense of guilt that was almost crippling.

The EST experience was intense. It gave participants the opportunity to get a good look at themselves and take responsibility for their choices. They could then get rid of the barriers and excuses that had prevented them from living transparent, productive, loving, and joyous lives. It helped me to process some of the guilt issues I had with Carol, and I got to work out other issues I hadn't resolved in the past. It was all timely. I kept getting more involved. I also did special leadership programs and staffing. The benefits were massive, but the moment it started feeling like I was in a cult, I disassociated myself, which has been my principle throughout my entire fool's journey—not to attach myself to anything in order to keep growing.

Undeniably, the benefits were obvious. But over the years, I've witnessed some people do the "basic" training alone and misinterpret its essence. In some instances, I've seen more harm done than good. Dennis Wilson might have been an example. Part of what you "get" in the basic training is the relative dichotomy of "good and bad." When you go through the advanced training and so on, it balances out to a more complete, holistic, and responsible perspective. Being exposed to the relative aspect of good and bad, without understanding the full scope, conveniently appealed to Dennis—it gave him license to get in deeper trouble. A gradual wave of "justified" mischief became a pattern for Dennis that would eventually strip from him everything he loved, including his life.

Back home between Beach Boys tours, there was always plenty of social action at the Chateau Marmont, my old stomping grounds, and around its vicinity in the West Hollywood Hills. When partying in LA, "When in Rome, do as the Romans do" was pretty much my motto then, but with a twist: "Feel as the Romans feel." I would get the gist and enjoy the high-profile company, but I didn't have to do every stupid thing they did. Sometimes I found myself in the company of celebrities like Marisa Berenson, Priscilla Presley, Penelope Tree, and Bill Wyman, but it was best experienced in the context of "It's just another day—hello and goodbye." Of course, rubbing elbows with known celebs is quite a bit of fun, but in truth, no more fun than perhaps eating an amazing taco with a buddy near skid row—or anywhere off the beaten track.

I think that what we put a special value on is the memory. It is the memory that others also get to enjoy when you tell the story. It's not the same telling my grandchildren, "I hung out with superstars and top Hollywood models," compared to telling them, "I had a delicious taco from a truck somewhere in downtown LA." But the actual experience is not much different in how you feel at the moment.

Elton John had been hanging out with the Beach Boys on one of our East Coast tours, so I was invited to a party at his Beverly Hills mansion celebrating Elton and his protégé, Kiki Dee, having a No. 1 hit with "Don't Go Breaking My Heart." The party was just as you would expect it to be: completely over the top. Each table on the vast lawn had a bowl full of cocaine as its centerpiece. Luckily, I didn't feel the need to get blasted to fit in. I had been down that road before, a decade earlier.

I liked Kiki Dee. She was traveling with us and opened a few shows for the Beach Boys. I remember one time in Saratoga Springs, New York, we were all staying at the hotel on the grounds and partying big time. I had a breakfast date set up with Kiki for the next morning. But as I left the room—after some serious partying with groupies 'til sunrise, and from my appearance it must have been obvious—Kiki was morning-fresh and heading toward me down the corridor where I had no escape. She greeted me with a kiss, but by the look on her face, there was no breakfast to be had!

One of the least exciting things about touring was the bland uniformity of the towns, airports, and hotels, especially in the Midwest. To reap some benefit from being in this region, I sparked an interest in collecting antiques and handcrafted knives. We had rental cars available, and I knew where to find the most notable knife makers. These master craftsmen usually worked out of their homes in converted garages in rural areas. It was a refreshing way to get out of the hotel routine and do something different out in the country, especially getting a real taste of grassroots living and hanging out with traditional folks. One time I ran into David Crosby, of Crosby, Stills & Nash, who was also a knife collector. He wanted to buy a knife I had that was the only match for his rare "swing folder," a pair from a brief but historic collaboration between Bob Loveless and Barry B. Wood. I was into collecting as well, so I chose not to sell mine.

In contrast, arriving in cities like New York City, San Francisco, New Orleans, and Chicago provided a greater variety of options. In New York, there was never a dull moment. Local personalities who were fans of the Beach Boys would often drop in to entertain us. One time John Belushi took us to his cozy Blues Bar on Greenwich and Warren, with an old jukebox that was his pride and joy playing everything from Sam and Dave to hardcore punk. The place was vibrant, with lots of people and typical fiddling conversation. It reminded me of Al's Bar, the West Coast's oldest punk club, across from where I had a loft on Traction and Hewitt in downtown LA. There were amplifiers and some other musical instruments, and you could jam. The Blues Bar was the where Dan Aykroyd and John Belushi developed their Blues Brothers act in the late '70s.

Another time, after our concert, Andy Warhol approached me backstage at Radio City Music Hall and invited me to come to his studio, the Factory. I refused—something I've been questioned about by many of those I've shared the story with. When he asked, my mind immediately raced to, "Why me?" At the time, I was still rebuilding my life from the drug scene and debauchery in New York in the '60s, and much of it ran through my mind—I still felt somewhat vulnerable at the time. I was aware of who Warhol was and had an idea of what his world was like. Besides what I knew from the media, I had additional insight from Chuck Wein, the associate of Andy Warhol I'd befriended in LA in 1969. The invitation was solemn rather than casual; it evoked a familiar dilemma of potential fame, but at a price—a high one. Unfortunately, or perhaps fortunately, that evening I said I had other plans—never a dull moment in the Big Apple!

In Boston the night before our concert, musician and producer Andy Paley, a close personal friend of the Beach Boys, threw an after-hours party for the group. It was the most amazing party. Andy was living in a house built in 1905. The gorgeous property was located on Beacon Hill and was owned by the Museum of Fine Arts. The party went on all night. We were on an East Coast tour, and during a break the following day, we all met again in New York at Max's Kansas City on Park Avenue. Andy Paley and his brother Jonathan, Dana Buckley, Ricky Fataar, and I came along. William Burroughs, Lou Reed, and numerous members of the glam rock scene were on hand that night and gave the club its usual pizzazz. Later on, some of us ended up at Studio 54, where we watched the giant half-moon in all its glitter scoop a toot of cocaine amid an overt display of private parts with couples openly fucking at the gallery of the gods to the beat of disco music. We were on tour, so we only had two nights in the city—two nights better forgotten!

In 1975, Elton John headlined an all-day concert at London's Wembley Stadium with the Beach Boys, Joe Walsh, and the Eagles. David Cassidy was in our limo. Best known for portraying Keith Partridge of TV's *The Partridge Family*, he was the teen idol of the moment and at the height of his fame. When we arrived at Wembley, the fans went crazy. I could only imagine an antediluvian frenzy looking like that! It was scary because they were all over the vehicle with us stuck inside and nowhere to go. "Damn, the Beach Boys are so popular here!" I said, but we soon learned it was David Cassidy who the fans were reacting to. David had been traveling with us on a US tour and stayed for the UK dates. He was a great guy to hang out with, and we had tremendous amounts of fun on the road. When we finally arrived, Elton John, Paul McCartney, and other high-profile rock 'n' rollers were backstage. Later, McCartney wandered into the dressing trailer, backstage where I was, looking for "the boys." We had a small chat, mostly about the whereabouts of Carl and Dennis and whether Brian was with them. Wembley had turned into Penny Lane!

The routine backstage while waiting to perform wasn't always so glamorous. Most of the time it was monotonous and made us a little antsy. We'd have to get creative, which sometimes got us into a bit of trouble, mostly when Brian was around. One time before the show, Brian found a bottle of Robitussin with codeine that Carl, who had a cold, had left on top of a locker. With no one taking notice (except me), Brian grabbed it and instantly gulped the whole thing in one shot. The infamous Dr. Eugene Landy was there, supposedly "looking after Brian," but to no avail. Dr. Landy's presence always made matters worse. Landy had isolated Brian from his brothers, and even his mother, Audree, and the rest of the group. Besides that, he was doing all kinds of unethical and horrible stuff with royalties and other issues.

Carl Wilson was the most sensible of the brothers. His primary concern was to keep the music at the highest level, and he was also the peacekeeper. Carl concerned himself with the group's image and general well-being. From a young age, Dennis enjoyed pulling pranks on people. Not everyone enjoyed them, and no one was spared from his shenanigans. Even Al Jardine, a co-founder of the group who did his best to stay out of Dennis's way, got bullied. Dennis used to call Al "Lightweight" and mocked him by kneeling on a pair of shoes and saying "This is Al" in a tiny voice.

Dennis and I met in the middle. We started doing pranks on each other. Dennis wouldn't miss a chance to poke at me, and I didn't lag too far behind. One day, Dennis invited a super-cute girl traveling with the group—she was gathering stories for some publication—to come up to his room. I suppose he invited her under the pretext of being interviewed. Dennis suddenly had a brief meeting to attend to downstairs in the lobby, so he excitedly asked me (we had connecting suites at the hotel) to let her into his suite. I said, "Of course, Dennis!" Looking for a way to get back at him (I owed him one), I saw the leftovers of a plate of chili beans left from the night before outside the door. I picked up the chili beans and dumped them in his toilet, didn't flush, and left the bathroom door wide open with the light turned on. The rest is up to the imagination. I let the young and beautiful interviewer in from my adjacent suite, led her to Dennis's room, and said, "Make yourself at home. Dennis was just here and will be back in a short while." He didn't forgive me for that one!

I paid the price—but the saga continued another time while backstage waiting for our show to begin. I brought Dennis a Heineken beer, which he liked, but earlier I had pissed into the bottle. This time I had to run for my life.

Sometimes the tours seemed long, and out of boredom we acted like kids having fun over the silliest things—we had to keep our sanity. One of those was a daring, stupid thing Ed Carter and I concocted. The challenge was to see if we could answer with a stone face "I don't care" to anyone who would come to us with a compliment. I know...

horrible! But that's how boring it could get. We did it several times, but I'll never forget how we did it to a lovely man holding hands with his little daughter. True to the spirit of that silly challenge, and regretfully, we did it anyway—that was the last time.

We even made wacky films to kill time. Someone had brought us a video camera. This was in my early touring days. It was huge, and it was still only black-and-white. It had a thick umbilical cord with a space-like backpack attached on its end for the reel-to-reel video recorder. It was one of the first portable video camera-recorder combos. The first film we did was called *Big Dick Bonnaroo*. Carl Wilson was "Big Dick," and I was "Joey," a thug, and we had the participation of a dozen female groupies. I can't recall Dennis's role, but he had one (probably in the bathroom casting the groupies), and Billy Hinsche may have been the cameraman. The film content was entirely legal—well, sort of. But before the tour was over, Carl ordered the footage destroyed.

Unfortunately, on-the-road pranks and silly movies became a thing of the past, and more disturbing events became more frequent. A lot of it had to do with the tumultuous relationship between Dennis and Mike Love. I was napping once mid-flight in the back of the plane when I was suddenly awoken by Carl's manager, Jerry Schilling, urgently telling me that there was trouble on the flight—Dennis and Mike were about to get

Carli with Jerry Schilling in Hawaii

into a fistfight. My thoughts were: On the plane? Why me??

"You're needed in the front," Jerry went on. Another idea that ran through my mind was that Jerry, a big guy who was Elvis Presley's best friend, and also had served as his bodyguard, was there along with plenty of other guys. *Why me?* Jerry urged me to come on.

"Carl is afraid Dennis won't let anyone else near." Carl had sent for me. So I went to check the situation. Dennis and Mike were in the middle of the aisle, nose to nose, ready to do battle, and everyone else was freaking out. My thoughts then were, My god, we are up in the air in a small plane. This could get seriously dangerous!

I quickly got behind Dennis and wrapped my arms tight around his arms and chest; I knew that Mike would back down if I disabled Dennis. As I was holding Dennis, I whispered close into his ear: "What the fuck are you doing?" Dennis turned his head and whispered back, "I'm just fucking with them." Dennis was just terrorizing the group, part of his not-so-passive aggressive nature. Dennis relaxed, Mike relaxed, and we could all breathe again.

Now I could finish my nap—kind of.

Dennis and I first met in a men's room, backstage at a Southern California venue, but I didn't see him again for a while after that. His life had gotten pretty crazy toward the end of the decade. Between his involvement with the notorious Charles Manson, with whom he had lived at one point and collaborated with musically, to his acting debut in *Two-Lane Blacktop* in 1970, Dennis wasn't around much. At first glance, Dennis gave me a puzzled glare. It was a common thing with him—he would test you right away. Then he said, "What are you?"

Assuming he was asking about my nationality, I replied, "Puerto Rican." I don't think he knew what to make of it. He nodded and left. After that, a fair distance remained between us except for an occasional glare or a stupid, unintelligible comment. We were always competing for the cutest girl on the road, which added a little more fuel to the fire.

It wasn't unusual for Dennis to walk into a room and challenge everyone to arm wrestle. One time I saw him beat everybody, including a bodyguard nicknamed "the Mole" because he was a construction digger, whose arms were as thick as my thighs. Subsequently, Dennis wanted to arm wrestle me, and I won. I was a skinny guy with a big afro, and he just couldn't believe that I beat him. I think I beat him because he didn't scare me as he did everyone else. People got fired so quickly and often by the

Beach Boys that it terrorized them—for some, being around Dennis was like walking on eggshells. Dennis had psyched his way into outwrestling those guys. After I beat him, we became closer. He knew I'd hold my own, that I wasn't afraid of him and that I'd be a worthy adversary.

Dennis and I were now competing even more for the attention of the same women. One night in Akron, Ohio, as we walked out of the hotel's restaurant where we were staying, Dennis referred to a sexy waitress we had both noticed, telling me they had a date after the concert. I said to Dennis, "Funny, I asked her out, too, and she said yes." Dennis got all worked up and replied something like, "No, she's coming with me, and if you mess this up, you're fired." My reply was, "Well, fuck you, Dennis, fire me then—that's low." Anyway, the argument escalated, and as we reached the sidewalk it became a scuffle. As we got tangled up in the fight, we suddenly stopped, looked at each other straight in the eyes, and in our best ingenious and resolving spirit, we both said, "What if we ask her to come with both of us?" We went back in and asked her, and she said yes. After such a brilliant and creative resolve, from then on we always worked as a team. I am almost too embarrassed to admit that we nicknamed ourselves the Macaco Brothers. (Macaco is a slang term referring to a monkey that's well-endowed and sexually voracious.) From then on, our corrivals didn't stand a chance in the survival pursuit of our species.

Something was missing in Dennis that he couldn't replace or fill— no matter how many thrills or conquests. We had frequent intimate talks, mostly about our childhoods and about life after death. We'd talk about our youth, his in Hawthorne, California, and mine in Ocean Park. After I shared some of my stories, he wanted to meet my dad. During one conversation, Dennis insisted that we go to a small airport nearby where the Beach Boys were keeping a leased jet between tours and order the pilot to take us to Puerto Rico to meet my dad. He implored. But I had to convince him that it was a bad idea and that I wouldn't take part in it. The mess that would have caused with the rest of the Beach Boys would have been the last one, for both of us. Fortunately, I kept him from taking the plane. But it made me realize how much a loving and supportive father figure—which he never had—would have meant for Dennis. I felt sad.

Dennis was curious about the afterlife, and it became a frequent topic between us. On that account, Dennis would later resonate with a song I wrote, "Constant Companion," which we would produce for *Bambu* later on. "It's Not Too Late" also had afterlife overtones. He believed that there was "a high road and a low road," leading to the same outcome in the afterlife. By that, he was referring to the idea that regardless of your pious or mischievous nature, you were a child of God, and if your heart was kind, you would reap the same heavenly rewards.

Over the years, I was curious about why cousins Dennis Wilson and Mike Love constantly clashed. I patiently waited for the right intimate moment to ask Dennis. He had the following answer: "One time when I had taken LSD and was very high, Mike took me for a ride on the back of a motorcycle and freaked me out." Knowing firsthand what it is to be on LSD, I understood. Much later, on a rare occasion when Mike and I hung out, just the two of us in Puerto Rico, I asked him the same question. Mike's reply: "Dennis fucked my first wife."

Understood.

Their early relationship with their father Murry sealed Brian's, Carl's, and Dennis's shortcomings. Much documentation about Murry's dominance and bullying has come to light, but none of it was apparent to me when I met him and the few times I was around him. Audree, their mother, couldn't have been a sweeter person to be around, and she was around often. A little over a month after Murry died (on June 4, 1973), the band was back on the road again.

On the first day of the tour at a hotel in Cincinnati, Ohio, Carl approached me carrying something strange. Audree was with him. He stopped me and said he had gone to the hardware store and bought a gift for me. It was a yellow extension cord with a lamp on its end— the ordinary kind that everyone has in their garage. I knew his dad's passing had distressed him but had no clue what to make of the lamp deal. For all I know, Carl had never been in a hardware store in his adult life, much less while on tour. Carl's strange gift of the extension cord baffles me to this day.

After the concert, back at the hotel, Carl, Dennis, and I were on a sofa in Carl's suite, talking about Murry, when first Dennis burst out crying, then Carl. We all got up, and we group-hugged as tightly as we could, very emotional and heartfelt. It was like a life of resentment melting away. The shows that followed were incredibly moving. Brian, as expected, seemed aloof, but wasn't. Brian didn't need a tragedy to withdraw, so his mood didn't seem to change much—he was already there. Carl and Dennis's grief, and even Brian's, was private and perhaps awkward, but it was real.

Having Brian around on tour in his depressive state was frustrating. It was painful seeing him in a constant state of suffering. On the 1979 tour of Japan, Brian remained most of the time hunched up with his head down throughout most of the tour, and it was heartbreaking to watch. To think that a man of his talent and abilities would remain in such pain and self-isolation made me feel helpless—there was nothing anyone could say or do to bring him out of that state. There were some hit-and-miss attempts afterward to try to help Brian, but for the most part, much of it was sadly based on self-serving manipulations.

Various relatives and acquaintances have claimed that they "saved Brian." I believe that some of them had good intentions. I witnessed at least one such claim from his cousin Steve Love, Mike's brother, who was managing the Beach Boys at the time. But in my view it was when he found his love, Melinda, that Brian ultimately really began to resurface—at least partially—out of his deep gloom. A few decades later in New York I saw the premiere of *Love & Mercy*, a movie version of Brian's life. Many people have asked me if I thought the movie told the real story. My reply has always been yes. But while it portrayed the real story, the reality was even more dramatic. Most of all, the three main nemeses—Murry Wilson, Mike Love, and Dr. Landy—were well portrayed.

After Murry's death, Dennis quickly snapped back into his usual mischievous nature. One time shortly after, during an East Coast tour approaching New York City in a private Falcon jet, Dennis ordered the pilot to fly between the Twin Towers in New York City. He did this as we were about to circle the towers while approaching the city. I was sitting in a jump seat (slightly behind, between the pilot and the copilot) in the cockpit as Dennis was hollering at the pilot from behind—it scared the shit out of me. I lowered my head to my knees and went blank. I must assume that the pilot refused, but I'll never know.

Meanwhile, Carl, being the most resilient and level-headed of the Wilson brothers, promptly got busy with his responsibilities as the bandleader. But a day didn't go by without some kind of struggle. The rest of the traveling musicians weren't so interested in the internal conflicts and issues, which were escalating. We called it "the Love factor" (we pinned all our daily miseries on Mike Love). Being close to Carl and Dennis made me an accessory to their ongoing feuds with Mike Love and also Al Jardine, who at the time acted like Mike's lapdog. Part of the reason I was caught in the middle was that history was repeating. Years ago, I had gone through the same thing with TM meditators vs. non-meditators cynically jabbing at one another when I was with the Living End. The same polarization was part of what caused the breakup. Apparently, the Beatles had similar internal conflicts, as I imagine many other groups have.

Being on the road was like living together. Eventually, there was inevitable segregation within the Beach Boys because of the difference in lifestyle between the TM meditators and the "others." I had become a TM initiate in 1968 in New York, even if I demanded my money back. However, within the Beach Boys, I was still one of the "others." The segregation got so intense that, for a time, the Beach Boys leased two jet planes to keep the two groups apart. The TMs were non-smokers, non-drug users, vegetarians, sober, and uptight. The "others," us, smoked cigarettes and weed, drank booze, were meat-eaters, and had fun. The TMs spent a lot of time criticizing the "others." The "others" didn't give a rat's ass.

Still, despite our differences the group remained at peak form on stage. For me, some of the most exciting times touring with the Beach Boys were when Ricky Fataar and Blondie Chaplin were in the group. The level of musicianship was at its highest—not to mention all the fun we had. We clicked right away, bonding both musically and personally. Blondie, Ricky, and I all shared the similar experience of coming from hot touring original rock bands. And with me coming from Puerto Rico and them coming from South Africa, we had some common idiosyncrasies.

There was a song from the Beach Boys' *Holland* album we'd do during performances, "Leaving This Town," where our influences would really come to life. In that song, Blondie's lead vocals were genuine and soulful, and Ricky's drumming was at its peak. It was also in that song where I was unleashed to do a free-form organ solo. More than any other song in the repertoire, "Leaving This Town" felt different every time we played it, each time taking it to the next blissful level. That was because the song had room for expression. I still get goosebumps every time I hear a live performance of "Leaving This Town." Fortunately, one of those awesome performances was caught live and released for posterity on the 1973 live album *The Beach Boys in Concert*. The lyrics to "Leaving This Town," written by Fataar, Wilson, Chaplin, and Love, epitomize the emotional struggle of being on the road away from your loved ones.

STRENGTH.

STRENGTH

With this tarot card, you are reminded that even if you are going through tough times, you are strong enough to handle whatever you are facing. You can accomplish anything you set your mind to and will come out of it with even more power than you had before. The Strength card is about the fortitude of your heart and the ability to overcome obstacles.

Sometimes being on the road was a test of wits. In spite of the sameness of the airports, the hotels, and the venues, especially in the Midwest, which could be downright gray and depressing, meeting new people, especially girls, always brought an element of hope. We were almost always invited to a party at someone's house after a concert. But more often than not, traveling while on tour was a bit rushed, and we'd have to get back on the plane after the concert and arrive late in the evening at some small town where everything was closed.

Still, there was a great deal of energy to be channeled after a concert. The way for some of us to cope with that energy was just by visiting each other's rooms, smoking some weed, drinking beer, playing cards, watching comedy shows on TV, or just becoming silly and laughing about Mike Love's antics. Sometimes we would make up games. One time in Carl's suite, I think Dennis came up with the idea of a game of telling the most embarrassing truths ever. Christine McVie, Dennis's girlfriend at the time, was there, too, and it turned out to be a roar! We all took our turns telling our OMG moments. I only dare to share mine because it wouldn't be right to share other people's most shameful and intimate moments. My story went something like this:

"One afternoon my mother caught me jerking off in the bathroom,"

I began, getting everyone's undivided attention. "I must have been around thirteen or fourteen, and hands down (no pun intended), the most embarrassing moment of my entire life. I don't know what got into me," I went on. "I was at my parents' house and went into a small guest bathroom we had downstairs at the end of the hallway. It was in the middle of the day, and I just stepped in but forgot to lock the door. I don't remember if I had gone there to pee or just for a matinee selfie (I probably didn't use the word "selfie"). But there I was in the bathroom, taking my time, slipping into a piquant moment of self-appreciation, buried in concentration and building a mental scenario in crescendo. What followed was a hodgepodge of images collected and concocted from my fertile imagination, leading to an apex at that highly anticipated instant. I must have been hunched up and half pretzeled in front of the bathroom mirror..."

By this time, the moment-of-awe silence was broken by Carl with a burst of uncontrollable laughter. I continued, "My veins were popping out of everywhere while still squeezing and thumping the last breath out of 'Old Boy' for the last jollies, and my mom just walked in! I froze, evidence in hand. My mom also froze."

I went on. "As we both stood there in a catatonic state, all she said was, 'Oh...I'm sorry.' Then, just like a movie in reverse, she retracted, shutting the door behind her. Making matters worse, I think I was tickling my prostate with my other hand."

"Oh god—that must have looked contorted and disgusting!" Yeah, *disgusting*, I heard Christine say.

"All I know is that after that infamous bust, I could have squeezed myself out of the bathroom through the six-inch gap in the small Miami window in the bathroom. I just wanted to disappear—forever! I waited in the bathroom, hunched up, silent and in disbelief. There wasn't any way I could face my mother for the rest of that day, or ever! I think she got it and made it easy for me to sneak out of the bathroom without the dreadful encounter of ultimate shame. So, I sneaked out and stayed away and faded into the night."

There, I just shared the most embarrassing moment in my life...*I'm free!* Carl, Dennis, and Christine got to share theirs as well, but I always thought they were holding back, except for Carl's story, which was pretty darn juicy, but mine surely topped the bill.

Games went on, and also role-playing, some of which were recorded on video. One time I played a psychiatrist and Dennis was the patient—it was hilarious! Both Dennis and Carl liked playing games. Once, while staying in a hotel in Denver, Colorado, Ed Carter and I filmed a funny skit about Mike Love. One of us had a bunch of lit cigarettes in our mouth (Mike was against smoking), and we did an interview mocking Mike. It ended up in a wild fight as we threw ourselves, along with furniture, all over the room. Silly games and skits like these happened often, just to break away from the daily monotony.

One time, while Dennis was "at it" on his bed with a groupie, I was playing a piano against the wall within a few feet in the same room, and the rest of the band was there surrounding me and singing along. It went on for hours while Dennis engaged in a variety of statuesque Kama Sutra positions with his mating partner. Carl eventually showed up with a boombox at full volume playing a song over and over, with a sticky chorus that went something like "Who Cried Wolf." Carl tried getting in on the action but couldn't, and suggested that we trash the room.

I'd never seen Carl in that mood before. I think he must have been on alcohol and some other substance and was frustrated by not being able to join the fun. A TV went out the window, and couches were turned upside down. I remember everyone trying to lift the piano, but fortunately it was too heavy to throw out the window. We made a mess of the room—all of it—not in anger, but to the rhythm of the song that was playing full blast on the boombox, with Dennis and the girl still humping away in the middle of the room. It was the only time I was involved in room trashing, which I never saw any point in, but I have to confess that it was fun.

At some point during the mayhem, the girl went to take a shower, and during this time everyone left the room, leaving her in the bathroom. It was Dennis's room, and he got scared when he saw what was left of the room, and he ended up spending the rest of the night with Carl. The next morning, the Beach Boys' management had to pay big bucks to take care of the mess and to keep it hush from the press, not to mention getting a major reprimand from Mike and Al. They were always out of the picture; perhaps they were the adult ones, staying in their rooms meditating or whatever, but they never got silly with us in any way. There was a clear segregation then.

A few people have asked me if I ever felt discrimination while being with the Beach Boys. No, not really. The closest thing that comes to mind is a brief encounter with Jim Guercio. Jim and I became acquainted when traveling with the Beach Boys. Besides being the group's manager for a short time, Jim was also often playing bass with the band on some of the tours. One time there was a conversation about Brian not writing or producing new material for the group. The conversation with Guercio took place somewhere in the Midwest, while killing time before an outdoor concert. Jim and I had a rare moment of rubbing shoulders, and he was grumbling about Brian being noncooperative and the Beach Boys being in the doldrums because no one was writing, and there were a certain number of album commitments to keep. Neither Carl, Dennis, nor anyone else in the group were at the time writing anything worth their salt, but I was. I had already composed songs like "Constant Companion," "All Alone," "It's Not Too Late," "Under the Moonlight," "Follow Me," "Wake Up America," and "Hold On," and I was writing new songs—my creative juices were flowing at their peak.

Guercio seemed frustrated. I told him that I could cover that gap, that I already had plenty of material, and that if needed I could write more in the Beach Boys' context. I offered myself passionately and with enthusiasm, saying, "Jim, I can do this—why don't you guys try me? Let's give it a chance." Guercio's reaction was the first and possibly the only time I ever felt belittled and undervalued around the Beach Boys. He didn't say much. Just the way he looked at me and left the scene was enough.

There were always plenty of exploiters under different cloaks around the Beach Boys, supposedly "protecting them from outside influences." It happens all the time. There must be a zillion stories where close friends, even family members, are kept away from artists by their managers, allegedly "in their best interest," when it is really all about self-preservation, self-importance, and control.

One time in Chicago with Dennis Wilson (we must have been on a Beach Boys tour), I don't know what came over me, but in a spontaneous rage I blurted out, "I'm Puerto Rican!" It just came out of the blue like a visceral realization. Perhaps it was the first time that I either had the realization or the admission that I belonged to a group of people perceived as less, or lower class in the white social structure. I remember feeling better after the utterance—it was cathartic and liberating, I could almost say an epiphany—but more like a flash realization. Dennis didn't have anything to do with that moment, but afterward I shared it with him. I was shaken.

I never felt the least trace of disparagement from Carl, Dennis, or Brian, or from Mike Love and Al Jardine, although there may have been some light rub with the latter. I could agree that Mike was harsh, annoying, greedy, and a plain asshole. (We all were, except for Carl, who genuinely cared about and was considerate to other people. I think that now in his late years, Mike is becoming the man he always wanted to be—we all do.) But I couldn't say racially prejudiced or biased when it came to interacting with someone from a different nationality. To his credit I believe he embraced diversity. Al was hard to figure out, but he never gave me any reason to think he was prejudiced. He just never was one to shake things. If Al would take sides during the Mike vs. Dennis saga, it was most likely for pragmatic and moral reasons.

Al didn't make waves on his own, but Bruce Johnston was like a crafty feline who would step in and out at his convenience. When you first meet Bruce, especially with the rest of the guys around, he would appear to be the nicest of all—"too nice," one might think. My conversations with Bruce were always like that, "nice." But behind the scenes was another story.

Carl and Dennis were my confidants, and I knew more about what was happening behind the scenes than any other Beach Boys member realized. I'll always remember when Carl came to me excitedly, saying that he had splendid news. I was outside in the back at Western Studios on Sunset Boulevard, on a break from a session, leaning on a car smoking a cigarette when Carl came to tell me that the group had picked my song, "Constant Companion," for their *L.A.* (*Light Album*) single. I distinctively remember my reaction; I was excited, but still not betting my life on it. I knew that there'd be powerful forces against it. "Constant Companion" made the final track list on the album mix. Still, Jim Guercio insisted on bringing back Bruce Johnston as producer and collaborator with the Beach Boys. It was a desperate measure for Guercio because Brian had not been taking part in the studio—no cash cow to milk.

The *L.A.* (*Light Album*) was the band's first release after signing a new $8 million contract with CBS, and Guercio, being in the middle, reacted. With producer Curt Boettcher, Bruce brought along a disco version of "Here Comes the Night," an old Brian Wilson song originally released on the 1967 *Wild Honey* album. According to Carl, Bruce not only opposed the Beach Boys' decision to have "Constant Companion" as the single, he didn't even want it on the album. He wanted to remove it altogether and replace it with the disco version of "Here Comes the Night." Bruce and Guercio did their best to convince the group this was the way to go. They were right—it was the way to go: further into the shithole the Beach Boys already were in. There were four other attempts by Jim Guercio's Caribou Records to revive the dead horse by releasing various DJ versions. Decades later, the media immortalized the record as flop of epic proportions:

> "The Beach Boys' Eleven-Minute Disco Atrocity from 1979 Will Take You Straight to Hell"
> —Dangerous Minds

> "CBS and the Beach Boys ate dirt when the disco single not only failed to make the Top Forty, but the album failed to make the Top Ninety-Nine!"
> —The entry on "Here Comes the Night" from the book *The Beach Boys FAQ*

> "Lost in the '70s: The Beach Boys, 'Here Comes the Night.'"
> —Pop Dose in 2009:

> "'I hate playing this song': when rock stars go disco."
> —*The Guardian* in 2018 (about "Here Comes the Night"):

> "'Here Comes the Night' is not so much a sellout as it is simple padding."
> —*Rolling Stone*, 1979

Because the fans who heard it were aghast, the Beach Boys performed the disco version of "Here Comes the Night" in concert only once, and to a disappointed crowd. This performance took place at Radio City Music Hall in New York City in 1979 in support of the newly released *L.A.* (*Light Album*). This was the first time I witnessed the audience unanimously booing the Beach Boys, and it was very embarrassing.

New Zealand must be one of the most beautiful countries I've visited. We played a concert in the city of Auckland and then crossed over to Christchurch. Both places had their unique charm. In Christchurch, a river ran through the town, bordering parks and beautiful homes. There were children and adults peacefully playing and sailing in the river; it was picture perfect. In Auckland, diverse bodies of water also graced the scenery. I won't forget being at a park where all the women were wearing skirts and sandals. They looked very feminine at a time when most women in America were stuffing themselves inside jeans. New Zealand was just the beginning of a 1979 spring tour that included the main cities in the southeastern and southern coast of Australia, beginning in Brisbane, then to Perth, and ending in Sydney. Before the tour, internal trouble within the Beach Boys had been brewing up to a boiling point. The Wilsons and the Loves both hired bodyguards to protect them from each other while on Australian soil.

The emotional stress had its peak moment toward the end of the tour, at our hotel in Sydney. As I was walking down a long hallway toward my room, I saw Carl coming my way accompanied by British television personality David Frost. It was a strange scene. David aided him as if Carl was having trouble walking, and Carl was laughing hysterically while holding his jaw. We all stopped and I asked Carl what had happened. Still hysterically laughing, Carl responded that Rocky had punched him in the jaw. I looked at him with a bewildered expression and he continued, "No one ever hit me before!"

As the mood shifted from laughter to seriousness, he explained that he had been slugged at a meeting with Mike Love and others. Mike's younger brother, Steve, then the Beach Boys' manager, had hired his cousin, Stan, and a goonish old school buddy, Rocky Pamplin, to babysit Brian throughout the tour. During the meeting, Rocky accused Carl of giving heroin to Brian; Carl told Rocky that he was full of shit, and Rocky slugged him. (Pamplin would later write a book claiming that he and Stan Love were the ones who saved Brian from self-destruction.) From that moment on, I knew that there was a tough road ahead of us.

After that episode, my biggest concern was how Dennis would react. The group's separation was now more than clear. Fortunately, Dennis remained calm and reasonably clearheaded. Later that evening, I found an intimate fine dining restaurant where Dennis and I spent most of the night. At first we talked about the incident, but it was soon forgotten, and we had the perfect dinner. The restaurant was located in an upscale residential area, and the food and the wine were terrific. Both Dennis and I had duck's breast for the main course, and we took our time. After a succulent dessert, the chef, a South African, came to sit with us with a bottle of a fifty-year-old cognac and Cuban cigars. The only way to seal that special evening was by standing on the lovely neighborhood sidewalk and peeing in unison into the gutter. As we were in prime gusto, cigars still in our mouths while finishing our urinary ritual, a police car drove by slowly. Fortunately, the two discombobulated policemen kept driving.

Oddly enough, during one of the Australian tour dates in Perth, it was Carl who compromised the Beach Boys' reputation by being stoned and acting knotty on stage. Now Dennis became concerned about his sweet little brother, which was quite a reversal of roles. On stage, Brian was performing professionally again, and Dennis was behaving himself. Carl later apologized to the Aussies on their national TV for his behavior, saying that he had a couple of mai tais before the concert.

We survived the tour, and business went on as usual—almost. The Australian event brought backlash to the group, but despite internal skirmishes resulting from the tour mishaps, the band's subsequent performances went off without a hitch. Performing on *Burt Sugarman's Midnight Special* the following year provided some sugarcoating to the group; at least the group looked coherent. But unfortunately, the executive powers had been shifting to Mike Love and Al Jardine. The decade culminated with a new deal with Reprise and the *M.I.U. Album*, and worse, the release of "Here Comes the Night."

Before the Australian tour, I played Dennis a cassette with some of the compositions I'd recorded at my home studio in Mount Washington: "Under the Moonlight," "Constant Companion," "All Alone," "It's Not Too Late," and "Sho-Ru-Bop" (later released as "Wake Up America"). There were other songs on the tape that we didn't get to work on. Dennis flipped. Right then and there, he said he wanted to make an album of my songs and wanted me to be his producer. I agreed, but I also suggested that he co-produce the record with me. Dennis went to Jim Guercio, still the Beach Boys' manager and the owner of the Caribou Records label, and got $100,000 to get the project started. That was the beginning of what was later released as Dennis's second solo album, *Bambu*. Caribou Records and Sony Legacy later rereleased the watered-down version again, along with *Pacific Ocean Blue*. (I say "watered-down" because I'm aware of the superiority of the original intended version. Many fans enjoy the released version, and by no means should my comment take away from their experience.)

The period between 1977 and 1978, when we planned and produced *Bambu*, was marked by Dennis's notorious torching of a Ferrari belonging to his third wife, Karen Lamm, and gunshots exchanged between them. Karen was an actress and the former wife of Robert Lamm of the band Chicago. Dennis's relationship with Karen was turbulent, to say the least. His indomitable spirit and Karen's controlling nature turned out to be a dangerous mix. Karen was extremely volatile and often violent, which often led to Dennis taking more drugs and going on weeks-long drinking binges. While she appeared to care for Dennis's well-being (she would complain to me often about Dennis's drug use), there were allegations from people close to them that she got Dennis involved with heroin. But that wasn't my perception.

They were married twice, in 1976, divorcing in 1977, and in 1978, divorcing again in 1980. I'm not sure how they met, but they had been dating since 1974, and it was the first time that I saw Dennis become obsessed and consumed by a woman. I always saw Karen as "the lamb who consumed the wolf." Still, amid all the turbulence, Dennis and I worked fine together at the studio. We respected each other's ideas. He knew what I could bring to the table, and I knew him well enough to know what to expect.

We had the blueprint for the new project, which was the demo I had made in my home studio, and now we had the budget and Brother Studios, the Beach Boys' facility in Santa Monica. Tracking was straightforward with a pool of musicians we were comfortable with: Ed Carter on guitar, Wayne Tweed on bass, Bobby Figueroa's great drumming, and Michael Andreas arranging and assembling the horn section. We also brought in a Baptist choir, a full string section, and other musicians when needed. I particularly enjoyed bringing Manolo Badrena of Weather Report to do percussion on "Constant Companion," a rare gem naively removed from the Caribou and Sony Legacy versions of *Bambu*. Later, Dennis and I would do the sweetening with synthesizers and various keyboards. Also, we would often get visitors at the studio when we were working.

One afternoon I was doing some Hammond organ work at the studio, and Roger McGuinn walked in with his twelve-string

Carli sailing with Dennis Wilson

Rickenbacker guitar. I asked him if we could jam to the solo section of "Eight Miles High." We did, and it was amazing! It was one of those times I thought to myself, "Now I can die happy."

The recording sessions usually started in the late morning or early afternoon. Either Earle Mankey or head engineer Steve Moffitt engineered the session, and I enjoyed working with both of them—we had a great rapport. If we took a break in the afternoon, Dennis and I would sometimes hop in Dennis's vintage Ford, stop at a small corner market to pick up some cold beer, put it in the rumble seat, and drive on to Marina Del Rey to go sailing on his fifty-two-foot ketch, *Harmony*.[5]

5   The *Harmony* was built in Japan in 1950 by the Azuma Boat Company for George T. Folster, a New Englander whose ancestors had sailed the Pacific in the days of the great whaling ships. The craft was christened *Watadori* (Bird of Passage), and the theme set by the original name was reflected in the carving of a bird under the bowsprit, as well as in the hand-carved designs in the cabinetwork belowdecks. Starting from blueprints

Dennis loved that boat so much! It also thrilled him to be working in the studio—and we were making progress.

There was no resolution to the bad blood within the rest of the group—it was now on the back burner. The real problem lurking around was his still-volatile relationship with Karen Lamm, a sure mood-changer and a catalyst for Dennis taking a sudden emotional dive with grave consequences. On top of that, Dennis and Carl hadn't been talking to each other. I will never forget the night when I called Carl to ask him if he would do a guitar and vocal part on two tracks we had been working on that day. Carl agreed to do it. When he showed up that night at the studio, he and Dennis embraced and gushed with emotion. I wanted Carl to lay a vocal track on the chorus of a song called "It's Not Too Late." Once he did the first pass, we knew there wasn't any sense in doing more takes. We might have done one or two more passes, but that was all we needed—it couldn't get more real.

Dennis's vocals were all scratch—on *Bambu*'s release, there wasn't a single final lead vocal track. I often thought he could do better, but Dennis never seemed to be happy with any of his vocal tracks. His lead vocal on "All Alone" *especially* wasn't final. "All Alone" was the most challenging for Dennis, yet the most gut-wrenchingly heartfelt.

One night I got a call at home from Christine McVie and Dennis, at 4 AM., from a recording studio—I believe it was from Tom Murphy's recording studio in Hollywood—asking me for the lyrics to "All Alone." Dennis appeared obsessed with redoing his lead vocals and was going from studio to studio taking a shot at it, and Christine was trying to help. I felt sucked dry trying to keep Dennis functional. I just wanted to be with my children and have a healthy, productive life. The project dissolved as Dennis was falling deeper down the abyss. The situation got hopeless, and I had to pull back. Incidentally, the name I had originally picked for the album, which Dennis loved, was "The End of the Line."

It was heartbreaking seeing Dennis deteriorate so fast. Christine McVie, I believe, in her own way made her best effort to help Dennis,

drawn up by an American yachtsman, the craft was built from materials from all over the world. The wood includes teak from Burma, mahogany from the Philippines, and camphor wood from Formosa; the sails were imported from England; and the brass fittings were made in Scotland.

but also to no avail. At this point it was impossible to "guide" Dennis Wilson. I often lured him toward family life by having him over at our house for dinner. Brenda would cook and he'd play with the kids. It must have been around 1980. We then had three toddlers—Marcel, Myles, and Marlon. Dennis would also fiddle with the piano, and he'd let Brenda take his Ferrari for a spin. He loved clowning around with the kids, and we had some wholesome fun afternoons, but inside he was a very lonely man. Within him was an internal solitude that could only be quenched with over-the-edge thrills. Everything about Dennis was bigger than life. He lived in the fast lane, desperately searching for something possibly missing from his childhood. I can only speculate this from the talks we had about his youth and the relationship he had with his father.

Brenda and I went to visit him once in Malibu. It was the last time I saw him. I remember him in bed, surrounded by hundreds of boxes of Nike shoes. He mumbled something about an endorsement he had made. Then he whispered into my ear a sexual dream he had—one I would rather forget.

While I was living in Pasadena, Jack Rieley came for a visit. Jack had been spending most of his time in Europe since he left the Beach Boys in 1973. It was now the beginning of the '80s, and I hadn't seen him for several years. By then, Brenda and I were settled with children. Jack had just returned from Europe and brought along Christoph von Plettenberg, a tall, good-looking kid who Jack claimed was connected to some royal family in Holland. They needed a place to stay, and Brenda and I accommodated them in our home.

Jack explained that his new friend was a count, and I would jokingly say to Jack that he was a cunt. Jack was now clearly gay. Throughout all the acid tripping we did and living together, I had never thought of Jack as gay. Maybe he hadn't either, or I was naive, or it just didn't matter. Jack told me that after a visit to San Francisco he realized he "had other preferences," so I congratulated him and asked him what else was new—no issue. I loved Jack dearly—he could have told me he was the Zodiac killer and I would have still loved him. Our friendship was uncompromising. I loved Jack, and I still do. My life without him wouldn't have been as rich at all levels. The way we exchanged ideas was grand, and anything was possible.

Jack called me frequently when he was in Europe, inviting me to come and stay as long as I wanted. He invited me when he was living in Amsterdam, in Paris, and in Berlin. He always offered to pay all my expenses, and I knew he needed me there, but I always declined his offers. Jack was also too consuming, and I had a new family to look after, which was my priority. But I still missed our all-night talks about saving the world, the songwriting, and just goofing around—we had plenty of laughter and awe-filled moments.

That same year, 1980, I started having thoughts of leaving the Beach Boys. The Wilsons vs. Love war was peaking, and I had three little toddlers. Leaving them to go on tour was becoming too painful—and Dennis's abysmal decline wasn't helping. In early 1981, I played on my last tour and resigned.

JUDGEMENT.

JUDGEMENT

 The Judgement card prompts you to review and to reflect on all of your previous decisions and your actions. You must ensure that they, and especially any new decisions, are in line with where you ultimately want to go. You will be inspired by your own self-reflection, and any actions you take once you find yourself will change the course of your life.

Leaving the Beach Boys was a calculated risk, and I was willing to take a financial dive if necessary. Brenda and I had discussed it, and we agreed. My Beach Boys saga centered on Carl and Dennis Wilson. It was all about the laughter, the pain, the music, and the whole gamut of emotions that made us vulnerable and human. Carl and Dennis gave me a lot—a lifetime of memories and reflections. They both embodied the extreme—the yin and the yang—and we remained friends. But I was then happy to move forward from anything Beach Boys related, not out of resentment or animosity, not at all—just to move on. Leaving the Beach Boys was my new freedom.

Thanks to the diligence of the Beach Boys' manager during that time, Steve Love, the Beach Boys had established a pension plan a few years back where I would get a lump sum of money when I'd retire from the group. With that money, I could take some time to reflect on what to do next without having the pressure of immediate economic burdens. The Beach Boys' pension helped and bought us time. But by then, Brenda and I had three toddlers: first Marcel, then a year later, Myles and Marlon—two identical twins. The jackpot, lovely Melanie, wasn't born yet.

I'll never forget the ride back home after Marcel was born. It was winter, and the three of us took the train just to enjoy the comfort and

*Brenda holding newborn
twins Myles and Marlon*

fantastic views. There were so many precious moments during the journey—the sight of crystal-clear lakes and the snowcapped Olympic Mountains while crossing the Pacific Northwest was grand. I remember holding newborn Marcel along the way, looking at the panorama, and talking to him as if he understood everything I was saying. Together we would look at the majestic white mountain landscape during the day, and at night the stars would put up the most graceful spectacle. It was magic!

The pension plan savings helped, but I needed steady work to keep from depleting our savings. It wasn't long before I got work calls. Soon after leaving the Beach Boys, I got a call from the renowned jazz pianist Les McCann. Les assembled a quartet with three keyboardists and a drummer to play some concerts in the Los Angeles area. I'll always remember the drummer, who was fantastic. His name was Kevin Calhoun, and he was from Tulsa, Oklahoma. On Moog synthesizer was Andy Armer, a great keyboardist, and Les McCann and I alternated between Fender Rhodes and acoustic piano.

Andy Armer was a Grammy Award nominee for writing and producing "Rise," a No. 1 single by Herb Alpert in 1974. Andy, himself a talented keyboard player, who had also taken part earlier with my group Your Own Space, had recommended me to Les McCann's new experimental keyboard group. A call from the leader of the Jazz Crusaders, Wayne Henderson, followed. Henderson had heard about me and was producing an album for the iconic jazz drummer Chico Hamilton.

After the call, our first encounter was in the hallway of the recording studio, the Total Experience, in Beverly Hills. The moment we saw each other we both just started laughing and hugging—it was as if we had known each other forever. Wayne was medium height and stocky, had a raspy voice, and was as black as coal. During the sessions, every time he wanted someone to go back to the top, he'd say, "Take it to Jump Street!" He was a funky dude in the best sense of the word, and I just adored him! I had a tendency to hold back during recordings, and he always pushed me to open up and play more aggressively—he was a great musician and producer.

After having me on the sessions and completing the album, Wayne called me back to play on a George Benson album he was making for Warner Brothers. Henderson raved to Benson, his peers, and the other members of the Jazz Crusaders about my keyboard skills during the sessions. He must have been more aware of my talent than I was—I felt embarrassed and undeserving when I heard Wayne talk that way about me to these artists I admired so much.

Playing and recording with George Benson was a most rewarding experience. When we first met at the Ocean Way studio on Sunset Boulevard, he asked me to jam with him before the session. His playing was mesmerizing. Throughout the whole process I learned that jazz is a balance of power and humility. Being in the jazz world is like being inside a quiet storm—a certain restraint is part of its power and beauty. It was happening; jazz was back in my life. But the money I earned from these sporadic jobs wasn't enough to sustain our way of life, and my pension fund was disappearing fast.

At some point between sessions, I flew back to San Juan for three weeks to visit my parents. During that time, I missed calls to do other mainstream sessions; I then learned how fragile the position is to remain a top choice for jazz studio work in LA. When I came back, I had already been replaced on the circuit of sessions I had been getting the studio calls from. All it took was breaking the flow by having to decline some additional sessions being offered. When I came back, I was no longer in demand for jazz keyboard studio sessions. I got calls for scattered, mostly rock sessions, with Peter Cetera, Evie Sands, and others, but the jazz circuit at the time was fast-track, demanding, and highly competitive.

As a pianist, I regarded jazz as the ultimate challenge, and I was eager to engage myself in it fully. Also, I knew that I had talent and passion for photography and film. I bought my first 35mm still camera during a Beach Boys tour of Japan in 1979. It was a Canon A-1, and I loved it. In my mind, I had become an instant photographer, but I was far from it. Being so eager to learn, I enrolled at Pasadena City College, close to where I lived. There I took courses in television production, learning the basics of professional video production but not much about filming.

The next year I shifted to Los Angeles City College, which had just completed an $8 million renovation of its film department. LACC was a novel experience for me; it was more about cinematography and filmmaking. Studying filmmaking was a gainful experience. I was the best student in the class because I was already a professional in the field of music; therefore, my focus was real and passionate. I enjoyed every moment, absorbing every bit of information. Lighting and directing were my favorite subjects and remained the most useful later. I needed to learn how to "light" my world and "direct" my living scenes—my life's metaphor.

I'd only stay in college for a little over a year because I kept getting calls for professional paying jobs filming commercials for a small local advertising agency—we were running out of money, and I had to grab any job that came my way. I also found myself pondering the idea of doing some local gigs so we'd have some steady income. From across where we lived in Pasadena, Frank, a neighbor, timidly approached me to ask if I'd be interested in playing with a country-western band. It seemed interesting to me—something new I'd never done before. So I said yes. We weren't making ends meet with the occasional jazz gigs, and it was too soon in my new career to make steady money in film.

Frank's band played at a club in Anaheim, a grueling forty-five-minute drive from Pasadena. The Cowboy was a huge venue, with three bars, a large dance floor, a mechanical bull, gift stores, fully staffed professional sound and lighting equipment, an ample backstage with dressing rooms, and a humongous stage. There was a set of double metal doors in the back where a half dozen roughneck bouncers would violently kick out drunk, brawling cowboys several times a night—the real deal. I played at the Cowboy for two years. The attraction for me was the music.

Besides my early musical background, including profound jazz experience from age fourteen, the two years I dedicated to playing country swing and bluegrass music were rewarding for my craft, especially for my chops (finger dexterity in jazz jargon), by keeping up with the fiddle and the mandolin. My background in boogie-woogie and honky-tonk was perfect for the country experience, as it was also grassroots for jazz because of all the improvisation—every song had at least two rounds for each instrument to solo, especially in old-time country swing. I also had deep blues influences from accompanying blues performers in New York and Los Angeles, such as Etta James and other great blues singers, which undoubtedly integrates very well with jazz and other genres. The rock and soul added brilliantly to the mix in the way of drama and many quirky nuances.

Later I also realized how beneficial my early days of Latin dance combo playing were. The simplistic early dance combo experience opened my ears to logical sequences in chord progressions—in a more developed sense, I came to call this musical intelligence. Semiclassical music gave me a repertoire and a clean delivery, and finally, my early exposure to the avant-garde expanded my emotional and intellectual creative palette. So, at least in a musical sense, I didn't feel I was prostituting myself, as long as the music remained interesting.

The new experience playing country and bluegrass was fun, but still not what I wanted to do long term. Still, I feel very fortunate to have spent two years of my life with these guys playing music. Sometimes I get the urge to contact my old friends and try to arrange a visit to the old West. Hmm, wouldn't mind gathering the old cowboys for a midnight session...

"What do I got to stay around here for?" as Joe Buck said in *Midnight Cowboy*.

XII

THE HANGED MAN.

THE HANGED MAN

The Hanged Man tells you that you are at a crossroads and that you need to take a break from what you've been doing. You may soon have to take some risks and make small sacrifices in order to succeed. It also means that doing something new will be beneficial to clearing your head and seeing the big picture.

Brenda wasn't too happy with my new career whims. Also, the gig alone wasn't enough to support our previous lifestyle. It seemed natural for me to pursue something that I thought I'd be good at and have passion for, but she was right; going to college for film at that moment was a luxury. Eventually, we had to sell our comfortable Pasadena home. We sold it for double what we paid for it, but it was still the worst deal I could have made. One of my few regrets—ever.

After selling the house in Pasadena, a financial advisor conned us into buying a property we didn't like in a nearby area we didn't like so much, which she covertly also owned. While I felt that I was making personal progress in learning a new craft, I neglected our finances. Our once-comfortable lifestyle went into a spiral. Our spirits lifted with the birth of my first daughter, Melanie, but our dire financial reality was still lurking behind the scenes.

We moved from house to house several times, each move more depressing than the previous one. My passion for filmmaking distracted me, but I pressed on. I was putting time-consuming studio work and touring on the back burner because studying film took much of my time. Doing local gigs was my only option while I kept busy attending every seminar available at the movie lots in Hollywood and related extension courses on cinema, lighting, direction, writing, and acting that UCLA offered. Even with the losses, I was optimistic and started getting calls for film jobs.

One call I got was to produce a music video for Dean Martin. One of the performer's sons, Ricci, approached me to make a video of his father's version of Ivory Joe Hunter's "Since I Met You Baby." Then I got a call from the elder Martin's management, securing my participation. I can't say that I knew how things worked in Hollywood, but film-related calls started rolling in. Filming and editing the Dean Martin video was a tremendous learning experience, for I had never done a music video of that magnitude before. The video was well received by Warner Brothers, and a press party was arranged at a Beverly Hills restaurant. Canadian actor and talk show host Alan Thicke, Warner Brothers CEO Mo Ostin, and of course Dean Martin, Ricci, and many other celebrities were there.

After the release and the hullaballoo of "Since I Met You Baby," Ricci mentioned that he soon would be traveling to an intimate setting in a private jet with his father, along with Frank Sinatra. He suggested that we come up with a theme for us to make a video to pitch to Sinatra. Ricci came up with the idea of a black-and-white parody of a boxing match with Jerry Lewis to accompany the song "I'm Beginning to See the Light." I loved the idea, and we started brainstorming and quickly

Dean Martin's "Since I Met You Baby" Warner Brothers release party, Beverly Hills, Ca. L to R, Alan Thicke, Ricci Martin, Mo Ostin, and Carli Muñoz

came up with a sketchy storyboard with a storyline to present to Sinatra during the flight. Frankly, Sinatra didn't jump out of his pants at the idea, nor did he reject it, but he never responded. That was the only shot we had at it—it was a good try. Ricci and I remained close, participating together in music recording projects, putting together experimental rock bands, and performing our original music locally.

Although I would still see Carl Wilson occasionally, by this time I had fully distanced myself from the rest of the Beach Boys, including Dennis. Carl was now dating Gina Martin, Ricci's sister—and they would frequently show up at gigs we did around town. My distancing from Dennis wasn't for lack of affection but to avoid entanglement in his hopeless self-destructive mode. On the evening of December 28, 1983, I learned from Carl's manager, Jerry Schilling, of Dennis's drowning at Marina Del Rey. For those close to him, me included, Dennis was a tragedy waiting to happen, and it was just a matter of when. Still, it was a devastating blow to everyone who knew him and loved him—he was only thirty-nine years old.

After his passing, the many conversations we had had about the afterlife surfaced for me. Dennis, being extremely competitive, rarely expressed a liking for songs or groups outside of the Beach Boys, especially contemporary ones, but there was a song that he liked very much and would mention to me often—"Time," by The Alan Parsons Project. That song is Dennis. It is no coincidence that he wrote songs like "The River Song," which had "Farewell My Friend" on the flip side. A strong association between Dennis and bodies of water is undeniable, considering his first solo album was titled *Pacific Ocean Blue*, not to mention his influence on the Beach Boys. As the only surfer in the group, it was Dennis who pushed to do surf music early on.

Dennis died in the water, at his old slip in Marina Del Rey, and was duly buried at sea. In addition to his metaphorical affinity to the water, Dennis also expressed a deep interest in the afterlife. Two of my songs on his second solo album, *Bambu*, that embody the afterlife in their lyrics are "Constant Companion" and "It's Not Too Late." The vocal duet with his beloved brother Carl on "It's Not Too Late" epitomizes their lofty soul connection.

Filming the Dean Martin music video opened doors to other projects. I also got a call from the American Film Institute to be the lighting director for a movie starring Zelda Rubinstein. More calls came in, including assembling editorials for the Beach Boys and photography jobs in fashion and portraiture. I had a friend, Lesley Paget, who had modeled for *Italian Vogue* and could not model any more after an accident she had in a Jeep. She was still beautiful and slender, but she had some scarring and some stiffness in her neck. Lesley thought I had talent and much potential for fashion photography and connected me with swimsuit designers and other high-end models.

Another industry I was breaking into then was music scoring for film. I had recently done a special project score for actor Vince Edwards and a full score to two B movies: a sci-fi flick by Robert Marien called *Sojourn Earth* and Michael Elsie's *Citizen Soldier*, with Dean Stockwell, who would go on to a long and successful acting career, and Toni Basil, best known for the worldwide hit "Mickey" in 1983. But my priority now was my wife and children. Right or wrong, we had made a firm decision to raise our children around extended family, or at least close to family, and that meant moving somewhere away from Los Angeles.

Meanwhile, the western fad trickled down from the mainstream. The Cowboy's owner, Jack Wade, built another club in Anaheim called Crackers, where I was also hired as part of the house band. It was a brilliant concept where all the waitstaff were performers, mostly singers who would drop their trays from time to time and get onstage, high on a platform in the middle of the large room, and perform Broadway show tunes. There was a balcony high above that surrounded the entire room. A large kitchen and the dressing rooms were upstairs behind the bandstand, and the performers would parade down using the open stairs, which descended from the rear to the stage where the band would be playing. Someone in the group would be the master of ceremonies and announce the performer, and then we'd back their show. Every detail was well-rehearsed and well-choreographed—very professional. The club was always filled to capacity.

While I was working at Crackers, Brenda went with the kids to visit her parents in Vancouver. I opted then for renting a commercial loft in the downtown Los Angeles area, where I set up my photography and lighting equipment. There I'd do photography jobs, castings, and testings. Eventually I fully moved into my studio loft on 800 Traction Avenue and Hewit Street. It was a century-old commercial building where various young artists lived and worked. I leased from George

Rollins, an artist himself, and we became lifetime friends. There weren't many other artists yet in the area, so integrating with them was easy. Since then, big-interest and developers have taken over the region. Now it's gentrified for yuppies and called the arts district.

While I was living there, a full-size Cessna single-engine airplane, painted psychedelically, was nailed with a huge iron stake straight through its center to the wall of the old the American Hotel, the building across from where I lived. Below the Cessna was the entrance to Al's Bar, the West Coast's original punk club. Another popular late-night bar and eatery nearby was the Atomic Cafe. My favorite place to eat and sit for hours brainstorming and writing scripts with a friend, movie director Michael Elsie, was Gorky's, a Russian cafe by downtown's flower district. The booths were comfortable, and they had a self-service food bar where you could also have the most delicious omelets made. The ambiance made it easy to spend the entire day there doing our work, fueled by coffee, beer, or wine. The loft on Traction became my last home in Los Angeles.

The commutes to and from Crackers in Anaheim were still brutal, but now that I was living alone, it didn't matter much. My wife being away for the summer gave me a false sense of freedom. Besides playing at Crackers every night, I was doing photography jobs at my studio. I had frequent access to beautiful models, and the lure for side flings was always there. I had a long-standing pact with my wife to not mess around in the same town. The loophole in this agreement, which was part of our wedding vows, became my excuse for extramarital affairs. This time, we were in different countries, and it was easy for me to justify my actions, but eventually it took its toll on us. Hurt and resentment will always be imminent in an open or quasi-open relationship, unless you are, of course, Jean-Paul Sartre and Simone de Beauvoir.

Living in LA had become a struggle. My false sense of freedom, even if justified, was weighing me down. Now we were in a downward spiral, moving from house to house, and my family was falling apart.

Although it gave me a certain sense of mobility, the absence of Brenda and the children weighed on me—I missed them terribly. By the time they returned from Vancouver, Brenda and I had almost become strangers. We had no home to speak of; we were living in a rental property, and family-wise, everything was crumbling. On top of that, bulky antique furniture from the old Pasadena home was darkening our space and adding more weight to our lives. We knew we needed a substantial change—for the children and for us. Brenda knew all about my flings because she would always ask me, and I would tell her the truth. It was my odd way of being honest—I couldn't be faithful, but I could be forthcoming. What I couldn't figure out was that she never showed either anger or hurt from any of it. It all seemed like part of an agreement we had made when we got married.

Going back in time about five or six years earlier—a few days before our wedding, I got cold feet and called the whole thing off. As I explained to my new bride at the time, I realized I wasn't ready to settle down in a relationship. I was still touring and couldn't guarantee that I'd never have relations with other women. I honestly felt that, and I dreaded the idea of having to lie about it. I've never been one to live a double life. The whole marriage deal was constantly twirling around my head.

I even spoke with a friend, the only friend I had then in Vancouver, a saxophone player named Patience. We planned for him to pick me up just outside the church for a last-minute swift rescue operation before the ceremony. Fortunately, I didn't have the heart to go through with it. The night before the wedding, I reached out to Brenda. We had a talk about it, and she calmly told me that it was OK for me to feel that way and that everything would eventually work out.

I will never forget that conversation. It gave me the courage to go ahead with the marriage. Still, my unrelenting concern was that I didn't want to be a liar. So I went along with the ceremony, except for the vows of faithfulness, which must have been a bit shocking to the pastor and her family.

In hindsight, I could argue the merits of what I did as well as the failings. On the positive side, we built a family, remained together for eleven years, and were separated but still married for another eleven years. There was virtually no lying in our relationship, and best of all, we had four beautiful children whose lives I can't imagine being without for a single moment. My lack of commitment had nothing to do with Brenda. I loved her, and it wasn't that she lacked anything in any way. It was just my own personal issues; it was about me not being ready or lacking the courage for that commitment. Later I was ready because I'd matured enough through hard knocks to have the capacity for commitment while still being honest. I just wasn't then.

Brenda remained supportive despite my shortcomings, and we did our best to talk it out and find the best solutions. We decided that the best thing was to sell all our possessions and leave Los Angeles. A vast patio sale took care of getting rid of all our furniture and other items that proved weighty. Whatever we couldn't sell, we gave away, making some acquaintances and neighbors very happy. What we wanted most was a high standard of living for our children. We agreed that the children needed to be close to extended family, which neither of us had in California. We knew it was time to make a tough decision: Vancouver, Canada, or San Juan, Puerto Rico? With little hesitation, we booked a one-way flight for the six of us to San Juan, where my family was.

THE TOWER.

THE TOWER

The Tower often comes up when everything in your life feels like it's crumbling, and you have no way out. What doesn't work your life must be torn down in order to build something strong and sturdy in their place—something solid that can last a lifetime. But this card is a reminder that change is a natural thing in life, and it's one that we must embrace.

Once I returned to San Juan, I realized I had changed too much to have a complete sense of belonging. The culture shock was just a small aspect of readjusting. I also carried a cultural deficit. And if returning to San Juan after twenty years was a shock for me, I can't imagine what it must have felt like for Brenda. Our root cultures were so different. When people come to Puerto Rico, they either fall in love with the island and its way of life or they hate it. By far, most people love it, but Brenda didn't adapt well. Perhaps our particular circumstances of having four little ones while staying with my parents—which we had to do at first—made it hard for her. But as much as I tried, there was no way to make it right.

I also felt that I had fallen behind many of my local peers who had made a life in a higher academic environment. So I forced my brain to learn about the things that I'd neglected most and thought were the most challenging for me. I began studying deep and complex mathematical concepts, astrophysics, and quantum physics. At first, I wasn't able to understand a lot of it—especially the equations—but I stayed with it. I called it mind jogging. One of the many challenging books I read at that time was Douglas Hofstadter's *Gödel, Escher, Bach: An Eternal Golden Braid*. I understood the concept well, and it was revealing and fascinating, but the equations were a stretch for me. I studied everything

I could about business, and also delved into poetry and classic literature and art.

Looking back, my biggest battles have been about belonging and fluidity. I have struggled with both. I started drifting away from my roots since I left home, and taking drugs alienated me even further. While my initial intention for using drugs was to explore the world and myself from a different perspective, there were times that I got caught in its ugly grip. At some point, it became a hit-and-miss situation until I was fully absorbed. Then my identity was sucked up, everything became blurry, and I lost flow—lost fluidity. Everything became a struggle. But while going through the process, I felt that I was gaining something more profound. Perhaps becoming self-conscious is the price of the process of attaining higher consciousness. There were times when I felt I had to relearn everything anew—that's how far I had shifted perspective.

After almost a year of struggling with readjusting to island life, I finally got a job. I had an impressive resume in regard to the music and film industries. I got interviews for work related to these fields, but I was always rejected as "overqualified." I sensed that the real reason was fear. I was genuinely looking for work to feed my family and was willing to start at any level and ultimately contribute to wherever I'd be working. But I suppose the level of my professional experience might have been threatening to some.

The only film-related job I could get was working for an advertising agency. Although there I had an opportunity to film documentaries, the advertising world further stripped away any passion and love I might have had left for filmmaking. I had to use my talent and hard-earned knowledge to make commercials—little movies telling lies to the audience, persuading them to part with their hard-earned money for something they didn't need. Is there anything more undignified than sitting around a large conference table, with men and women with college degrees, wearing expensive suits and dresses, spending half a day of their life discussing how to push a toxic rubber ducky on an otherwise healthy kid? I despised it; still, I had to work, had to pay my bills, and had a family to feed.

Regardless, I took another chance and left the agency. I was the head of a department, and Raul, my most direct assistant, shed tears upon learning of my intention to leave. Despite my fair warnings that he wouldn't be making nearly as much money, he also left the agency to work with me. We ended up prospering, and Raul remained my loyal right hand for many years.

I tried mitigating and keeping some familiarity by buying a comfortable full-floor penthouse apartment in Condado, near where my parents lived, in an area where most people spoke English, but Brenda and I still weren't happy in Puerto Rico or with each other. Our future together on the island didn't hold promise. We also felt that our children weren't getting the best options, and being close to family didn't turn out to be the panacea we had hoped it'd be. Our eldest son, Marcel, had the hardest time adjusting; he was already showing signs of going astray. Again, we analyzed the overall situation and started looking back to the mainland and looking for better options, another place to build a nest. To remain close to family and my work in San Juan, this time we chose Florida, a lot closer than being on the West Coast.

The six of us got on a plane and arrived in Miami. There we rented a car and set out on a tour of the state of Florida, looking for a place to settle. After scanning both coasts and central Florida, we opted for Orlando. Part of the mission was locating a top school district for our four young ones, and Winter Park/Dommerich had it.

We bought a house in Orlando, and the plan was for Brenda to move in with the children and I would follow. It didn't happen that way. Brenda and the kids moved into our new house, but as much as I despised the advertising world, it paid the bills. I will always remember the deep pain in our separation, especially being far from the little ones, but there didn't seem to be another solution. I would join them regularly with frequent commutes and live with them as a family in Orlando whenever I could. The commutes at the beginning were weekly, but the intervals between commutes eventually widened. And as much as I wanted it, establishing a business in Orlando wasn't happening—there were a lot of promises but no action. It was becoming a major uphill struggle. I soon realized that living in Central Florida wasn't my cup of tea.

As the time between commutes expanded, little by little we drifted apart. We both eventually ended up having new lives. While Brenda and the children made their life in Orlando, I remained in San Juan, and eleven years would go by before we finally got divorced. To our credit, it was an uncontested separation, and to this day Brenda and I get along fine. For me, separated or divorced parents maintaining a good relationship is vital for everyone's well-being, especially the children's.

There has always been mutual respect, cooperation, rapport, and even requited admiration between my first wife Brenda, and my second wife, Katira. That alone has been empowering and a blessing for the entire family—not to mention convenient at family reunions.

Meanwhile, the agency business became more meaningless by the day. I left but remained close enough to do freelance work, and some people I worked with remained lifelong friends. Still living in Condado, I rented a small division in an office building nearby, bought some used essential recording equipment, and established a studio for producing voice-overs and jingles. I continued directing commercials, which paid well. At least now, I could choose my work and make my own decisions. My first client was the agency where I had been working. Business flourished quickly. Now that I was living alone on a full penthouse floor, I could turn most of the space into a larger and more professional recording studio and a film production office with a small in-house staff.

Another thing that made the freelance agency work more bearable was working with my old school friend Vinnie. Vinnie owned one of the major recording studios in San Juan, and also had become a top sound engineer. We did a lot of sessions together, and he guided me through the idiosyncrasies of commercial jingle production. He also helped me feel back at home. Vinnie had purchased a thirty-six-foot Cigarette racing boat, the *Tequila Sunrise*, where we spent awesome weekends hopping around the Virgin Islands. One memorable time was when we went to Foxy's Wooden Boat Regatta in Jost Van Dyke on Labor Day weekend. Just knowing that I had something to do with the major world events that were now taking place every year on that tiny island since our visit over two decades ago during the 1960s was insane. When we gave LSD to Foxy for the first time, we had no idea he'd be inspired to go out and see the world, and upon his return create Foxy's Wooden Boat Regatta and Foxy's Old Year's Night celebration.

It was a full-moon night when we departed from the town of Fajardo, where we had spent the night preparing to sail. The *Tequila Sunrise* was powered by a pair of racing engines that Vinnie had installed. He had won some races recently, and he hadn't had time to swap to the cruising engines. We left the marina at 1 AM, and the sea was majestically lit by a full moon. The power of the boat was exhilarating while we skimmed above the incoming waves, 180 kilometers east to St. Thomas, where we had planned to spend the first night. But we didn't. After refueling in

St. Thomas, we went ahead and made the stretch to Jost Van Dyke.

When we sailed into Jost Van Dyke's Great Harbor late at night, we became the ultimate nuisance. The bay was filled with all kinds of sailboats, some of which had come from as far as Sweden and Denmark, and we were one of the few motorboats. On top of that, our racing engines had a ferocious roar even when idling. Suddenly we were flooded by searchlight beacons. We weren't welcome, but we quickly shot the engines and claimed our stake in the gorgeous horseshoe harbor. At sunrise the scenery rivaled any possible dream of utopian fantasies. Beautiful European damsels were swimming naked in the water. True to our now obnoxious reputation, we disrupted the quiet morning by plugging in our electric pianos, guitar, and amps and jamming from our boat. The result was gainful. A handful of beautiful girls swam to our boat—they welcomed the break from being stuck in sailboats for long periods of time. Also, the *Tequila Sunrise* was fast and furious, hence exciting. In no time we could get to any of the sweet spots on different neighboring islands in the Sir Francis Drake Channel, for breakfast, a picnic, or a glorious, secluded dip in paradise.

Back in Jost Van Dyke, the level of partying was exponential. The number of kiosks casually serving huge Caribbean whole lobsters, the alcohol, and other party favors, along with amazing calypso music, was heavenly. I made sure to go and find Foxy and remind him that I was among the young musicians who had visited the island twenty years ago and given him acid. He lit up to the story and welcomed me back to "his" island.

At some point in the evening, I swam back to the boat for a short nap. Later, I felt the boat bobbing in the water, and what followed was seeing the front deck hatch door being opened and a pair of legs coming down the hatch. The rest of the body got stuck, so there was a pair of gorgeous legs and a naked butt trying unsuccessfully to slide down the hatch. I was baffled at the sight, but I went ahead and assisted the young lady down to the cabin. She explained that she was swimming away from her fiancé, whom she had had a fight. She then took off to the water and saw our boat in the dark of the night and decided to take refuge in it. While she was an intruder, I felt an obligation to protect her. I gave her a towel, and she relaxed. She went on explaining that she and her fiancé had plans to get married upon their return to mainland USA and that they were excited to be on an adventure, but that he was "being an asshole." Vinnie eventually joined us, and we welcomed her to stay with us in the boat. Her fiancé also caught up and asked permission to board. She agreed, so we let him join us. They were an all-American sweet young couple on their "dream vacation."

We all remained together drinking tequila, listening to music, and having a good time. At some point I noticed that she was hitting on me. I wanted to take a break from the drinking, and also to give the couple some space without me being around, so I went in the cabin to lie in bed for a while. Unexpectedly, she followed, jumped in bed with me, and we made out, but I felt uncomfortable about the situation, so I stopped her. What followed is that she took off the little bit of clothing she had on and with an alluring gesture, dove into the dark night water. At this point I was feeling concern for her fiancé, so I chose to stay in the boat with the guys instead of dipping with her. After a swim around the boat, she climbed back onboard from the stern side over the transom, looking like a sea goddess with her light-golden hair dripping water on her blooming breasts and naked siren figure. We then searched for the charter sailboat they had come from and returned them safely.

It was insanely exciting revisiting Jost Van Dyke, especially after all the time that had passed since our first encounter. Forty years later, the memory was still vivid in my mind, which prompted me to write a brief memoir describing that first magical visit in detail:

"Caribbean Sunshine"
A psychedelic adventure in the Caribbean waters
by Carli Muñoz

One of the most memorable and transcendental music experiences I had was on a tiny island located just north of St. Thomas, Jost Van Dyke. This happened during the mid-'60s when our rock group The Living End created havoc during the summer in St. Thomas. Toward the end of our sojourn in St. Thomas, two local friends, Tutsi and Mario, invited the group to go to Jost Van Dyke, which we had never heard of, as a personal invitation from its "governor," Foxy. Without hesitation and animated with an adventurous spirit, we accepted. Soon enough, an old fisherman with his small outboard fishing boat boarded us and took us on the roughly twenty-kilometer stretch from St. Thomas' north end to Jost Van Dyke. Other fishermen took the rest of the group in their small boats. The vessel we were in didn't make it to shore due to motor failure just short of about three hundred meters from the shore. I was accompanied by a girl I'd just met in St. Thomas, and had a matchbox with four tabs of Owsley Orange Sunshine in my pocket. Being true to the adventurous spirit, I didn't want to wait for another fishing boat to come and tow us, so I took two tabs, gave my friend the other two, and off we dove into the pristine emerald-blue waters of the Caribbean Sea.

By the time we swam to shore, the perception of being there on ultra-heightened senses defied any common sense or normality. Forty natives of African descent, who were fishermen and British Crown subjects, inhabited the island. Besides the fishermen, there was a tax collector and the "governor"—his name was Foxy. As far as dwellings, the only concrete structures were the remains of a small one-room jail and the facade of an equally small chapel in ruins. The other solid structure comprised Foxy's house, a cozy wooden shack where he kindly lodged my friend and me during an unexpected storm on that evening. There were some other sparse small shacks made of wood and palm inhabited by the other natives. My girlfriend and I were the only ones who took the dive. Soon after our wet arrival, the rest of the band arrived on boats at the shore. That meant that some other Sunshine tabs had also come on land dry and safe.

It was beyond intense observing how an ordinary day in the Van Dykeans' lives would turn into the most dynamic, passionate, colorful, and aggressively prosaic, but cleverly poetic form of RAW calypso extravaganza—the calypso I never knew existed! It all started with our humble visitors' offering of the only treasure that we possessed (besides our green adolescence) to share: Orange Sunshine and a little weed for a chaser.

The prelude to the music was a game of dominoes between Foxy and his closest competitors on a makeshift wood and driftwood table under some dry palm leaf. This served as a catapult to the Sunshine effects experience. While the Orange Sunshine was covertly performing its breach on the senses' gateway, the game gained its own energy level. It became strangely aggressive with overtones of a struggle for life and death. Amidst the heavy sweat pouring out of charcoal black skin, the Sunshine evoked such adrenaline levels and tension that the half-naked gladiators took arms. Fortunately, the choice of weapons was musical instruments—most of them homemade. The only classical musical instrument was an old guitar with a few strings missing that Foxy played. Other musical instruments were a broomstick attached to a washtub with an old rope and a homespun tambourine, as well as other improvised percussion instruments.

The aggressiveness that had started during the domino game morphed into the musicians' own form of calypso. As they picked up their instruments with a vengeance, they started playing what seemed to be an eight- and possibly nine-bar cadence reminiscent more of jibaro Puerto Rican mountain music rather than calypso. The intensity, though, was in the verbal improvisation that each combatant engaged in. One would utter verses to the other about "how good I fucked your mamma," or how "your wife moaned louder with me," etc. How I wish I had a Sony Walkman Recorder then, although it was the intensity of the moment and the raw expressions that added to that singular and priceless event! What troubled me most is not remembering the structure of the music. I remember being highly impressed by it—it wasn't like any calypso I've ever heard before. Unfortunately, Jost Van Dyke is not the same as forty years ago, but Foxy is still there, playing and singing his music, not as prosaic as before, but profound. I can take you there—come rain or come shine.

Four days in paradise didn't change the fact that I was now separated from those I loved most. Big money was flowing in, but being without my family created a gap that I could only fill by being a workaholic. I was still emotionally devastated and remained like that for the next couple of years. I lived and breathed work at the studio with little to no social life. There was a restaurant, the Green House, a few blocks away, where I could have a late dinner and breathe out a day's work. Eventually, I found a quaint bookstore/cafe within walking distance, where I would regularly go to spend late afternoons with a coterie of friends old and new. Inadvertently, I found myself attracted to a young lady who ran the store.

One of her employees confided that her boss had been curious about me. Once I learned who she was, and knowing that a relationship with her would be impossible or disastrous, I tried keeping my emotions to myself. She was young and beautiful; her big black eyes were haunting, but kind. There was also a certain innocence she cautiously guarded. Her family was extremely rich, which made her less accessible. Besides, I had a self-imposed rule to never, ever get romantically involved with the daughter of very wealthy parents—it is about the likelihood of the relationship being controlled by the parents. But I was bewitched and bewildered.

One time, I gained her attention by buying an expensive collection of Cuban poetry from her store. To make my deed even more impressive,

I bought it for my friend as a gift, which I didn't fail to mention. The redeeming side was that I genuinely enjoyed giving my friend the collection. I believe he appreciated it immensely. When I was buying the book collection, with a beaming smile that could melt iron, she innocently asked, "Do you like poetry?" From the little I remember, I felt a momentary Lilliputian triumph from her words. Still, a bit of anxiety dominated, making me scramble for something to say, something that might sound meaningful. I lied. I said that I liked poetry. I remember saying it with a conviction that compounded the lie. At that point, I could appreciate poetry, but I was far from being knowledgeable or passionate about it.

I felt like an enchanted fraud (almost a frog) and channeled my feelings into music and writing. Although a distant and cordial friendship would have been sublime enough for me, which remained a possibility, I blew it. Even after learning about the young lady's engagement plans, driven by a false sense of hope and temporary madness, I handed her a cassette and manuscript with a series of songs and improvisations I had composed and recorded for her. The next day, she elegantly but solemnly gave them back to me, letting me know that she couldn't accept the gift. The message was unmistakable, and that should have been more than the end. But wounded egos don't work that way. It was then a transitional period in my life, and everything seemed to collapse around me. So I did the unspeakable. I buried my emotions, but instead of quietly and elegantly fading, I still frequented the bookstore inebriated and may have misbehaved. I will always regret my actions. But in that world, apologies of that nature are expendable.

Other significant flings took place during the next few years—one possibly being of a masochistic nature, which after pulling me up to the skies, released me on a free fall to dooms-land, deeper than ever. It never ceases to amaze me how powerful intuition can be. I was attending an O'Brasil[6] concert/dance activity at the Vanderbilt Hotel in Condado, across from where I lived, when I passed by a group of girls chatting. One particular voice caught my attention. It was in English. An entire world of ideas passed by in seconds, as if the universe knew what was about to happen. Two things were evident when I heard that voice; one,

---

6   O'Brasil was a very popular local band headed by composer and bandleader Roberto Figueroa. They played authentic Brazilian pop music and did frequent concerts for a large and faithful following.

I had to captivate that woman's heart, and the second was that I was going to pay for all my sins with that relationship. It all happened in a matter of seconds. It was fateful and happened just like I perceived it. Did I create it that way? Or did I see the events to come?

All the "coincidences" in the world aligned for us to end up together. It was as if there wasn't any choice, and it felt as if I was walking on air. Everything about Megan and I being together was beyond-this-world exciting. There was an energy level that was continuously driving us to the next exhilarating moment. We were silly; we were kids; we were knotty, adventurous, and unapologetically irresponsible—only in the moment. As much as our love was on fire, there were protective barriers on both sides. Despite being separated, I was still technically married, and she also had issues with a past relationship. Eventually, I found myself off balance and outspent. Events followed that were almost too much for me to handle. We were together for perhaps two intense years. Truthfully, time then was of no concern. Megan was quite younger than I was, and I was basically keeping up. But I was hovering and savoring every moment.

Megan's beauty, the way I saw it, came mostly from a tomboyish, adventurous nature she had, which at that particular time in my life was impossible to ignore. I had been drowning in my work and was far from anything remotely adventurous. In addition to her outgoing personality, she was physically stunning. She had beautiful thick, long, amber hair and compassionate yet adventurous blue-green eyes, full lips, dimples on her cheeks, and a radiant, almond-shaped face. The sexual attraction was insane, and every single moment together was beyond intense—even in regard to the silliest things. I remember one time we were at the beach in the water, and I said, "I just peed," and she excitedly responded, "Me toooo!!" with the wide-eyed and mouth-to-ears excitement of a nine-year-old. We traveled constantly, sometimes penniless, and still we had tremendous fun. It was the adventure, not knowing what would happen the next moment, that made it all the more exciting. Every moment, even the most seemingly insignificant event had meaning.

But what goes up must come down, and our relationship was no exception. Although separated, me still being married was in a way a safety net for not remarrying, and I suppose it was the same for Megan by hanging on to an ex-husband that she claimed she still had ties to. There's nothing

I could really point to, but somehow we began drifting apart. Perhaps I lost sight of my own needs and responsibilities. Distancing between us was imminent, and like a vulture waiting for the right moment, a higher bidder who was lurking around made his move and tied the knot.

The second part of my intuition, "Paying for all of my sins," came to be. The loss at first seemed unbearable, and it took at least one year of pondering on "what I did wrong" to recover. But what a lesson! The loss tested every bit of emotional strength I didn't know I had. Perhaps it is what I needed most to master the art of sustaining a future thriving relationship. But it wasn't my last heartbreak. Still after, I kept going through a string of failed amorous relationships, each one teaching me a different, much-needed lesson.

At some point I was still so distressed about the loss of Megan that a friend recommended I share my grief with a professional. There was a psychiatrist who lived near me in the Condado area who my friend highly recommended. Although I didn't think I needed to go that route, I booked a session with him anyway. His name was Archer Johnson, and he confided to be the discreet psychiatrist for both the rock artist Prince as well as Princess Stéphanie of Monaco, and frequently flew on private jets to treat them. I loved Archer from the start, although we only needed two highly productive and fun sessions. After sharing my grief and agony with him, he asked me point-blank: "What is it about Megan that caused you to lose so much sleep over her? Why?" After giving it a good amount of thought, I answered, "Well, she had a great butt." At that moment Archer, who was a big fat man, broke into a roar of laughter, so much that we both ended up on the floor in tears, almost choking to death from the laughter. Pain over.

Not long after, with the help of a dear singer friend, I wrote the words to a song called "Tujunga Waltz," which implies letting go. The music I had composed long ago, in 1969 or 1970, while I lived in a house at the north end of Tujunga Canyon in LA. It is the words, which I adapted to the song, that expressed the sorrow and then the letting go. There is a depiction in the bridge of the song of a time when Megan and I were crossing the mountain range between Arizona and Southern California. There we climbed a peak, where we danced to the moon and the stars. The song was first released on *Love Tales*, my first instrumental piano solo work, and then on *Follow Me*, with the vocals and full ensemble:

"Tujunga Waltz"
By Carli Muñoz

The coffee makes the break of dawn; it wakes me; I'm out of bed.
The pastry is sweet but not enough to fill me; I'm in the red.
You filled my heart with new love, and then you stripped it away.

Pretend I'm nothing to you, but baby, I'm just the same.
Now I can see through you; I no longer take the blame.
My cup was filled with sorrow but now is vanished away.

We danced the Tujunga Waltz. Right above the skies,
gliding sweet and flying.
Where the sun and the moon and the stars, they all watched
as we dance.

I want to seal my broken heart away from this empty nest.
For love for life for all it's worth, to win or lose; it's all the same.
And now I can see clearly—it's just me and my Tujunga Waltz.
I can see; clearly, I can see clearly—just me and the Tujunga Waltz.

Then came Hurricane Hugo. I was still living at the penthouse in Condado, and the loss after the Category 4 hurricane was enough to cripple my business and eventually drive me to bankruptcy. I learned when submitting a claim for the damage that the insurance company had canceled the mortgage insurance four days before the hurricane. Their declining coverage was not just financially devastating, but a puzzling situation. No one knew how that had happened, and I spearheaded a lawsuit on behalf of the building against the insurance companies, the brokers, and the banks—twenty-two entities in all. We won, but it took ten years to recoup any money. Meanwhile, I had lost my commercial film business when the near 160-mph winds destroyed twelve of my windows and most everything inside. I was in the apartment trying to film the atmospheric event with a thick towel wrapped around my head. The building was swaying, and there was glass flying all over the place, even scarring the concrete interior walls. The impact of Hurricane Hugo was a major setback, mostly to the many people left homeless and jobless across the island. For me it marked the end of an era and a new beginning.

Not long after Hurricane Hugo, I lost my mom. My mother was the rock of the family and the light of my life. She was a quiet person, but always kind and alert, observant and wise. I loved especially being alone with her. A sense of peace and joy was inevitable when you were around her. One day, after a visit to her dermatologist, we got the alarming news that she might have cancer. Once confirmed a few days later, we were informed that her lymphatic system had been compromised—it was no more than three weeks from the news of her condition to her passing away. It was devastating and frustrating news for all of us, but she was graceful all the way through. At some point and even without much hope, the oncologist suggested chemotherapy to my mom, along with the warnings of losing her hair. All she said, with an innocent and kind smile, was, "It's OK, I'll just wear a hat." That's my mom! After another week at the hospital, and just minutes after cracking a few jokes and a kind smile, she quietly passed on.

My mom's passing was a moment I had dreaded throughout my life, and I didn't have any idea how I would respond. I was surprised to find that when the moment came, I was at peace. I just had a warm and delectable sensation of my mom being all over and even closer to me, more than ever before—it filled my whole being. She remains close in spirit, but her physical presence was still a major loss for me. At that point all was lost—physically and emotionally.

Carli's mom, Melania, circa early 1940s

Carli and his mom, circa 1956

Carli at 15, dressed in a suit
for a night out

Carli playing his first organ, 1959

Carli's first Steinway D, with Diana and concert pianist Royer Williams

*The Living End performing at the Condado Beach Hotel
with the Diosa Costello Revue, circa 1964*

Carli with Diana

The Living End with Tessie Coen after replacing Diana

*Cover of the Space album, as released by Capitol Records
(notice the hand logo of the sub-label)*

Jack Rieley

Carli at Topanga House

Carli at far right, with The Beach Boys, posing for Dennis, Halloween 1970

Carli on the left with bluegrass band, early 1990s, California

The Beach Boys at their best—with Carl,
Ricky, Mike, Kenyatta, Al, and
Carli—early 1970s

Carli backstage at Wembley,
photo by Annie Wilson

Carli performing at an outdoor concert with The Beach Boys

*Andy Warhol and Christine McVie backstage at a Beach Boys concert at
Radio City Music Hall in Manhattan*

*Kiki Dee at a party celebrating her
and Elton John's No. 1 hit*

Carli playing a solo during a Beach Boys concert, flanked by Mike Love and Bruce Johnston, with Ed Carter and Mike Meros in background

With Brian Wilson in an arcade

The Beach Boys on stage in Japan, 1979

In the boarding line with The Beach Boys on tour

Carli performing during a Beach Boys
concert, flanked by Mike Love
and Bruce Johnston

Carli playing percussion at
The Beach Boys' free concert
in Central Park, New York

Carli during the filming of Dean Martin's music video

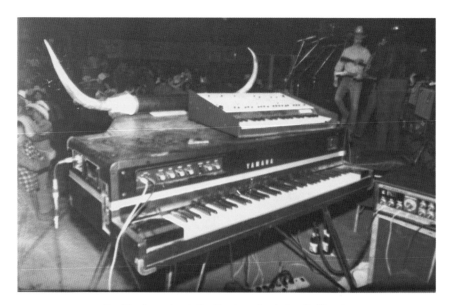

Carli's piano rig at the Cowboy, Anaheim, California

At Carli's artist studio, work in progress

Carli with Breaker, photographed by James Lynn

Katira at the Chantry in Vermont, in front of
Andy Warhol's Queen Elizabeth II

Eddie Gómez, Jack DeJohnette, and Carli

*Carli with Roman Klun and Justin Sullivan at recording studio, Brooklyn, NY,
Wangari Maathai session—a singular-moment-of-completion*

*Pen drawing by Jeremy Steig of Carli (cat), Eddie Gomez (monkey),
and nude waitresses, at the Elephant Castle in West Village
after doing a recording session in the city*

Carli playing piano at Carli's

Cruising Venice Boulevard with Dennis Wilson between recording sessions

With actress and model Marisa Berenson at the Chateau Marmont

PART 3

IX

THE HERMIT.

THE HERMIT

 The Hermit knows that the only way to process what is happening in life is to withdraw from the noise of the world and create a quiet space of solitude where you will encounter the innermost knowledge of yourself. The answers will come from within. Be very still, and listen, listen, listen...

The aftermath of the hurricane and then the loss of my mother created an emotional vacuum. I missed her soothing presence and everything about her. I missed seeing her quietly at home painting near an open picture window with the ocean's breeze caressing her hair. I felt my children's absence more than ever, and my string of failed relationships depressed me even further. I was also back to square one financially. I still had a mortgage, a car loan, and living expenses for my family in Florida, and suddenly no income. The hurricane had crippled the island. I then made a firm decision; my advertising-related work was over. From that moment on, regardless of the financial pressures and consequences, I was just going to play the piano—acoustic jazz trio, specifically. I took a substantial financial hit, but I didn't mind starting over.

Amid all the significant losses—the hurricane, my mom's passing, my bankruptcy, my family being away, and all of the failed relationships—I regained a sense of strength and the will to move forward. I put myself at the helm—placed all bets on me. I'm a believer, also a tried-and-true example of the power of intention. Every major black-and-white life decision I ever made and stood by eventually brought me beyond the desired results.

The path was narrow because jazz wasn't for most people, especially in Puerto Rico. Second, clubs couldn't pay for a live trio.

To make it more challenging, part of my pledge was to play only acoustic pianos—no synthesizers or electronic keyboards. Besides, the bass had to be upright—a real classic jazz trio, no compromises.

Despite all the demands, I put together my first trio and had my first gig. The only places that could afford to pay for a jazz trio and that would have a decent acoustic piano were the big hotels and resorts. Fortunately, it was a time when there were a lot of renovations, and new hotels were on the rise. Thanks to a local booking agency, which filled the moribund Local Musicians Union gap, my jazz trio never stopped working. I had built a reputation for being on time and for consistency, and foremost, the music was the real deal. The agency got behind what I was doing, and there wasn't a new hotel in its first year without the Carli Muñoz Jazz Trio.

The era of opening hotels with my jazz trio lasted eight years. It was a very significant and valuable period because for me it was the perfect workshop. The level of freedom I had for experimenting, learning, and practicing new material and ideas on the job was perfect for my development as a jazz pianist. Since the '80s, I have felt sometimes that I wasted twenty years dedicated to playing rock music. But I know they weren't wasted. You can inseminate jazz with all kinds of influences because it is fertile ground, and every musician's trajectory is different. You want your voice to stand out, and that only comes from who you are and what you've been doing. It is always unique.

By around the time of Hurricane Hugo, I had inherited a partially abandoned five-acre prime property with a nearly four-thousand-square-foot home on a hill in Palmer, a Rio Grande sector. The property belonged to the Shwardetles. Arthur Shwardetle had been an industrialist friend of my dad since the mid-'50s, a German American, big-framed man who was as red and jolly as he was kindhearted. His appearance was as you would expect a wealthy American industrialist to look like in the '50s. He was also a brilliant chemist.

One day about three decades before, in the early summer of 1959, Arthur asked my dad if he could bring me to his estate in Vineland, New Jersey, to spend the rest of the summer with him and his wife, Miriam, known as Mimi. I was there when he asked, and I started jumping up and down with excitement. "Please, please, Dad, let me go!" Arthur explained that he and Mimi could never have children and that it would make them over-the-moon happy having me as a guest. That was a summer I would always remember!

A wooded area of fifty-four acres nested their estate in Vineland, including a lab, a chemical factory, and their residence on the property—a large American Colonial two-story white wooden house. Although the house was big, they built it for a couple, so besides the kitchen it had just their bedroom and a large office. I slept on the couch in the living room.

Arthur and his wife were opposites, at least physically. Mimi was tiny. She was Jewish, while Arthur was of German descent. They were both exceptionally kind and did everything to make me feel at home. There was a brand-new Steinway & Sons walnut grand piano in the living room, which I later inherited, along with furniture, books, and other items after they passed away.

Upon our arrival, one of the first things Arthur did was to show me his collection of vintage and modern handguns and rifles. Then we went out to shoot cans in the woods. The next day he took me to a small runway nearby to fly an old single-engine airplane he had. I had been in small planes before, but his plane was different. I'm not sure what it was, but it had the look of a Vultee BT-13 Valiant, a WWII fighter airplane. Arthur allowed me to take the controls—big mistake. Not used to the faster-than-expected response of the pitch control, I took the craft into a violent dive, which turned my stomach, putting me in bed for two days. As soon as I got back on my feet, we went shopping for a bigger airplane to add to his fleet—this time, a twin-engine six-seater Cessna 310. Arthur and I went puddle-jumping through the major cities on the East Coast in the Cessna while visiting leading museums in Philadelphia and Washington, DC.

Having a son is what Arthur and Mimi had wanted all their lives. And me being there inspired Arthur to go on an airplane- and motorcycle-buying spree. One morning we went to a motorcycle shop. He bought himself a new black R50 BMW and insisted on buying me a brand-new red and gold Ducati Bronco to ride alongside him. The thought of that bike in my mind, even now, is still thrilling! But when I called my dad for permission, he wouldn't allow it. The same day that Arthur bought his BMW, we took a turn while gravel racing a train, and we fell. (I later inherited the R50 but never picked it up.) After returning to San Juan, my dad bought me a red and gold Ducati Bronco. I suppose he just didn't want to have that joy taken away from him—lucky me!

I returned to San Juan sooner than expected. My parents had gotten a letter from the Shwardetles wanting to adopt me, and they immediately pulled back from them. Knowing the Shwardetles couldn't have children, and that for them I had been the closest thing to having a son, my parents sympathized with the older couple. But their request to adopt me was way over the top. Some years later, Arthur sadly died from heart failure, and Mimi, who was irreconcilably heartbroken, contacted me saying she wanted me to keep the house in Puerto Rico.

Vineland Chemical had been battling a superfund lawsuit from the EPA, holding the company responsible for improper disposal of toxic waste. As a result, there were conditions regarding inheritances and any transfer of wealth, and a conditional deal was made for my use and having first bid on the property. The deal was that while Mimi was alive, I would rent the property for $1 per year. Also, I could buy it for appraisal value. For me, it was an honor to give life to that magnificent property, which belonged to such dear friends. The house still had some of their furniture, which gave me a sense of continuity and familiarity with the Shwardetles.

The view from the house was magnificent. On one side it faced the rainforest, and on the other Las Picúas—and pristine Luquillo Beach and beyond on the northeast coast. Three pavilions—two cylindrical and one diamond-shaped—overlapping at different heights were part of the design. The round pavilions had large glass panes all around, combined with sliding glass doors. There were only thin concrete columns between the glass, turning two of the pavilions into octagons. The diamond-shaped module blended into a massive open kitchen, with a picture window facing the Atlantic Ocean. Two wings sprouted from each side of the center: one housing a studio and a multi-car garage, and the other, two large bedrooms with a full floor-to-ceiling glass door with an ocean view. Extended open-arched corridors and terraces followed the house's contours on both sides, surrounded by green grass and a blue horizon on the coastal side, and the peaks of the rainforest on the mountainside.

There I became a hermit, the fool on the hill with my dog, Breaker. Those were peaceful times. I embraced the solitude and reveled in the natural beauty surrounding me from all directions. It was the tranquility I needed for reflecting on my shortcomings and allowing self-reconciliation after a roller coaster life and all of my recent losses. Only an occasional visitor, often unexpected, would break the isolation.

One such visitor was James Lynn, a photographer friend who came to visit me with his professional equipment. He took an iconic shot of me playing piano and making eye contact with Breaker. The time spent with visitors was often high-quality. At night, the magic of the sky and infinite horizon would be overwhelming. It would be common to see satellites orbiting from the deck, among other unexplainable sightings in the sky and in the infinite horizon. Sometimes I would have sleepovers, which there was plenty of room for.

There I had some memorable parties. For one of them I invited all the ex-girlfriends and lovers I had had in recent years, which got a little hostile toward the end. As the evening progressed and the liquor took effect, the exes got progressively virulent. The animosity was at first subtle until I began to feel ice cubes running down on my back under my shirt as I played the piano. That was it—party over, everyone go home—well, almost everyone. Then, I threw another huge party for the entire staff and participants of Life Spring, a training seminar that followed in EST's footsteps.

Life Spring in Puerto Rico had been a great success, and I was among the first to participate in the workshop. Having done EST in the '70s, I knew it worked as a life-changing catalyst, and I welcomed the boost. After my involvement, I threw a big party on the hill with multiple tents, bar stations, and bands at different areas of the property. I still bump into people I don't know telling me they had been to that memorable party at my house on the hill.

Both EST and Life Spring came from the same source, Alexander Everett, a remarkable Englishman with plenty of history behind him. Werner Erhard with EST and John Henley with Life Spring carried the torch further. Both seminar trainings had a significant impact on American society from the '70s through the '90s, as they certainly had on me. Like in EST, Life Spring divided its vast program into sections. There was the "basic" training, which took place on two weekends. The more intense "advanced" training also took two weekends to complete, but with half of the capacity, it was more intimate. I did the first weeks of "basic" in San Juan but chose to do the "advanced" training in New York. I figured that there must be more significant challenges in the Big Apple than in San Juan, and I wanted it to be as brutal and meaningful as possible.

IV

THE EMPEROR.

THE EMPEROR

The Emperor is an authoritative force who has been through many experiences to achieve this status. It is a card of leadership and power. It is the archetypal father figure of the tarot and the symbol of masculinity, which brings structure, authority, and strength, and holds immense amounts of power over the outcome your life.

As I expected, the two weekends of "advanced" training in New York were industrial strength. The group was diverse, as always: businesspeople, actors, poets, Wall Street traders, clergymen, Jews, Catholics, Protestants, atheists, young, old, rich—you name it. We all were there for the long haul. From the beginning, the trainer and the staff paired each person with a buddy from the group. They paired me with Keyla, a young Black woman from Washington, DC who had AIDS—she remained my buddy throughout the entire experience, and our task with each other was to give unrelenting support in getting through the experience.

The training was intense from the start and built to a crescendo culminating on the final day of the second week. Because there was an oath for graduates to not reveal the content, no one knew what to expect. (Since this particular script for the seminar no longer exists, I find no harm in sharing this event.) The last exercise of the second weekend was highly anticipated because of the announced preparations. The trainer assigned everyone a role opposite to their personalities. That meant that if you were, for instance, afraid of sexuality, the role assigned would be of a stripper, and you would have to act it out with music and all its particulars in front of the group. Or if you were overconfident—cocksure—the role assigned would be that of a quiet character of a taciturn nature.

You had to play the role and go out in the city within a one-hour break and rent a stripper's costume, or a librarian's, or whatever your costume would be. Everyone had to play according to the rules—except me and my buddy. They separated us from the group and took us to a room in the back. The instruction was to remain still and silent—we were not allowed to participate with the rest of the group.

Meanwhile, the trainer, Candice, a powerful and assertive, full-framed, strikingly beautiful red-headed woman who must have been in her late forties, was in the principal room (a large convention room) assigning the roles. Although this last exercise was meant to reveal more profound truths about yourself and letting go, the group was having fun at this point. It felt more like a big costume party—a welcome shift after the revealing but grueling two weeks of self-confrontation. I could hear the roar and the laughter from the back room where we were to remain quiet. Thoughts of anger and disappointment ran through my mind: Why me? Why us? Why are we are being singled out from everyone for the most fun event—the grand culmination of two weeks of hard work?

Then, adding insult to injury, the trainer came into the room and gave us instructions: Our role was to be the servants for a lunch that would take place after the role-playing event. She ordered us to go to a costume store and get a classic butler outfit for me and a French maid outfit for my buddy. She gave me $150, collected from the group, to put together (in one hour) a lush buffet for the seventy-five participants plus the staff. We were instructed to serve everyone formally, without speaking to them or looking them in the eye—we could only look at them from the nose down.

Those were the instructions. My buddy and I scrambled out, taking a cab to a costume store I had seen in the West Village and got our outfits. Then we took another cab uptown, closer to the venue, where we stopped at a deli that seemed to have much of the stuff we were looking for. There we bought trays of healthy salads, various meats, lots of fruits and vegetables, and fresh flowers for decoration. We got in another taxi with all the stuff in large trays and made it back on time and on budget. We set up a dining room with tables and chairs from a storage room back at the venue. I can't remember where the silverware came from, but everything was perfect. While we were in the back with doors closed making all the lunch preparations, we could hear the music and the roar of the event, but we weren't allowed to go even near the door. With resignation, my buddy and I both played the role to perfection. Knowing how challenging our part must have been while serving, some participants expressed pity and compassion. Still, I wasn't permitted to even look at them to thank them or acknowledge their sympathy. I tried to contain a few tears of self-pity after one of their heartfelt comments.

After dinner, we were instructed to tidy up the back area where it took place, while the rest of the group was led back into the ballroom. While still in the backroom, some staff members came in and asked me to sit on a chair from the dining set. There, someone from the staff blindfolded me, took off my shoes and socks, and rolled my butler's tuxedo pants almost to my knees. If there was to be a depiction of The Fool at the peak of his journey, that was it! Everything had turned quiet. Now as I was blindfolded, barefoot, and flanked on both sides, two staff members lifted me by each arm and carefully led me to the larger room.

There was an eerie silence during the slow and long walk. I could perceive the room was dark, and I could vaguely see some flickering lights through the cloth of my blindfold. Then they assisted me up two or three short sets of steps, turned me around, and seated me on a chair. This time the chair was comfortable. What I felt next was my feet being placed in a bucket of lukewarm water. Someone removed my blindfold, and I realized that I was sitting on a throne in the middle of the vast room. The rest of the participants lined up on the path I had just walked, holding torches (hence the flickering lights), all with all their attention on me. Candice was kneeling, reverently washing my feet with the lukewarm water and a soft cloth below in front of me. By that time, I could hardly contain my emotions.

The trainer stood up and turned around to address the group, telling them something to the effect that I was the chosen one to play the server role, symbolizing humanity's server, because of the potential for leadership and humanity I had displayed throughout the two-week training. I could never express what I felt then. What followed was all the participants gathering forward and lifting my body over the top of their heads, passing me from hand to hand—I felt like I was levitating across the room—while Sheena Easton's "When He Shines" played. The song had been picked by the trainer and staff to characterize me. It is hard recalling a more rewarding experience—ever! As for my buddy, it appeared that she knew ahead of time what was in store for me and was all smiles. We hugged profusely. After I left the training, the city of New York was mine once more!

A few years after introducing Life Spring in Puerto Rico, the same group created a series of events where they brought influential authors and leaders related to the New Age movement, including Deepak Chopra, Brian Weiss, Wayne Dyer, and Alexander Everett, the father of EST and Life Spring. Although I was not directly involved, I was close to the group that was bringing the celebrities, so I often assisted during the talks. Having met Werner Erhard in the '70s, I was familiar with the movement's history and origins. And since Werner was a Beach Boys fan, we once met backstage at a Beach Boys concert at the Anaheim Stadium in California. He landed in a helicopter behind the bandstand before the concert. Jane Fonda was also there and joined in the huddle. In particular, I wanted to have an intimate conversation with Alexander Everett regarding the roots of EST and Life Spring, which had had such a significant impact on my life.

When the group brought Alexander Everett to do a two-day event seminar in San Juan, I was at the peak of being "the fool on the hill" in Palmer. I had adapted to the secluded life, with only my dog Breaker and my old CJ4 Jeep. I asked my friends who brought Alexander to allow me to spend an entire day with him. They agreed that I would pick up Everett in the morning and that we would spend a whole day together on the hill. If I didn't miss the property in Palmer after I left it, it is because it served its purpose well while I had it. My day spent with Alexander Everett on the hill was transcendent.

We spoke of many things, but it was mostly the Merkaba meditation that caught my attention. He described how, during his world travels, he had come upon the practice of Merkaba, and then he demonstrated the complex meditation process. I recorded the whole thing on a cassette, which I must still have somewhere. On some occasions I performed the meditation as described by Alexander, but at some point I had to stop— it was frighteningly powerful. The practice involved visualizing complex three-dimensional geometric figures, like tetrahedrons, spinning in regions of your spiritual body in counter-rotation, turning oneself into a vessel.

Later in the afternoon, we got in my Jeep and headed back to town. Alexander had a small group conference that evening, and I had promised to return him on time. I rushed through the scenic route of Loiza, Vacía Talega, and Piñones, a bumpy and curvy backroad along the coast back to the guesthouse where he was staying in Ocean Park. At the conference, he mentioned how scared he was on the ride back from my house—everyone laughed. I then commented, "But I got you back on time."

XIV

TEMPERANCE.

TEMPERANCE

Temperance is a card about balance, patience, and moderation. It reminds you to go with the flow of your life instead of trying to force its pace or direction. You have been calm and you can help others, so you need to reflect on your priorities and then create a positive flow with a balanced life.

In the years since Arthur Schwerdtle's sudden death, Mimi had been suffering insurmountable grief. I was still living at the house, and Mimi and I talked almost every day on the phone. I was able to visit her a couple of times in Vineland with my daughter Melanie, but Mimi remained inconsolable.

One dreadful night in May 1997, I got a call from the Schwerdtles' estate attorney telling me that Mimi had been murdered. She was shot four times in her home while she was dragging herself to the telephone. The police investigation concluded that her maid had killed her. I never believed that story. The maid was convicted, but there were higher powers at work. I spoke on the phone with the Vineland chief of police, who advised me not to come to the funeral. He informed me it would be dangerous and that they couldn't guarantee my safety. It was a tremendous shock to me, but there were signs that something terribly wrong was going on at the estate. In our most recent calls, Mimi had expressed a tremendous amount of fear, especially of the Feds who were stationed at the property surveilling her calls. She had gone through a recent episode of being bullied by them, being physically pushed, threatened, and accused of hiding large amounts of cash in her yard. In addition, shortly after Arthur died, Mimi told me that lawyers from a sinister local Vineland law firm, the one assigned to handle all their insurance policies, ransacked their house, taking the gun collection with them and other expensive personal items.

Tragically, as of 1966, the EPA had unleashed a superfund multimillion-dollar lawsuit against Arthur and his company, Vineland Chemical, for improperly disposing of large amounts of arsenic that eventually entered nearby rivers and lakes. The suit would take all of their assets and worst of all, their lives. There was also a Philadelphia law firm, Fox, Rothschild, O'Brien & Frankel, handling the superfund case's legal representation. My father later revealed to me that during the Cold War with Russia, the US Defense Department had approached Arthur by asking for his participation in a biological warfare program. But Arthur was a pacifist and refused. It is possible that that decision later brought Arthur dire problems with the Feds, prompting them to target Arthur for the worst kind of lawsuit. A superfund lawsuit demands that those found guilty of violating certain environmental laws either clean up the damage or aid the EPA in doing so.

I had gotten involved with the case after noticing the Philadelphia attorney's exorbitant fees—so far close to $2 million—plus much harassment of Mimi, and very little progress. I reached out to my cousin Karen, who lived in Philadelphia. Her husband, Anthony J. Drexel Biddle III, was well connected in the region, and he recommended a young lawyer he knew, Steve Rabner (a fictitious name), who specialized in environmental law. The young lawyer's father, a judge, had been one of the EPA's founders in New Jersey. He took the case.

After Steve and I met with Mimi at her Vineland residence, we went to Philadelphia to fire the law firm. There was a dark cloud at the attorneys' meeting from the unexpected termination, but we had to do it. I admired Steve's brilliance and courage. About four months later, someone found him dead for no explicable reason at the Philadelphia men's club where he was a member. He was only in his mid-thirties. Since then, I have reached out multiple times to Vineland journalists and cold case detectives in New Jersey to no avail—the case remains cold.

About a year after the murder of dear Mimi, the state executors in New Jersey had taken possession of all the Schwerdtles' properties. Soon after, they would have to liquidate the house on the hill with its five acres. Regardless, as much as I enjoyed the house, I missed being in the city. Being a hermit would not be permanent if I could help it. Still, losing the house was a great loss.

I still had the penthouse in Condado, but since the hurricane, it was more a shell with a bed and a few storm-damaged furniture pieces. I had replaced the twelve broken windows, but the studio wasn't operational. I parked the Concert Grand Steinway piano at the home of an artist friend, Dafne Elvira, sold the penthouse, and moved to a small apartment in Old San Juan, next to Capilla del Cristo, a chapel built in 1753, and Parque Las Palomas (Pigeon Park). The apartment was small, but rustic and cozy, with an open loft upstairs with spiral stairs connecting to the bedroom and the bathroom. There was only one window, but it was a picture window overlooking the entrance to San Juan Bay over a Steinway Grand I had inherited from the Schwerdtles—you could see gigantic ships slowly drifting in and out of the bay. The adjacent wall from Pigeon Park had been built in the eighteenth century. The other piano that I parked at Dafne's home was a nine-foot Steinway D Concert Grand that my dear friend Vinnie had given to me when I returned from California. He had two Concert Grands and must have sensed the nostalgia I had from our youth when I had a perfect Steinway Concert Grand piano at my parents' house, which he had so often played at when we were kids.

Carl Wilson had been on my mind frequently. He had been diagnosed with lung cancer, and I had recently gone back to Los Angeles to see him for what would be the last time. Carl was the sole purpose of my visit. We had a lovely, quiet dinner along with his wife, Gina, at their home in the hills of West Hollywood. Carl's friend and personal manager, Jerry Schilling, and his wife, Myrna Smith, a session singer and member of the vocal group Sweet Inspirations, were also there. I remember stopping for flowers on my way from the hotel and picking the most beautiful and meaningful bouquet I could find. He knew his days were numbered, but he was in good spirits and at peace with his condition. Naturally, he tired easily, so I kept the visit short and returned to San Juan the next day.

On my flight back to Puerto Rico, I got to fully ponder the impact of Carl's imminent passing. (He died months later, in February 1998.) Like Dennis, Carl had been my friend and ally. He was the first member of the band to believe in me, and we remained close through thick and thin. Now I really knew that with Dennis and Carl gone, a chapter had been closed. I loved Brian, but the connection wasn't there. Brian barely connected with himself, let alone with others. But the Wilsons were different, no question about it—they weren't ordinary people.

One time in a conversation, Dennis or Carl mentioned that they hadn't gotten to grow up like normal kids, that they missed a certain youth because of their early fame. That makes all the sense in the world, but it doesn't explain their extraordinary talent. Also, their relationship with their father Murry must have been a huge influence on their character. But that is no different than with anyone else—we are all in one way or the other influenced by our parents. The Wilsons made their mark in the world, in our generation, and beyond, like few brothers have done in the history of music.

Back in Old San Juan, I met many talented people and made lots of new friends. Being centuries old and charming, the old city is the preferred home for artists, galleries, and creative people. Also, it is where many influential businesspeople live or have a second or third home. The properties in Old San Juan can be deceiving by looking at their facades alone. Their playful and cozy Spanish colonial architecture from hundreds of years ago often conceals massive amounts of living space. The homes often feature very high ceilings, exposed wooden beams, interior patios, and various levels of roof terraces. The walls, built thick and sturdy to withstand constant cannon bombardment from galleons, have survived centuries of wear.

One thing I liked best about living in Old San Juan was that the moment I'd walk out to the street, I'd be in a city alive with people, restaurants, and stores, and most likely I'd bump into someone I knew. You could walk anywhere—like walking around in a large mall—but it was the real deal, and in addition, charming. Most of the streets still in use today are the cobblestones initially built for horse carriages. Unfortunately, in some areas, boneheaded politicians replaced the original cobblestones with newer and inferior facsimiles. The new ones are far from the aspect, weight, and quality of the original ones, which were used as ballast on ships en route to the island in the early 1700s.

Meeting new people while living in the old city was fun. House parties were frequent, and it widened my circle of acquaintances. Eventually, there was a nucleus of friends who I'd enjoy most and whose friendship I knew would be genuine and lasting. That initial group of friends made living in the old city so much more unique and would eventually inspire me to open a restaurant.

You might think that by growing up in Ocean Park and having many friends and an active social life in my youth, I would have tons of friends now that I'm back home. But it's not that way. When I left, I didn't look back, and the experiences I had are not in line with most of those of my old friends. The fool's journey detaches you from your past. You have to choose your friends anew. Most past friends and acquaintances operate from a different perspective, often far from relating or connecting with mine in a deep sense. I have music fans, restaurant fans, and plenty of acquaintances. I also have friends, but I choose them.

While living in Old San Juan, I played at the El Convento Hotel, a recently renovated Carmelite convent, dating back to 1651. I played there just one night a week. But there I built a sizable local clientele. Playing at El Convento was the springboard to opening my restaurant. There I met many of the future critical players in creating Carli's. Some of these new friends were visual artist Dafne Elvira, Jorge Zeno, chef Patricia Wilson, sommelier Angel Valentín, and Jim Bonbright—who became my business partner. Also in Old San Juan, I met Nildín Saldaña, who would become one of my dearest friends and play a huge role in the making of Carli's.

Once we secured the locale at the iconic Banco Popular Building, transforming the space into a fun and artistic fine-dining restaurant was my priority. My group of friends and I got to work on it. I didn't have a formal design, just my hand drawings and pure intuition guided me. I had never owned a restaurant or worked at one other than playing piano in some corner. Interestingly, I had learned a lot from being tucked in those corners without knowing it—mostly what not to do. When the Ritz-Carlton came to Puerto Rico, I played in the lobby with my trio for its first year. I was there when the waitstaff was being trained, which seemed rigorous. Yet the service I observed was mediocre. I would often have to get up from the piano in between songs to get a server after seeing a guest twisting their head around hoping for service, and I'd be the one to tell the waitresses to pay attention. Those little but meaningful experiences made me a better restaurant owner.

My travel experience with the Beach Boys, staying at the top hotels and dining at some of the world's best restaurants, was also helpful. But most of all, it was the people I surrounded myself with who made all the difference. Since I was thirteen, I have been a bandleader; I know how to lead, set the example, and delegate. It was my new friends who, by sheer love and belief in me, engaged selflessly in creating something beautiful and lasting. We also had fun doing it. It all started with

Aparicio, El Convento's accountant, asking me, "Carli, why don't you open your own restaurant?" Then, a year later, a complete stranger, Jim Bonbright, stopped me on the sidewalk and offered his partnership and financing. Local artist Jorge Zeno had a revelation about the name and created the logo. Banker Richard Carrión gave his blessings and became my landlord. Dafne Elvira generously shared her artful musings. Chef Patricia Wilson recommended the perfect chef, Jorge Cruz. Sommelier Angel Valentín brought a joyful spirit and expertise in wines and service. My dear friend Nildín Saldaña provided meticulous details. Finally, Jim West's masterful carpentry made the vision reality. Fausto and Katira came later. Voila—perfection!

Nildín was infinitely supportive and helpful in creating Carli's. She also assisted me when Carli's was in its infancy. I will always remember when, Nildín invited me to a get-together at her apartment in Condado on my fiftieth birthday. When I arrived, it was a *big* surprise. All four of my children were there. She had flown them in from Florida. I had the time of my life. I couldn't have been happier!

I loved Nildín so dearly, and as little boys do to girls, I was playful but perhaps overly puckish. Shortly after opening Carli's during high season, the restaurant was filled to its capacity, and Nildín offered to help by being the hostess. She would be more than a perfect co-host with her impeccable classy looks and natural charm. Her refinement, being second to none, came from her upscale upbringing during a time and place where such virtues were most valued. Additionally, she had a natural beauty that Hollywood movie stars of the heyday would have coveted. So, there is Nildín with a packed house, at her best in every detail, unassumingly exuding pure elegance.

Most of the diners were North American, and although Nildín's English was grammatically correct from her privileged education, she wasn't aware of the everyday nuances. To assist the servers during rush hour, Nildín asked me what the evening's featured main course was so she could go gracefully, table by table, greeting the guests and recommending our best option. The special for that evening was duck breast with lingonberry sauce. But knowing that Nildín wouldn't notice the difference, I told her that the sauce was "dingleberry." Yes, I know. Not to mention that I'd be risking my reputation with customers, let alone Nildín's.

Since I knew that she would make the infamous offering in the most charming and sincere manner, I thought she could get away with it.

By all means, Nildín didn't know what a dingleberry was or needed to know, ever! So, with all her grace and poise, she went table to table with the smile of a thousand suns, proudly announcing our special entrée for the evening: "Good evening, if I may, our special entrée for tonight is duck breast with dingleberry sauce." The startled look on our elegant patrons' faces was priceless, but no one dared say anything nor ordered the duck! I still get an earful about this every time I see Nildín.

Carli Cafe Concierto's motto from the start was "Una historia de amor, a punto de comenzar" (A love story, about to begin), and we lived up to its promise. Our goal at Carli's wasn't to make a ton of money, but to make people happy. It was typical for a happy camper to leave the restaurant floating and saying, "Don't know what was better, the food or the music." I couldn't count the number of folks who met there and then spent their lives together; either they met, got engaged, or got married at Carli's.

Carli's tenacious Cupid even helped my partner Jim, and eventually me, to find the loves of our lives. Besides finding a perfect mate, many folks claimed to have had their most profound musical experiences there. I will always remember many magic moments performing with various jazz trios I had at different times, and solo piano performances, sometimes "à la *Casablanca*," to a pair of lovebirds, or to one solitary customer at the end of the evening.

By this time, even as busy as I was with my new restaurant adventure, I felt that I had drifted away from one of the most significant people in my life, Jack Rieley, and I missed him—he was a root connection to my past. It seemed like a lifetime of events had gone by, and somehow I needed to reconnect. I still didn't want to go to Europe, but as destiny had it, he called me to let me know that he had come back to New York, and I went to see him. Jack had returned from Europe with his young boyfriend, Jaye Muller, and rented an apartment at the Police Building in Lower Manhattan. They also bought a chateau in Brattleboro, Vermont. Jack didn't feel comfortable with long drives or flying, so they would travel back and forth from New York on their private caboose on a train during the chateau's refurbishing. The caboose was set up like a home, with all the amenities, a fireplace, and even a balcony. It was a way for them to travel in privacy and comfort.

Jack had met Jaye in Berlin, and they became partners, both personally and professionally. Instead of writing songs and saving the world like we did in our days, their focus was rather on making a fortune, and they did. Seizing the moment with the digital technology and communications boom and the necessity for a portable fax system, Jack and Jaye hired a team of techies from Australia to work for them. The project became JFAX Personal Telecom Inc., a digital platform that made a lot of money for them. Later they sold JFAX, and the company went on to be included in the Fortune 500.

Their new home in Brattleboro was a 1916 Italian villa previously owned by a famous opera singer, soprano Stella Brazzi. It was designed in the tradition of grand European estates, complete with a columned entryway and a fountain in the center of the forecourt. Jack called his new villa The Chantry, meaning "an endowment for the chanting of masses"—also, "an intimate place of worship." As a concept, the name suited well the original idea of being a shrine for music, art, and beauty. I loved the extensive sculptured gardens.

The living room was dominated by a Fazioli grand piano and an original carved fireplace, and the walls were filled with fine art, mostly photographic art by Ryan McGinley, who would frequent the villa and do photo shoots. I remember an original Andy Warhol of Queen Elizabeth II by the stairs landing. I particularly loved the sunny, enclosed "orangerie"—a conservatory with skylights and a wall of windows filled with citrus trees and flowering plants—and the library with double doors leading to a balcony. The wine cellar in the basement, the pond with a waterfall, the greenhouse, and the carriage house were grand. When I visited, there were young adults all over the house and the estate. During the day the property's fifteen acres were a playground with live naked nymphs and bouncing satyrs flying off a giant trampoline in the middle of the forest, and after dinner the indoor heated pool and jacuzzi were a nightly bacchanalia.

I enjoyed the visit, but it was far from "old times." By then Jack seemed to be happily surrounded by young skateboarders from the Lower East Side in a quasi-hedonistic kind of setting—it was almost like being in an X-rated amusement park. Most of them were truly talented kids—artists, musicians, and photographers in the prime of their youth. Jack's boyfriend, Jaye, was welcoming. During my visit, he organized a rock concert for the town, and I played. Jaye, being a talented musician and songwriter, put the band together. I did miss having quality time with Jack. His new mien had him partially removed from being grounded.

While I visited Jack, I naively lent my apartment to my motley kitchen staff for a few weeks, and when I came back it was trashed beyond recognition. I was homeless again, but that didn't have to be a tragedy. In fact, this time I thought it could be an adventure. I was looking for a small room to live in, while sorting out my life once more, a new phase. One day I was walking on Ashford Avenue in Condado when I saw a familiar face. She was a young, beautiful, blond surfer lady whom I had seen around the Condado area. We engaged in a conversation, and when she asked me how I was doing, I told her I was looking for a room to rent. She took a deep breath and excitedly said, "I recently got divorced, and now I live alone in a huge two-story penthouse on the beach in Isla Verde." She went on, "The only thing that I have to warn you about is that I wear no clothes when I'm in my apartment—if that's OK, I have a room I can rent to you for only one hundred dollars per month..." *OMG* is the only thing I could think. Could it get any better? With little hesitation, I agreed. It turned out just as she described—or better. Not a bad landing from a "fool's journey"!

VI

THE LOVERS.

THE LOVERS

 The Lovers card represents the close relationships in your life. It means that the intimacy you have with your significant other is a rock-solid and you're happy together. As a couple you are confident and have the strength to empower each other. It is also a card about your values and decisions.

Nature, life, or whatever doesn't cease to be sobering, if not convoluted. As much fun as I was having, my attention now would have to take a serious turn. About a week before moving to the glorious "naked surf bunny's" penthouse, I had met someone special. We were seeing each other every day, and the excitement was exponential. If I had learned anything from my past failures, now was the time to prove it, and this time my better sense prevailed. It was now time to strap on my imaginary chastity belt.

We had five encounters in which I foolishly didn't realize it was the same woman, and they were all in Old San Juan. As I remember it, I took a walk from Carli's to a health food store to buy a carob candy bar I liked. On my way back on Calle Fortaleza, I saw a gorgeous woman alone, walking in my direction on the opposite sidewalk. Maybe she wasn't, but I remember her wearing an enormous hat and a long skirt, and as she walked, her gait swayed gracefully in slow motion. She appeared to be looking at the store windows along the busy street. I stopped in my tracks and just stood there, frozen, savoring my candy bar and watching her every move. She didn't acknowledge my presence, or so it seemed. What was racing through my head was, "Oh, my god, she's so beautiful. She looks Italian—a starlet—and her husband must be parking his Ferrari; then he's going to buy her diamonds." I even saw an image in my mind of a skinny, hungry dog, dreaming of a string of sausages—that was me! I watched as she went into one of the little boutique stores. After she came out and kept on walking nonchalantly, I walked away, defeated, thinking I would never stand a chance. Or that I would get slapped, laughed at, and be humiliated if I approached her.

The second time, it was in the evening. I was walking with a lady friend toward the El Convento Hotel and saw a gorgeous woman walking toward us—this time accompanied. They stopped, and the woman said hello to my friend and had a light conversation. I stayed two steps behind—it was a brief conversation. Mesmerized once more, I asked my friend who she was, and she said she was her husband's cousin. At the time, I didn't know that it was the same woman I had seen at Calle Fortaleza.

The third time was when Carli's used to be open for lunch. I sat at the bar and noticed, sitting at the banquette across the room, a breathtaking woman accompanied by two other young and one elegant middle-aged lady. They were the only customers left from lunch and were there talking and drinking wine, champagne, and martinis. For a moment, the older lady looked my way as if wondering who I was. I went to the table and introduced myself. Somehow, in the conversation, the lady mentioned her son, whose wife and I had lately spent time together. I let her know that her son was my friend and told her I held him in high esteem. The conversation was amicable. I remember I was squatting all the time while talking with her. I do that out of respect to be eye level and not impose myself uninvited by pulling up a chair—I believe it's the right thing to do, especially when you are the owner on a brief visit to a guest's table. The whole time we were talking, we were eye to eye, and not for one moment did I dare to look at the young lady who had taken my breath away just minutes earlier. I couldn't look at her because my eyes would have betrayed me, right there and then. At that time, I didn't even know that she was the same woman I had seen at Calle Fortaleza or near El Convento.

The fourth time it happened during an afternoon when I was walking with my business partner Jim on Calle San Jose going toward the restaurant. I saw a sunny smile from a stunning woman coming from inside a clothing boutique store called Hecho a Mano. Again, she stopped me in my tracks. I said to Jim, "Please, let's cross the street and wait for me; I want to meet the woman inside that store." Jim crossed the street with me and stayed on the sidewalk, smoking a cigarette as I went in. I thought the young lady at the store was a manager, or maybe the owner. I just smiled at her, and as I was approaching, she got on the phone—she appeared to be talking to a customer.

Meanwhile, while she was on the phone, I checked her out discreetly from all angles, silently admiring her beauty. Even when she appeared to be talking to a customer, the beautiful smile on her face never abandoned her. Being on the phone seemed to last forever, and I was feeling a bit anxious. Finally, she hung up. I then did a very brief introduction and mentioned that my friend and I had just rented an old stately house in Old San Juan and we were having a Halloween bash that night, which I invited her to attend. I still had no clue she was the same woman I saw on Calle Fortaleza, or on the way to the El Convento Hotel, or at Carli's having lunch with her aunt. She didn't show up at the party.

The fifth time happened one night at Carli's when the restaurant was full. As usual, I made the rounds, making sure everyone was happy and had what they needed. I noticed two girls sitting at a cocktail table near the front door. I noticed they were both young and beautiful and had a bottle of wine on the table. Seeing young people at Carli's, especially drinking wine by the bottle, always catches my attention. I think it's sweet. What goes through my mind is that they are in college or hard working, and they are treating themselves to a memorable evening with their hard-earned money. There was a spike in orders at the restaurant, and the kitchen made an extra tempura jumbo shrimp by mistake. I immediately ordered a server to take the freshly made shrimp tapa to the two girls sitting outside by the door with the bottle of wine—nothing more to it.

About ten minutes later, I walked past the two young ladies and asked them if they were enjoying themselves. They thanked me for the shrimp tapa. Before leaving the table, I looked straight into the eyes of one of the two girls, who seemed familiar, and said, "Haven't we met before?" I realize that that might be the most common and cliché phrase you could say, but I meant it! By now at least I had a subconscious notion that I had seen her or even met her before. But I couldn't associate her with any of the previous singular encounters, which probably happened within one or two months. From that moment on, we were never apart. It wasn't until about six months later that Katira told me she knew I was the same person all along. She even confessed that she was angry when I wasn't looking at her during lunch at Carli's while talking with her aunt. That's when I finally realized that she was the same person all along.

Since the day Katira and I met, we were always together, but our courtship was relatively long. It took many weeks before we got intimate in the slightest way—not even holding hands or goodnight kisses. There was a considerable gap in our ages—Katira must have been twenty-three at the time, and I was forty-five—and we were both smart to get to know each other well before going too much further. Everything flowed naturally. We laughed a lot, our conversations were intellectually stimulating, and we even discussed our political differences.

I believe women mature much more quickly than men, so for me it is natural for men to be much older—I'm terribly immature! Despite our twenty-two years of age difference, there was a genuine rapport and growing emotions toward each other.

Our new life together was good, but we had a nest to build. I was still living at the hedonistic penthouse, albeit not a participant, where Katira would visit and stay with me on occasion, but it wasn't the healthiest ambiance for a newly formed couple, so I left the little paradise. What happened next is that my dear friend Nildín lent me a couch at her apartment in Condado until I could get my own. Katira and I were now spending all our time together, so we finally found an apartment we liked and could afford and moved in together for the first time. It was a lovely three-story sunny apartment, but the location wasn't great. It was near the Children's Hospital, and the area was too noisy. We thought of Ocean Park, but it was becoming overcrowded and would never be the same—the Ocean Park that I once knew.

Curiously, Katira had lived in one of the two apartments right beneath where my bedroom used to be at my parents' house in Ocean Park. Being worlds apart in distance and age, we hadn't known of each other's existence. Little did I know that all of those times I dreamt of my ideal, the girl of my dreams would someday be sleeping right underneath my old bedroom where I grew up and had so many grand romantic fantasies! The odds are astronomical! And if you add falling in love at first sight, five times, letting her go each time, and still ending up together, the odds become insane. My family loved Katira, and to add to the insane odds, my aunts and her grandmother knew each other and had even worked together in the 1940s. Sadly, my mom had already passed away when I met Katira—how I wished that they had met! They would have loved each other to no end. But my dad remained always close to us.

Meanwhile, it had been five years since I'd seen Jack Rieley, and he was often in my thoughts. He would still call me from time to time and he had grown fond of Katira from our phone conversations—he was genuinely happy for us. But from our recent talks, I could tell there was something going terribly wrong with Jack. He seemed stressed and unhappy in his relationship with Jaye. Katira knew how much Jack meant to me, and we decided to pay him a visit at The Chantry. Sadly, not long after our visit, Jaye left Jack and moved to London, an event that Jack never really recovered from. Jack was truly heartbroken. After Jaye left, Jack sold The Chantry and moved to Montreal. From Montreal, Jack would call me at least once a day expressing his sorrow. I did my best to bring him peace—it was heartbreaking. Eventually, he moved back to Berlin.

Jack invited me to visit him after he returned to Europe, but there I anticipated a similar bacchanalian scene and declined again. He liked being surrounded by young kids, albeit not underage—I believe it kept him from facing his loneliness. Our relationship was different. But also it may have been a burden for him with me not being gay. I was just a friend—his friend whom he would always get a good laugh and a straight answer from. Everyone else around him was trying to please him for something in return. At first, we talked for hours weekly on the phone until we faded away from each other once again.

I felt helpless about Jack, as did Katira, who had grown to love him as well. All we could do was take a deep breath and go on with our lives. Our relationship kept on thriving.

Many years later, Kat and I laughed about a conversation we had when I told her out of nowhere, like on our third or fourth date, that I didn't use Viagra and never would. Also, from the beginning of our relationship, she knew I already had four grown children. I added that as our relationship evolved, if she wanted, I wouldn't be opposed to having more children, as many as she wanted. I just thought that would be fair to her, and now I couldn't imagine my life without having had my second lovely daughter, Mía.

The moment I saw the first sonogram early during Katira's pregnancy, I was smitten. I'm not sure if it was from the first scan that we could tell it was a girl, but knowing I would have another girl, I was over-the-edge-of-the-universe excited. Having my first daughter was such a joy and a blessing, and to have another girl in my life made me beyond happy. From later sonograms, I could tell that she had big round cheeks on her face, and when she was born, it was the first thing I noticed. The birth was by C-section, and the surgeon, being my wife's cousin, allowed me in during the surgery. I was doing some filming, but I remained focused on the real-time event, which included comforting Katira.

As I watched Mía being pulled out of the womb, it was love at first sight! Lifting the uterus, which was about the size and shape of a football, and placing it over Katira's chest for cleaning after the birth was impressive. Mía was gently placed on a table. My thoughts were that, after the comfort and security of a warm womb, she was now lying on a cold, steel, and stiff table. But she was well wrapped like a bean burrito, and I went straight to her. I held her tiny hand and whispered a few verses of the song "My Romance" to her delicate ear, which along with "My Funny Valentine" I had sung to her while still in the womb. It was such a pleasure and proud moment to pick Mía up and bring her to Katira's loving arms. Knowing that no introduction was needed, I said, "Katira, meet Mía."

To get to the recovery room we had to take an elevator a few floors down from the third floor where the surgery took place. In the elevator was Mía inside a little wheeled cart, a nurse, and me. I will never forget that in a moment of silence with the three of us inside the elevator, I asked the nurse her name, then I said to Mía, "Mía, this is Carmen," then, looking at Carmen, "Carmen, this is Mía." I couldn't believe my eyes, as Mía was smiling at the nurse, with Carmen making eye contact and smiling as if acknowledging the introduction. Once on the reception floor, the three of us paraded between a multitude of paparazzi continuously flashing their cameras; my instinct was to protect her new set of eyes. Of course, the paparazzi were the grandpas, grandmas, uncles, aunts, and friends.

Before I met Katira, my relationships were ubiquitous. That gave me the reputation among her family and friends of being a *pica flor*, or hummingbird, flitting from flower to flower. I knew at least what I didn't want in a companion and wasn't about to compromise. I had learned how to enjoy living alone, and sharing my life with someone in intimacy would be far-reaching. I had been through enough and also blown enough relationships to know what I wanted and to nurture it when I had found it.

I've learned that there is great value in being on your own, just as there is in having a partner and being in a prosperous relationship. I've met many people who complain or constantly yearn for "the right companion" or a relationship, even when they've had it in front of them. I've learned that to feel loved, first, we must allow it. Many people sabotage themselves that way—searching for love but not letting themselves be open to being loved. There is a line in one of my favorite songs, "Nature Boy," which says, "The greatest thing, you'll ever learn—is just to love and be loved in return." So true! Some people will find excuse after excuse for not finding love, such as feeling undeserving. That's self-sabotage. I believe the same goes for success, wealth, and anything good one can have in life. If we are genuinely open to what we most desire, it will happen, period.

THE HIEROPHANT

THE HIEROPHANT

 The Hierophant is like a messenger from the heavens. He brings guidance and wisdom, encouraging you to follow pre-established traditions instead of unorthodox methods. This card reminds you to embrace the traditions and to find a spiritual perspective on your current situation.

Carli Cafe Concierto was a success from the start. Opening night was soft and unannounced, but being at the end of December, the beginning of tourist season, it worked very well, and it remained full until the end of tourist season in mid-April. Local and international celebrities visited us throughout the years, including Moroccan prince Moulay Rachid, Hillary Clinton, Michael Bolton, Al Jarreau, Kenny Warner, Gonzalo Rubalcaba, and Benny Green, as well as other movie, sports, music, and political personalities.

One visitor I had at Carli's possibly became the most positive and influential force from there on in my piano jazz career. Bassist Eddie Gómez, was at the top of the heap among the world's greatest jazz bassists, having been part of the Bill Evans Trio for over a decade, beginning in 1966. That alone was meaningful to me because of my admiration for Bill Evans. Throughout the years, I listened to him more than any other jazz pianist. Somehow, Evans's sound resonated with my spirit. The level of sensitivity and harmonic richness, rounded by flawless, effortless, uninhibited delivery, was refreshing and inspiring, and Gómez was the perfect match with Evans. Evans exuded an almost childlike vibe in his playing. He made jazz sound beautiful without taking away the genre's complexities and excitement.

I had met Eddie Gómez in the early '90s when I was playing at the newly renovated Condado Plaza Hotel. This time I had a duo gig with double bassist Freddy Sylva at the hotel's Dar Tiffany's restaurant. One night Eddie showed up with his lady companion, Carmen. Eddie immediately took an interest in the jazz music we were playing. On a break, he recognized my bassist, Sylva, who, as I understood, like Eddie, had studied double bass in New York with Fred Zimmerman. I asked Eddie if he wanted to sit in with me and play a few songs, and we played Bill Evans's "Waltz for Debby" as well as the old standard "How Deep Is the Ocean."

Close to a decade after our first encounter, Eddie Gómez visited Carli's, and we quickly became friends. We got to know each other better and started playing often. At first, playing with Eddie wasn't easy for me. That was because while we played, I'd listen to him instead of focusing on my playing. And his playing was so masterfully all over the place and sophisticated that it would enthrall me, causing me to lose my way and risk skipping a few beats or so. Eventually, I learned that the best way to play with Eddie was to focus on what *I* was doing—that worked!

One night when Eddie was visiting Carli's, I gave him a copy of *Love Tales*, my first solo recording. A few days later, Eddie came back to the club and excitedly mentioned that he had listened to the CD and liked it. After a bit of shop talk, Eddie suggested that we do an album, and I agreed. We partnered as producers, and for three months we went about the logistics of the studio and personnel selection. In between, I made a trip to New York to meet with Eddie and scout recording studios and try out the pianos. We selected two studios: the late, and last, of the large recording studios in Manhattan, Clinton Studios, and a more intimate one, the Studio, in SoHo.

The recording process, being relaxed and spontaneous, was enjoyable. Neither Eddie nor I enjoyed doing more than a few takes of each song. More than that, it becomes work. Playing music should be just that—*playing* with music. When we were recording Cahn and Brodszky's classic "Be My Love," somehow we ended up having to do a few more takes on the bowed intro than usual, and Eddie yelled, "This is torturing me!" It was funny!

Besides doing the recordings, Eddie and I enjoyed hanging out. We always had fun; we'd frequent a neighborhood diner in the West Village with great food called Elephant & Castle. I still have a drawing that Jeremy Steig did when the three of us were at the restaurant. He did a whimsical sketch of Eddie and me with a pen on the paper tablecloth. Steig made Eddie a chimp and me a feline symbolized by a cat on my head; the two waitresses were candidly serving us with their large trays in the nude. I treasure that drawing. Sadly, Jeremy left us too soon.

Whenever Eddie visited Puerto Rico, he'd first stop at Carli's, sometimes directly from the airport; it became almost a ritual. He would first fly in mostly to see his mom, whose health was becoming frail. He often just showed up, and other times he would call me beforehand, but it was always fun and joyful—we just played, drank, ate well, and laughed a lot. We'd also plan our next project. This time I proposed doing a high-profile trio album called . He suggested Jack DeJohnette on drums. Once I knew who was playing, I'd make song selections. But this time, the title song required a horn. Originally, DeJohnette suggested bringing in Don Byron, a clarinet player. He didn't work out for "Maverick," but I had him instead play on "Three Little Steps to Heaven." After the main session, I called David Sanchez, who played horn superbly on the "Maverick" track.

Recording the album was quite an event. I flew to New York with my Katira and her sister Lola, spent a day in Manhattan, and then drove upstate to Shokan, with Eddie Gómez impatiently following us in his car. Allaire's recording studio was a top-notch setup in an old 18,740-square-foot mansion on twenty-two acres at the top of a hill overlooking a lake in Shokan, in Upstate New York, close to Woodstock. It was snowing most of the time, and for a little fun at Eddie's expense, I kept telling him over the cellphone how lost we were when we really weren't. He was fuming, and we were laughing. There I was again, my puckish nature at work with those I loved most!

Once in Shokan, we had to drive up a narrow and icy winding road, up a steep mountain to get to the studio. When we finally got to the studio property, there was a massive old iron gate where we had to wait for a caretaker to let us in. We called the caretaker Lurch. After a short drive past the entrance, there was a Tudor-style mansion made up of two main wings connected by a covered walkway. We were happy to be at our new warm and cozy home for the next three days. The rooms upstairs were charming and comfortable. The gathering place was a large commercial, all stainless-steel kitchen, with an adjacent open space with a large dining table.

The mansion included three recording studios. I had booked the large studio, which housed two gorgeous Steinway Concert Grand pianos to choose from. The large studio was called the Great Room and had thirty-foot-tall floor-to-ceiling windows and sixty-foot-high vaulted ceilings—very impressive. From the massive glass window, you could see mostly the clouds moving, and when the clouds would clear, the view of the mountains and a lake far down below was breathtaking. Brandon Mason was the recording engineer. I had met Brandon during a previous session I had done for an old friend, Duke McVinnie, at the same studio. I fell in love with the place and enjoyed working with Brandon, who was already familiar with the studio. We just had two half-days to record the entire album, including any overdubbing. So I made sure we did as few takes as possible, which is how I like to work.

I wanted *Maverick* to be colossal. I had a minor concern of being outplayed and overshadowed in a trio of such top-tier players as Eddie Gómez and Jack DeJohnette, but on the contrary, it empowered me. I wasn't sure what to expect from reviews after its release, but it turned out much better than expected. Some of them even touched positively on the overshadowing issue, including this one:

> "Virtuosic without being superfluous, Muñoz' playing style matches his writing—direct, unassuming, and to the point. But he's also an interpretive pianist with wide-open ears, and he's never overshadowed by the more illustrious reputations and experiences of his musical partners on *Maverick*."
> —John Kelman, *All About Jazz*, 2005

The songs on *Maverick* were a combination of my original songs, some standards, and a Keith Jarrett composition, "Margot." In an NPR interview on Marian McPartland's *Piano Jazz* in 2007, McPartland asked if I would play Jarrett's tune, "Margot." After I played it, Marian excitedly commented, "Boy, this guy is really something, playing a Keith Jarrett tune—so nice!" That is the beauty of not knowing what I'm doing (i.e., not being formally trained): no fear.

Being asked to do an interview on *Piano Jazz* with Marian McPartland was a high point in my life. Every Saturday, I had been listening to some of the most candid piano playing and the best interviews with monumental figures in jazz such as Teddy Wilson, Bill Evans, Oscar Peterson,

Eubie Blake, Hank Jones, Dick Hyman, and many other classics—such an honor for me being among them! McPartland herself was a brilliant pianist with a vast history. She was designated a Jazz Master by the National Endowment for the Arts, received a Grammy Award for lifetime achievement, and was inducted into the National Radio Hall of Fame. Later, McPartland became a member of the Order of the British Empire.

The great reviews kept on flowing in. One that summed it up well with the fewest words was by Paul Blair, of the New York-based *Hot House Jazz Guide*, who wrote, "You might not expect to hear much in the way of great jazz from a pianist who played keyboards behind the Beach Boys for more than a decade—and who spends much of his energy these days running a restaurant in Puerto Rico. But Carli Muñoz is a revelation." Blair accurately referred to the fact that I split my time focusing on various disciplines. He was probably even not aware of my film and photography career, which widens the gap, not to mention that I am self-taught. "A revelation"—not bad amid the barrage of seeming handicaps.

I had a good vibe working with DeJohnette. He had some excellent ideas throughout the recordings and seemed to enjoy the sessions. I had recorded before with Eddie, and he was also very proactive during the process. It was an excellent flow. After *Maverick*, Jack offered to produce an album for me with him and John Patitucci on bass. Although I respect Patitucci's talent as a bassist, I didn't resonate with his style. Besides, DeJohnette's idea of using synthesizer programming also didn't interest me, so I declined.

By this time my father's health was declining. My father could have lived past a hundred; he had the genes and the spirit. But after my mother passed on, his self-care diminished, and so did his health. The emotional bond my dad had with my mother had been a force field, and with my mother gone, everything changed, even with our care and being there for him. He had a strong will, which may have excluded good health and longevity. He might have felt less reason for living now with my mom gone, and he appeared to be shortening his life by indulging in drinking Cuba libres and cigarette smoking, but my dad was still a force to be reckoned with.

"A man of his word" would sum up my father—a tenet he lived by and stressed upon others; dependable, unbendable, sometimes to a fault. I don't imagine attributes like that existing in a vacuum, old-fashioned trust and goodwill being part of the package. My father called that true nobility, and he expected the same from his son and daughter. His bidding was non-negotiable, for it carried the weight of generations, as it consequently did for me. Even when my life was a roller coaster and I was hitting rock bottom, I never violated this precept—at my lowest point, it still remained my north star.

Although my dad never went beyond social drinking, his drinking was at times unsettling. Perhaps I perceived his drinking as a flaw that kept my life from being perfect, from not having "the perfect dad." Here is this dad whom everyone looks up to and admires, but to me there was a terrible flaw. When he drank, he'd never become violent or abusive; it was almost the contrary, he became excessively patronizing and clownish. He would go on rants in my presence of how great I was, or he would start singing opera at the top of his lungs; this could be anywhere—he'd just be completely uninhibited. Sometimes it was funny, even to us, but other times, especially around strangers, it was embarrassing.

For a time, my mother, sister, and I fell prisoner to his antics—the continual embarrassments in the presence of family and friends. No one else would demonize him, for his clowning was a form of entertainment, and many people even loved him for his jollity, but it rocked our sense of being a well-grounded, normal family.

Once I had a dream. In the dream, my dad and I were both around a pit of flames. As he was sinking into the infernal fire, I saw how our clutching arms were slowly separating; I let him go. I had been suffering from his vice—meaning emotionally, because I didn't drink, and never had a problem with alcohol. From that moment, I wasn't going to be dragged along or affected by it any longer. I let go of his arm and was free. All the hellish drama may sound like overkill, but it worked—after all, it was only a dream.

Nothing seemed to change in our relationship. I simply would not be affected by my father's occasional but annoying drunkenness any longer; I still adored him, but I didn't have to go down into that "pit of flames" with him. After, I wrote this poem for my dad:

> I hid like a stowaway
> Teetering between pride and shame,
> To come to praise
> The man I loved

A staunch realist often broken—
Who navigated through his flaws,
Without demure

Antiquated, drunken, ridiculous,
And generous to a fault,
He stuck to his guns—
Always sure

Telling stories of paragon virtues
That no one would challenge
Or could endure.

DEATH.

DEATH

The Death card is a reminder that all things must pass. It speaks of cycles and endings, but beginnings too. This card just means that one phase of your life has ended and the next one will begin. It is a reminder that hanging on to relationships, feelings, fears, or situations from the past will hinder you from allowing new, and perhaps better things to enter your life.

Dads don't last forever. At some point my dad was diagnosed with cancer. At first, he had it in his bladder, and he managed to beat it. But he kept on chain-smoking, and soon enough he developed lung cancer, which eventually spread all the way to his brain. After a huge battle with all possible resources available, we lost him. But my father, born Carmelo Muñoz in 1919, lived to be ninety-six, and most of all lived a life full of joy and giving.

My father was an architect by trade, but he was also an artist, a writer, and a poet. In his later years he dabbled with inventions, but securing the patents was more work that he was willing to do. He left some really good pen drawings and paintings behind. With my father's guidance, my mom also painted in her later years. She began painting in her mid-seventies and left us with some magnificent work she created shortly before passing on. It reflected her gentle and peaceful spirit.

Late in his life, my father assembled a collection of prose, thoughts, and poems he had written over the years. From the collection, I made a small book for publishing, which my dad called *Así Soy* ("This is how I am"). There is a poem that my dad wrote and dedicated to me on the back of one of his oil paintings, which says it all:

Si cuando yo muera y volviera a nacer,
(If when I die I am born again,)
estudiaría letras,
(I would study literature,)
escultura, música, pintura y filosofía,
(sculpture, music, painting, and philosophy,)
las mezclaría todas de sabiduría,
(I'd mix them all with wisdom,)
haría un cocktail e invitaría a todos,
(of them I would make a cocktail and invite everyone)
a beber de el.
(to drink from it.)

Poem by Carli's dad, dedicated to him on the back of one of his paintings

Besides being talented, smart, and open-minded, my father was generous and caring; he would help anyone in need. His generosity started with us, his children, but expanded to everyone within the family and beyond. My dad always remained my most staunch supporter; he meant well, and his advice was more than often right. My tendency was sometimes to fight against his ideas, but still, we remained close and shared immense love and admiration for each other.

As if losing my father wasn't enough, when he passed away things changed dramatically for my sister Bruni and me. I then realized that I had been ignoring signs and never did anything to protect myself from the unfortunate events that would follow my dad's passing. Because my sister was the eldest by almost a decade, my father entrusted her with our inheritance. But after starting a meaningless charade of whether to have a wake or not as an excuse to shut me out from her life, my sister misappropriated for herself the entire inheritance my father left us. She kept for herself all $4.5 million of a Lotto first prize my dad had won, and on top of that, she kept his social security savings and all his bank accounts—all of it.

Still, life for me remained beautiful; though perhaps foolish, but I've never been materialistic enough to let money issues slow me down or contaminate me with bitterness—perhaps I'd be a greater fool to complain about the life I've had. I still love my sister and wish her well. After waiting for over a year for a response from her after my father's passing, I took the matter to court. I figured that just letting my sister get away with it would have been a complete disfavor to her—it would have been allowing and even supporting her misconceptions. At least by taking her to court, she might get the benefit of realizing what she had done. With luck, I thought, she might look in the mirror and see her dishonor and betrayal, not just to me but also to herself, her children, and to our entire family. Had she done that, a healing process and self-forgiveness might have been the result, making her a better person and preparing her for the inevitable.

My sister clearly and sadly made off with our family's small fortune, but I doubt it would fill her void. I still wouldn't want anyone to judge her as a bad person; she isn't. Perhaps she harbored some resentment toward me or developed a sense of entitlement when my father widowed and moved in with her. I was always free to do what I wanted, and she wasn't. I got a sports car from my dad when she wanted one, and she didn't get it, which she never got over. I flowed in playing music, and she didn't, and so on. But in the end, none of that really matters. Also, it doesn't matter how much one tries to justify actions that hurt or take away from other people, especially your kin; it won't change what one has become or done. Sadly, in the end, no amount of money will replace the love of a brother or a sister. I promised my father that in the event of his passing I would take care of my sister, but I had no idea what that would entail.

Toward the end of his life my father seemed concerned about my sister's intentions regarding the handling of the prize money. Unprompted, he would often write and hand me letters clearly stating his wishes regarding the Lotto prize inheritance, but he would come back a few days later and ask me to return the letter. He would say that my sister got upset if he wouldn't simply trust her word. But by providence, one of these letters survived and was found by accident in a closet in our house. The letter doesn't only state the yearly sum to be paid on my behalf, but also the unequivocal fact that my dad picked the numbers and also paid for the winning ticket. My dad spoke—clearly. This is his one surviving letter:

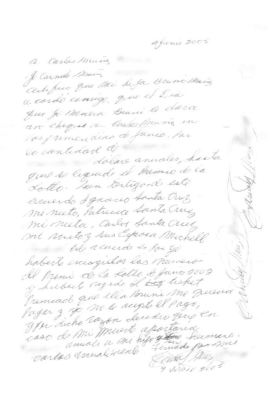

Letter from Carli's father, see facing page for translation

I, Carmelo Muñoz [third name undisclosed], hereby certify that my daughter Bruni Muñoz accorded with me that the day I die Bruni will give a check to Carlos Muñoz within the first days of June, for the amount of [undisclosed] yearly, until the liquidation of the Lotto prize money. Witnesses to this agreement are, my grandchild (all Bruni's children and a spouse), Ignacio Santa Cruz, my grandchild Patricia Santa Cruz, my grandchild and his wife Carlos Santa Cruz, and Michell [last name undisclosed]. This agreement is based on me having picked the numbers of the Lotto prize of June 2002 and for having paid for the winning ticket, which she, Bruni, wanted to pay for and which I refused to accept payment for. And for this reason, I decided that in the event of my death she would pay (the sum of undisclosed amount) to my son and her brother Carlos, annually.

Signed by me, [my dad's signature]
4th of June of 2005

XI

JUSTICE .

JUSTICE

This card ultimately means that the truth behind everything will come to light soon, and there will be repercussions. It is a reminder that karma is real, and there is a consequence for every action.

"Hey, Carli, this is Bruce, Bruce Ayers. How are you doing?"

"Wow...Bruce, such a blast! So good to hear from you!"

Bruce was a friend I hadn't seen nor heard from in over thirty years, since I left LA. His call came as a total and pleasant surprise. It was an invitation, an extraordinary invitation to be his guest that year at the Bohemian Grove.

I had never heard of the Bohemian Club, but I said yes. In three months, after a CIA check, all I had to do was to fly to Los Angeles and spend a night at Bruce's house in Santa Monica, and he would take care of the rest. I tried learning all I could about the place, but nothing prepared me for what it was like being there.

Three months after, I flew to LAX and, as instructed, waited downstairs outside the lower concourse to get picked up. A beautiful young lady wearing a silk scarf on her head and a large pair of sunglasses driving a convertible vintage sport XK8 Jaguar stopped and ordered me in. The radio or CD was playing operatic music full blast. Obediently, I dropped my small suitcase in the back, climbed in the front seat, and off we went. On our way to Santa Monica, we stopped at a Mexican restaurant for a delicious bite, but most of all, a double margarita. Melissa was Bruce's lovely wife. After we arrived at the house a little later, Bruce caught up with us. We spent that whole evening reminiscing about old times.

The next morning, Bruce and I got in his old Suburban truck, stopped in San Marino to pick up another Bohemian, "Old Guard" Carson, and continued north to Monte Rio in Sonoma County, San Francisco. After an eight-hour drive and passing the recurrent yearly picket line of angry protesters and local police cars, we parked and walked to a checkpoint before entering the Grove officially. We went inside a small wooden shack, where attendants verified our identity and checked our luggage. A sure sign of "no cellphones allowed" is when you see several of them nailed straight to the wall—right through each screen.

A vast parking lot with a loading dock to load the luggage on trailers surrounded the little receiving wooden hut. No cars were allowed past the parking lot. To get to our camp, we had to catch a ride in one of the vehicles they provided for constant transportation to and from the picturesque, 160-some grove encampments on the wooded property. Once there, I had to breathe in the exhilarating experience; it felt like what I would imagine being in a hobbit village would be like. The smell of firewood, the smoke coming out of the smokestacks, the scattered Davy Crockett-log cabin-like encampments on the sidehills, and the Indian tepees were a sight to be seen and felt. Just breathing the air was invigorating, and the canopy of tall redwoods towering above felt like being in Earth's cathedral.

I was a guest at an encampment called Tie Binders, named after the railroad moguls who populated the camp in the 1930s. After entering through the camp's gate, I walked into an open area with a walk-in stone fireplace, a fully stocked bar, and a grand piano on a stage. Surrounding the space, direct access to a fully equipped and staffed stainless-steel kitchen, a large bathroom with lockers and multiple shower stalls, and a comfortable living room handsomely furnished with another large fireplace completed the rustic but plush setting. The sleeping quarters were separate canvas-covered tent-like clusters,

Carli's luggage tag at the Bohemian Camp

or an array of wooden cabins, all equipped with cots. Everyone, even US presidents, slept on the cots. What redeemed the cots was that all were equipped with an electric blanket and first-class linen and pillows. The three weeks of Bohemian Grove usually took place in mid-July, under the tree canopy, so it tended to be a little chilly, especially at night.

Sharing daily breakfast and dinner in open space with two thousand or more bohemians was impressive. But lunch was a customary ritual at the camp—it was a sure way to spend time with your campmates. One day we were waiting to have lunch, and four Tie Binders campmates, another guest, and I were standing around having a chat. In the conversation, the other guest mentioned a keyboard that had once been strapped to his body. He also mentioned borrowing batteries from other instruments. I was curious and asked him where all of this had been happening. He replied, "Oh, I was at the MIR station, and I had to have a keyboard to play so not to get too bored, having to be in space for six months."

"The batteries," he went on, "I borrowed from some of the scientific instruments to replace the old ones in the keyboard." And the strap, of course, he needed; otherwise, the keyboard would have flown away, I figured. He was an American astronaut, Ed Lu. He also told me that he had had to learn to speak Russian in a matter of weeks to be confined in space with the Soviet cosmonaut Yuri Malenchenko for six months. I suppose the keyboard helped ease his stay.

Every day at the Grove, there were interesting programmed events. Two of them were recurrent: the smaller museum talk at around noon, and the more extensive lakeside talk, which was took place later in the afternoon around a lake. We would sit on the grassy knolls surrounding the lake, and a speaker, often a senator, a federal judge, or even a US president, would orate from a podium. Aside from those events, the concerts, plays, and lots of other happenings were first-class performances. For me, the lectures, especially the museum talks, were all a treasure to behold.

The museum talks, conducted in a semi-open all wood amphitheater, were more intimate. There were video monitors all over the place for everyone to see the slides or videos related to the presentations. And the speakers were the real deal! One talk that stands out was by Robert Ballar, who spoke about the discovery of the *Titanic* and the *Bismarck*. Ballard, also a Bohemian, discovered those ships, along with other great historic findings. He also located the aircraft carrier *USS Yorktown* and the wreckage of John F. Kennedy's PT-109. It can't get much more real or exciting than that.

But the most fun at the Grove was the spontaneous moments. While walking around with my friend Bruce, we heard a peculiar groggy voice from one of the camps on the hillside. I thought it sounded like Henry Kissinger, which wouldn't have been at all surprising—after all, General Colin Powell had just casually walked past us, going the opposite direction. It was customary to visit other lodges and join in for lunch. Following the curious and all-too-familiar voice of Kissinger, we wandered into the lodge. We sat in the same table with other Bohemians, listening to three United States secretaries of state, Kissinger, Shultz, and Baker, having a casual chat about things to come. After the lunch, I reciprocated by giving the camp members a well-deserved piano concert.

Since 1878, the 2,700 acres of Bohemian Grove have served as a playground for "masters of the universe." Some of that small one percent of humanity with the lion's share inhabits those woods for three weeks out of the year. Part of me felt guilty, another part felt like a voyeur or an interloper, and the other part felt privileged. The part that feels privileged almost brings me back to my childhood in Ocean Park when I was at the center of my universe—there was nothing above it. But now it's different. As I get older and wiser, it's all internal. I could break into tears at the awe and wonder of just being here on this planet while cleaning the dog's poo on my patio.

The following year, Bruce invited me back to the camp. An unforgettable event from that second year at the Grove was getting an invitation to the Wine Committee Dinner. Enough word had gotten around about my playing skills that the president of the Wine Committee requested my presence. Charlie Baxter, one of the Tie Binders camp members and an importer of French wines, approached me with the news. Charlie explained the privilege of the invitation. It was one of the memorable six tasting dinners of utmost prestige and exclusivity where most, if not all, the committee members are "old guard" Bohemians. I felt honored and flattered by the invitation.

The attire is very casual in the camp, meaning shorts, jeans, or chinos, and sneakers or hiking boots. There you would fill your heart's desire drinking great vintages, including bottles of Château Lafitte

Rothschild, or bottle after bottle of 1980s vintage Château d'Yquem, while proudly wearing your most casual outfit. I had made it a habit of always packing an extra you-never-know-what-might-happen outfit. They informed me it would be the one elegant and most prestigious event, so I dressed like a gentleman.

Late that afternoon, close to the beginning of the activity, Bruce accompanied me to the cabin where the dinner would take place, the Grove Clubhouse. It was a massive two-story log cabin, on a bluff overlooking the Russian River. Designed by Bernard Maybeck in 1903 and completed in 1904, the Clubhouse is also famous (or infamous) for the planning meeting that resulted in the bombing of Hiroshima and Nagasaki. In 1942 "the father of the atomic bomb," J. Robert Oppenheimer, who headed the Manhattan Project, hosted the meeting.

I'll never forget how I felt when I waved farewell to my friend from the balcony. I felt sad and almost embarrassed, not unlike an intruder, knowing that Bruce, and no one else from the camp, could be at that dinner. I was there early, as I would usually be before a performance. The committee made sure that there'd be a suitable piano for the occasion. After a brief wait, the first Bohemian to arrive (besides the staff) was the president of the committee. Right away, he stretched his hand out to introduce himself, thanked me for coming and said that he'd heard many good things about me and that I didn't have to play, that he had arranged for a seat for me at his table, the president's table—that I was a guest. I thanked him, but I had to take a deep breath after such a kind and honorable welcome. The dynamics of conversations at the dinner table, the food, the wines—the entire experience was an affair to remember.

After the dinner event, one of the camp trolleys was waiting to drive everyone to their respective lodges. I preferred walking, for I was floating on air and wanted to savor the experience. By then it was dark, and the dirt road was surrounded by hundreds of hillside camps with their chimneys devouring Douglas fir, signaling the beginning of a boisterous evening. During the long walk on the narrow dirt road, I heard a variety of music, overlapping from Americana to country, classical, and jazz. One particular ensemble caught my attention, which called for a detour to a trail where there were more scattered camps on the hills. Along the way, I ran into a wandering Boho and asked him if he knew which camp the music was coming from. He asked me to follow him, but I noticed the sound becoming dimmer. Instead, the man took me to his camp. The first thing I saw was a large stage with a Steinway Concert Grand piano and the rest of the stage filled with instruments, as if sitting there ready for a major concert. There were empty chairs in rows all around. The stranger (now my new friend) gracefully pointed to the piano, and I obliged.

I had already been walking on air after the most magnificent dinner ever, and still high from all of it. The alcohol from the beautiful extravagant variety of wines and spirits helped. Here was another piece of heaven. I climbed up on the piano, on the lonely stage, and started playing "My Romance." Before I finished, a bassist had joined, then a drummer and a guitar player, and as I finished the song, to my amazement, the array of chairs that had been empty minutes before were now being filled. A hungry and grateful crowd was cheering and applauding. It was the Steve Miller camp (i.e., leader of the enormously successful Steve Miller Band) and the kind man who had escorted me there was Steve Miller himself.

"Friends are the family you choose." —Jess C. Scott

One of the dearest and most influential people who enriched my life considerably was Lucille Dixon Roberts. I met Lucille at the Ritz-Carlton Hotel in San Juan in 1998 on a visit she made to Puerto Rico. While I was playing with my jazz trio in the hotel lobby, Lucille approached me between songs. We established a conversation, and learning that she was a bass player, I invited her to play. But Lucille hesitated, saying how rusty she was and that she hadn't played in a long time. Lucille was in her mid-seventies, but she was full of energy. I insisted, and we played "Take the 'A' Train." I thought she was good—old school. But mostly I loved her spirit when she played.

Four years later, Lucille showed up for dinner at Carli's, and I made her an offer to join me on standup bass permanently. She laid out excuses for why she couldn't do it, but again, I convinced her, and she stayed playing with me at Carli's until death did us part. Lucille developed an aggressive type of cancer, which swept her away swiftly, but she continued playing with me while on chemotherapy. However, at some point, as her condition worsened and she needed hospitalization, she went to New York to be near her family.

Lucille had performed with top jazz artists in the 1940s and '50s, including Fats Navarro, Buddy Tate, Sonny Payne, Taft Jordan, Tyree Glenn, Earl (Fatha) Hynes, Ella Fitzgerald, Eubie Blake, Tony Bennett, Frank Sinatra, Johnny Hartman, Billy Daniels, Billie Holiday, and Dinah Washington. But no one ever credited or featured Lucille on an album. When I learned of the possibility of losing her, I put together the first of a series of *Live at Carli's* albums, the first one featuring Lucille Dixon. Eddie Gómez also played on the album. I did everything I could to complete it, hoping to surprise her with a finished product before it was too late.

I went to New York with Katira to see Lucille at the hospital in early September, and she wasn't well. But on September 21, the doctors sent her home after she made a surprising recovery. On that same day, I got the final CDs in my hands, and Katira and I flew back to New York with a box of CDs to surprise Lucille. She was staying at her daughter's home in Manhattan, and there was a big gathering; her entire family was present, and Eddie Gómez and other musician friends were there. It was like a big celebration party—we played the record for everyone. Lucille was vibrant the whole night and over-the-moon happy listening to the CD! I was so happy for her! It was a splendid evening. The next day, Katira and I flew back to San Juan, and the following day Lucille passed away—her parting was beyond graceful.

One thing that always haunted me was unresolved issues, and Carol Banderas reacting badly to the acid trip back in the '60s never escaped my mind. An inescapable feeling of sorrow remained in me, and I had to try to resolve it. Forty years later I was still looking for Carol.

I had asked our mutual acquaintances if they could reach her and looked her up on Google, but no luck. One day I got an email from someone whose last name was the same as hers, Banderas. One of her cousins responded to a message I had left on a blog looking for information about Carol. I got some clues from her cousin, including information that led me to her father. I contacted him and told him the entire story of what had happened and said I still felt responsible and wanted to reach out to her. He said that Carol was in a local psychiatric hospital. The news made me sad, but I still wanted to see her and help in any way possible. At the least, I wanted to let her know how sorry I was about what had happened. Her father gave me the information, and I went to see Carol.

I had never been to a mental hospital before. It was the San Juan City Asylum at the Centro Médico complex. I remember bringing a blanket and a few other things to comfort her. Security was not as strict as it would be in a jail, but also not too far from it. They escorted me through a hallway to a large recreation room where Carol and I were going to meet. As we entered, the first thing I noticed was a stench of urine that was almost unbearable. The room was noisy. There were other patients, and some showed signs of severe conditions. Then, on the far end near a window, Carol calmly sat on a stiff metal chair, with a small square table in front, where her now-feeble arms rested.

The guard pointed to where Carol was, and I walked toward her. She had the beauty she had always had, only now her skin was pale, but her face wore well the nooks and crevices of time passed. Her hair was the same, but a little thinner and grayish-white. She got up from her chair and hugged me. I felt years of remorse going by before my teary eyes. We sat down, and while exchanging a soft smile, I held her frail hands from across the table and told her why I had come. I also mentioned that I had been looking for her throughout the years.

Her eyes were tender, and her lips now had a poignant but genuine smile. She was kind, expressing that none of it had been my fault. She went on recounting stories about how her mother had ostracized her before and after. She told me she had to move to San Francisco to get away as far as possible from her mother. She even had a brief marriage, but her mother soon after tagged along, moving to San Francisco to keep tabs on her. Even when she got to be Miss Puerto Rico, it had been for her mother's benefit. Her mother's manipulation was apparent to those who knew her, but it was more than anyone imagined.

I wanted to get Carol out of the asylum. To me, she didn't belong there. After the visit, I met with her father again and asked him if he would take her to live with him. I begged him. He was apprehensive but agreed to try. I then contacted an acquaintance who was a prominent psychiatrist and explained the situation. I told the doctor that I wanted Carol released to her father's custody. The doctor evaluated the situation and wrote a letter to facilitate my petition at the mental hospital. I already had the restaurant and would do whatever was necessary to accommodate her doing a simple task or just assist her in any way possible considering her condition.

After all the due diligence, with the letter in hand to secure her release, she gently refused. She felt secure where she was. I didn't press it; it was her choice. I visited Carol a few more times, eventually letting go. She had found her world, her safety, and it was not up to me to change it.

THE WORLD.

THE WORLD

The World is the last card of the Major Arcana, representing completion, success, and fulfillment. This card shows that you have been rewarded appropriately for your efforts with a feeling of wholeness and perfection. The World shows you that you are exactly where you are meant to be, with a greater understanding of who you are after all you've been through, and ready for the next phase of your journey.

By this time, I felt the "fool's journey" was coming to fruition, and connecting with Carol gave me a sense of completion. With Katira I now had a great companion, another beautiful baby girl, a solid business I liked, and authentic friends. And I was playing the music I loved. During my fool's journey I lost my mind too many times to remember (I know—sounds like an oxymoron; don't laugh!). How many people are willing to lose their mind? Perhaps for me having lucidity today is a miracle. Something is lost, and something is gained. That is something I still didn't know then, at the peak of going through life's roller coaster—a survival instinct kicks in, and only the moment remains, which doesn't reveal much at the time. I just knew that something fundamental was missing and there was a constant sense of yearning—like having an unquenchable thirst.

It all began with a quest for meaning, for some palpable truth about my existence. At first, wide-eyed curiosity led me to testing the boundaries of my outer world. But then, exploring my inner world is where it got intense and rocky, eventually becoming a narrow and dangerous path. Once I began taking psychedelics, a whole new world opened that was tantamount to an exploration of the outer edge of the universe. And then all of it being completely unexplainable was a very strange feeling unto itself; as social creatures, we have a natural instinct to want to share our experiences—especially amazing, otherworldly experiences. I was then further alone in my journey because now I experienced a world impossible to share, and the more I'd "see" of my inner world, the further away I got from the outside world most people call reality.

It all came to a point of crossroads where life-changing choices had to be taken. I could have continued to drift deeper into my innermost reality like a kite without a string, or I could choose to return to the world I once knew, but with a deep knowledge of my most sacred nature, knowing I would never be able to fully share or express to others. I of course opted for the second, which is the reason I'm still here.

Being back in the "normal" world wasn't easy or an overnight deal. I opted to create a balance where I could operate in a quotidian world discretely applying the knowledge acquired. But I had gone so deep into my inner sanctuary that I had to relearn many aspects of the ordinary, everyday world in order to adjust, often stumbling along the way. Coming back, I now felt like another kind of fool because I wasn't fully prepared; there was much to catch up on. Fortunately, I was blessed with the gift of music, and that was my constant. Music, being such a powerful carrier and means of expression, eased my transition back to solid ground. Music became the conduit, the closest way for me to relate and express the depth of my journey.

But I still yearned for more. There was so much to translate to our language of everyday living that a certain degree of anxiety remained. I knew I had seen the world from a privileged and unique perspective only available to a few foolish inward daredevils, and I had to *do* something about it.

In a way, I felt like a kind of impostor operating in the ordinary world. I knew that I wanted to share my experience, but I wasn't sure how. I had the music, but at times I felt that it wasn't enough. It wasn't until someone came to me to tell me how my playing spoke volumes of meaningful insights and imagery that I began realizing that I was already creating a bridge between both worlds by just playing music. It was a revelation that eased my anxiety about finding a way of expressing and sharing some of my innermost sentiments.

But still I wasn't fully satisfied. I then studied filmmaking formally in the hopes that I would someday use the craft to bridge both worlds further, but I got caught up in the web of making commercials and corporate documentaries to support my new family. That may have been foolish or not, but it took a wakeup call, Hurricane Hugo, and the total destruction of that little world for me to spring back to my essence, music.

Music remained my primary medium. I later dabbled in painting, which I enjoyed very much. It was a short period, perhaps no longer than a year, but it was revealing. I know I will someday revisit painting. Then, writing slowly became another passion that provided another conduit, and perhaps a more direct way of expression. All of it belongs to my fool's journey, a journey without a destination, just a path of infinite possibilities and discovery. But my life had now a clear path—it was all about the people I would encounter, the relationships and connecting in a deep sense. At this point I knew that somehow I was making a difference in people's lives and had learned to let people into my life and make me a better person—a high-yield exchange.

My life keeps getting richer, and sometimes I try hard to picture how it would be having a life of no care or concern past my immediate needs and surroundings. I suppose there are people who operate in that constant state, probably many. *Is that happiness?* I wonder. I see folks who seem to go about their lives unfazed by exterior events. Am I a fool to not just "operate" within my immediate bubble and let fortune be fortune for everyone else? That's a choice I believe we all have. The problem is that while we may just be self-aware as individuals, we are still part of a whole affected by every bit of action we take. There is a footprint. What we consume, the resources we use to consume it, our inertia on controversial social issues, and how our actions affect others are inescapable. Being conscious beyond our immediate adrenaline and dopamine responses is what makes us human. Wherever you go, always leave good scent.

Perhaps there is a window of time for most of us in our youth when we are spared from social responsibility. I do jealously guard a remote memory of impetuous youth, but having a high level of consciousness must be a sometimes painful aspect of maturity and evolution, I suppose. I'm brimming with character flaws. But I've found my greatest joy in serving—from serving my children, wife, family, and friends to serving humanity and nature at any measure I find possible. After all, at some point we must realize that we are as affected by the actions of others as they are by ours. Add reflection and self-awareness, questioning your own existence or role in life, and that's where the fool's journey begins, until it never ends.

My focus for self-expression still was jazz, mostly in the form of a trio, duo, but also piano solo—I could do anything I wanted. I would experiment with new songs or even sketches I had in mind at Carli's and bring them to life with an audience. There were many such experiments. One was a song whose melody I had been tinkering with, which had come to me in a dream. As I played it at Carli's, it took shape.

One night, an acquaintance brought a guest to Carli's who had just flown in from France. It was soon after the devastating earthquake hit Haiti in 2010. My friend introduced the Frenchman as Dr. Claude (I can't recall his last name.) He was the doctor who led or perhaps helped lead the efforts to eradicate the cholera outbreak that had been spreading after the devastating earthquake. All I could think of was the daunting task Dr. Claude had ahead of him. After the introduction, I went to the piano to play a second set. I had the trio then and announced that I would play a new song I wrote and had named in honor of Dr. Claude, whom I'd just met. I named my new song "Claude's Hope" and it remained "Claude's Hope" when later released on the *Follow Me* album.

I've often used songwriting to honor loved ones, friends, and people I admire. Among them, I've written songs to my two daughters ("Melanie" and "Portrait of Mía"), to my wife ("Katira's Waltz"), to my friend ("Tere"), to the memory of jazz pianist Bill Evans ("Remember Bill"), and most recently to my dear friends ("Duodécuple: Oda a Rafael y Gradissa Trelles"). I also wrote a song to commemorate Nobel Peace Prize Laureate Wangari Maathai.

When I was conceptualizing the *Maverick* production, the idea was to honor mavericks from past and present. That included some people I admired throughout history for their selfless contributions to humanity, and that is when Wangari Maathai's name came up. It was December 2004, and I was having breakfast and reading a newspaper at a local eatery near where I lived in Miramar, when I first saw Dr. Maathai's name in a column with her picture and a brief article about her winning the Nobel Peace Prize. The article briefly touched on what she had done as the founder of the Green Belt Movement in Kenya, and it moved me deeply. I included Wangari Maathai's name in the liner notes of the album as one of the living mavericks I had selected. When we finished the project, I sent a copy of the CD to her via her foundation in Nairobi. About a month later, I received a telephone call from Wangari thanking me for the music and for including her among my list of mavericks.

Around the time of our conversation, I was working on an idea for a new song. It was a simple bass line behind a powerful, soulful cadence, inspired by the music I had heard at the funeral of my dear friend Lucille Dixon, at St. Peter's Church (the jazz church) in Manhattan in 2004. After the service, I briefly heard a very simple but soulful cadence that never left me. It was what Shep Shepherd, Lucille's boyfriend, who passed away in 2018 at 101, was jamming on the piano at the church with his buddies from Harlem. Now I realize it was a gift from Lucille. She was someone whose love I felt—and still do.

My conversation with Wangari Maathai inspired me to press further into making a difference. I saw in her work the change that I idealized. Not only did I cite Wangari as a maverick on my album of the same name, she became the centerpiece of my 2018 album project, *Follow Me*, where music and images would come together to serve a common cause. On that account, dedicating my magnum opus to the memory of Wangari Maathai was an honor. It was a way to give all I had. It also allowed me to put myself on the sidelines and focus on something much bigger—the work of Wangari Maathai. It is the music project that I'm the proudest of.

The line I heard at Lucille's funeral over a decade before, the bass line and chord sequence for the song "Wangari Maathai," stayed with me—the more I played it, the better it felt. The groove now had a definite pattern, and interesting nuances were now taking place. Sometimes the level of creativity working off a simple bass line is not much more than working on a musical piece with many sophisticated changes. It could even be more challenging because to make it work, it is necessary to build on it and create transitions while maintaining a natural flow. The groove became a song, "Wangari Maathai." It was perfect because the baseline's soulful aspect evoked deep tree roots. Then, the universal folkloric language carried on the changes, and the melody made it an ideal way to honor the woman who had created the Green Belt Movement in Africa and inspired and improved the lives of so many.

It was a lot of fun playing "Wangari Maathai" at Carli's. I began playing it solo, but soon I started playing it with my trio, and the form continued evolving. I noticed that the public always reacted well to the song. One night while I was playing "Wangari Maathai" on piano solo, a man who walked into the restaurant caught my attention. He was tall Black man, extremely well dressed in a white suit, and I had the feeling that he would particularly appreciate the song I was playing. I played it a little longer, making sure he was getting the best of it. The man sat at the bar, and I knew he was engaged. It was the last song of the set.

As I got up from the piano, the man called my attention and commented, "What was that song you were playing—that was good." I explained that it was a song honoring a Kenyan Nobel Peace Prize Laureate, Dr. Wangari Maathai. He immediately lightened up and said that he was from Nairobi and knew Wangari. It was an exciting encounter. He mentioned that he was a doctor and headed a department at Johns Hopkins Bloomberg School of Public Health in Maryland. Dr Awari Hayanga was in San Juan on vacation. A very similar event happened later when I was playing the song, and a young, beautiful Black lady came in. She immediately went by the piano and seemed to enjoy the theme immensely. After, we talked, and she said that she was Wangari's niece—a small world!

People's reaction to the song "Wangari Maathai" went beyond music genre, race, or color—and it was always positive. By this time, I had released seven CDs that I had produced. There were three volumes of *Live at Carli's*, all jazz, and I had three studio jazz albums: *Love Tales* (piano solo), *Both Sides Now* (produced with Eddie Gómez), and *Maverick* with Eddie Gómez and Jack DeJohnette. The seventh was *In My Soul*, which was a rock genre album. *In My Soul* is the work I did in 2013 to set the record straight after Dennis Wilson's *Bambu* delusive version was first released in 2008. I recorded most of it in Nashville at Fred Vail's Treasure Isle recording studio, with some tracks done in New York and Los Angeles.

Now, almost a decade later, I was eager to get into the studio again, but it had been financially challenging. One of the positive reactions I had from "Wangari Maathai" made my next album project a reality. Justin Sullivan, a recent acquaintance who frequented Carli's, after hearing me play "Wangari Maathai," said to me, "That's a great song you just played—why don't you record it?" I believe I said that I would like to and eventually I would do it. He then responded, "No, I mean now—I'll produce it."

Justin's resolute demeanor surprised me—most of all, it intrigued me. I had been jerked around by so many empty promises in the past, and I had a good reason to be skeptical, but the sturdiness in his gaze made me believe he was for real. We agreed, shook hands, figured a budget, and I got to work on recording the song. Everything went well and according to plan. I remained aware that not just anyone takes a leap of faith that easily on someone they hardly know, so I committed to delivering the best I could. It helped to know that the song was great and worthy of seeing the light of the day, and I knew I would surround myself with the best to do an outstanding job. During the process, I realized that Justin was a man of his word and a visionary.

While the recording was in progress and taking shape, Justin suggested making an entire album. We shook hands again, worked out another budget, and got back to work. We did most of the recordings in New York. While doing some overdubs for my previous album, *In My Soul*, I worked with Roman Klun, a recording engineer I liked very much. He had just put a studio together in Williamsburg, Brooklyn. For me, even working out of a closet with an iPad, I would have still cherished recording the album with Roman. Working with him in the studio gave me some of the happiest moments of my life. It is almost magic when creativity can flow uncluttered and without limits to its expression. I feel that way working with Roman; it's just a joy.

The next album project, *Follow Me*, took about two years to complete. In addition to featuring "Wangari Maathai," *Follow Me* included a song that was its title track. Jack Rieley and I had written the song that eventually became "Follow Me" under a different name in the early '70s, and it gave me much joy to include it on the album. I always thought the lyrics were special. When Jack and I wrote it, we had been drawing from our own mystical experiences of being in nature in an altered state seeing through the eyes of heightened consciousness. To me the lyrics are a mystical poem. And the hallelujah chorus at the end hails the bewildering beauty of nature.

The curtain dropped for Jack in 2015, which put me in a long state of deep reflection. Before he passed, Jack and I had been back and forth on the phone for about a month discussing a strange illness he was struggling with. He was living in Berlin at the time, and he sounded paranoid and expressed fear about being treated by German doctors. He feared that the doctors had declared him unstable so that his fortune could be manipulated under German estate and inheritance laws. I never knew how much of it was delusional, but he sounded disoriented and seemed to be in constant, excruciating pain.

Given his suffering, I was partly glad his struggle was over. If I hesitated between the emotions of gladness and sadness at that moment, it was because while part of me was glad that his suffering had ended, I had never lost hope for a recovery, and it was hard to accept losing my best friend forever. Even when Jack and I were living on different continents for long periods of time, our friendship remained strong, and we would always share our individual accomplishments. Sometimes it felt like a competition of who was living the "better" life, but it was still a joyful, unbroken connection, even when we had almost opposite lifestyles. After he passed, I felt the loss, a permanent loss that turned everything gray for a long time. Michel de Montaigne expressed it perfectly when he wrote of his closest friend, Etienne de la Boètie, after his passing: "If someone were to ask me why I loved him, I feel that it could not be expressed, except by answering 'Because it was him; because it was me.'"

As the *Follow Me* album was completed, we were all proud of what we had done. I had never considered myself a commercial artist, so I wasn't expecting impending commercial success from the project. A Grammy, though, wasn't beyond expectation because I knew how good the album was. But it lacked the political backdoor push needed to generate a Grammy nomination. Justin went no-holds-barred with the budget, and we had an incredible vinyl run. Also, we produced a video featuring the song "Wangari Maathai." Being able to honor Dr. Maathai's legacy was greatly satisfying. *Forbes* magazine sponsored the release of the video, and Billboard the album's release. In November 2018, the video won an award of merit at the Accolade Global Film Competition.

Justin Sullivan, who had been funding the project and was the executive producer, arranged for an epicurean brunch premiere/celebration on the release's date at the Blackbarn restaurant in NoMad Manhattan. Instead of inviting the media, we opted to invite everyone involved in the making of the album and flew in the orchestra musicians who lived in Puerto Rico and everyone else who didn't already live in New York, with their expenses paid. It was a magnificent gathering. Sullivan made a heartfelt toast in gratitude to all present, and then I followed. The invitation also included attending the quintessential yearly American Jazz Foundation's Loft Party in Chelsea. It was a most memorable and rewarding weekend celebration of the culmination of a magnificent project.

Having the Wangari Maathai Foundation's approval was essential to the project, and we got it. A few years later, Dr. Maathai's daughter Wanjira Mathai, who became the organization's director and the movement leader after Wangari's passing, flew from Nairobi to host a brunch gathering held in New York at the beginning of the 2019 United Nations Climate Action Summit. I received an invitation from the foundation and went to New York to meet Wanjira. The brunch was an intimate and lovely get-together on a supporter's rooftop on the East Side near the United Nations building. I was most pleased to see longtime Wangari and Green Belt Movement supporters, as well as a younger generation, committed to a better future. And finally, meeting Wanjira in person was an honor and captivating.

Wanjira's gathering event was in mid-September. It was a beautiful fall weekend in Manhattan with blue skies and perfect temperatures. As always when I'm in New York, I didn't plan an agenda. I firmly believe that an unnecessary plan can ruin a good day. After the brunch, I thought I'd give a call to a poet friend, Robert C. Ford, whom I had met earlier that year at a party thrown by Mark Kostabi.[7] I would have contacted Kostabi, but I knew he was in Italy. Robert, who was known as "the Wall Street Poet," asked if I'd come and meet him downtown near Wall Street where he lived. The late-afternoon light was getting warmer by the hour, then by the minute, and I had my Fujifilm x100 street camera with me. Robert affectionately calls his apartment Sky Vault in homage to the thirty-five-story Art Deco building's breathtaking views overlooking the New York Stock Exchange. It used to be the headquarters of Chase Manhattan Bank. David Rockefeller even maintained his office there in the 1970s.

Carli's pic of 5-points intersection at Wall Street

After a brief tour, we took to the streets. Magic hour is unique in the Wall Street area because the fusion of modern high-rise and older low-rise

---

7   Mark Kostabi is an artist who rose to fame during the 1980s NYC East Village scene that included Andy Warhol and Jean-Michel Basquiat. Most notably, his paintings were used for the album covers of Guns N' Roses' *Use Your Illusion* and the Ramones' *Adios Amigos*. He is also an accomplished composer/pianist as well as a socialite, whose extravagant "Kostabi World" parties, featuring world-class musicians, are often featured in "Page Six," the gossip column of the *New York Post*.

landmark buildings is not necessarily on a square grid. There are obtuse street angles all over; there's even a five-street junction. Almost by now buried in the eastern horizon, the sun played hide-and-seek through the jagged building clusters, forming a shadow dance—a photographer's feast followed.

Following a shooting spree chasing light and shadows, Robert and I gravitated to Harry's in Hanover Square, where we indulged in perfect juicy burgers and drank old fashioneds. Later that evening, we met Ford's friends at a Composer's Concordance concert. As we were going up the venue's stairs, thinking we could still catch part of the show, we were late, and the musicians already were coming down and hungry, so we ended up at the Pig 'n Whistle across the street. There we gathered at a long table near the front window.

It was probably the first time that I was surrounded by so many pianists. There were at least four of them, including on my right who seemed older and more seasoned than the rest, David Saperstein. We engaged in music conversation, and it came up that he was a piano teacher. I would turn seventy-one in a few more weeks and had never taken piano lessons or ever had a piano teacher for more than two days. I candidly asked David if he'd be my maestro.

We started the class on the day after my seventy-first birthday. Since I lived in San Juan and David was in New York, the music lessons took place via FaceTime. The classes turned out delightfully more conceptual than technical—we discussed other composers, mainly avant-garde, and played a lot for each other. This was undoubtedly a new era for me—I had made a life's career in music, and yet it was only now that I was finally studying music. I love new beginnings—they make me feel young and get the creative juices flowing.

The same way that fall becomes winter, I was naturally shifting means of inner expression, all within the art realm. When I discovered drawing and painting, something new awakened in me that I had never felt before. Between sketches and paintings in acrylic, I produced a fair number of pieces in approximately one year of work. But then one day, the same way it began, I stopped painting.

Writing was different. What first lured me to creative writing was corresponding with someone special. It was Tere, a dear friend with whom I first exchanged creative musings in the early email days.

Tere, being a scholar and a journalist, empowered me to use my social network postings creatively. It wasn't much, but it was the beginning as far as I can remember. I also remember writing crafty letters to my parents at much earlier times to convince them I was making progress away from home. But being a late bloomer with writing also gave me new sensations at a time when I could most appreciate it.

After Carl Wilson's passing, I had some correspondence with his widow, Gina Martin. I remember trying to be as comforting as possible under the circumstances, and there was a fair share of lyrical writing back and forth. At another time, I was corresponding with Van Dyke Park. While the celebrated arranger/composer is best known for his work with Brian Wilson (he wrote the lyrics for many songs on the lost Beach Boys album *Smile,*) he's widely regarded as one of the most talented and admired behind-the-scenes figures in rock and pop music from the mid '60s onward. Van Dyke was such a celebrated wordsmith that I resolved to deliver worthwhile and stimulating missives to him during our noble exchange. American writer and poet Garry More, who wrote the liner notes to my album *Follow Me*, also became a major source of inspiration and encouragement to keep on writing.

Sometimes life isn't as polished as it seems. It's actually better. I believe there is an ever-present, inherent potential for order, beauty, and harmony. The one thing I can say for certain is that the clear choices I've made have been fundamental to tapping into that source and enjoying the benefits—I feel extremely fortunate for its outcome. I also believe anyone can tap into that source. It is just a matter of true intention and reflection, and having the courage to let go of toxic waste and old baggage.

Many dreams still remain on the horizon, but none cause me anxiety. As we age, the world keeps on rapidly changing: Jump forward to the near future, and my bet is on blockchain technology and virtual reality—perhaps it will evolve with different names, but in essence it'll be the same thing. A massive shift in the arts, commerce, business, and entertainment will drive a new generation forward.

But there will always be a wave of yearning for things past—the magic of naivete reclaimed, which will create a welcome balance from the synthetic nature of digital technology. Regarding music, I can't predict its future. But my tendency is to go in the direction of avant-garde piano improvisations, which is what fulfills me the most. The honesty, courage, and spontaneity required make it exciting for me to play this music. At this stage of my life, I can't imagine how much further I could go musically from free improvisation—it is liberating, and performing it is tremendous fun. Then, perhaps, recording a performance of some kind of asemic rhapsody would be in order.

Still, like everyone else, I have my bucket list. Spending quality time with all of my children and grandchildren tops the list. There are secondary whims such as riding a motorbike like my BMW 1200 GS alone throughout the Iberian Peninsula—that, I haven't done yet. I had an itch to own another Austin-Healey 3000 like the one I had as a teenager—that, I have done. I'm yet to participate with my Healey in a classic vintage car circuit race in England, like the Revival at Goodwood, or in Europe, the Mille Miglia—that's still high on my list. It would probably be a significant challenge transporting my Austin-Healey to Europe for a race. Instead, it would be ideal to buy, rent, or borrow a vintage racer in Europe to enter a circuit. Curiously, I almost got that one checked off my list, but then came the coronavirus.

I met a British businessman and car collector at Carli's, Ben van Grutten, who kindly offered me one of his exotic cars to join a classic race in England. Van Grutten extended an invitation to the Goodwood Racetrack Members Meeting and the Speed Festival. Being a friend of the Goodwood Racetrack owner, Charles Gordon-Lennox, 11th Duke of Richmond, Ben planned for me to stay at the Duke's residence and participate in the members' race. That would clear part of my bucket list. Unfortunately, all this happened just before the COVID outbreak, and it had to be postponed. But we remained in contact, knowing the COVID siege wouldn't last forever. Maybe by the time you are reading these words, I'll be with my friend Ben and the Earl of March sipping tea and savoring crumpets chased by a single malt Highgrove Scotch whiskey, or who knows, Jack Daniel's, getting ready to spin some old wheels around the old track.

I feel blessed with all the good and genuine friendships I've had. Perhaps I didn't focus my life on accumulating monetary wealth. Still, I've lacked nothing, and I can't imagine money replacing the wealth of love and camaraderie I've experienced throughout my life, not to mention the memories. I just hope that I didn't let anyone down along the way, for if I did, it was meant to be a mutual lesson to learn and grow from. I've found myself alienated from loved ones, family being the most difficult to reconcile. But the sun still shines—genuine friendships often fill the void of the emotional hollowness of family estrangements, and art and authentic relationships allow us to feel and express, which is the very essence of our existence.

For me the ultimate quest stands in a legacy, somehow leaving this world better than I found it. That is still my primary ongoing quest, one that will last until my last breath, for as long as I am alive. It is a never-ending task. Today I thrive on mentorship. I've assembled a small but promising group of high school students to teach them creative improvisation on piano. Along with the music mentoring, I try to share good values with them and encourage them to pursue worthy causes—I have great confidence in them.

Resolving issues with past relationships has been of tremendous value for me. And even though I'm in an ongoing legal battle with my sister, I'm not attached to the outcome. I have not forgotten the deed, but in my heart and mind I have forgiven her.

In my youth I didn't lack money or resources. Yet, my true journey began when I gave it all up: giving up a comfortable and secure life of privileges. When I glance at my entire life I can see the beauty of where I came from. I can also look back to the lows, the losses, and the poor choices I made along the way, all of that being part of my journey.

Looking over where I've been—from my happy and careless youth to going to hell and back—a sense of completion surrounds me. After all I've been through, I'm happy and proud to look back and see where I came from. Especially the love, values, trust, faith, and the hearth-stone education that stuck through thick and thin made the base for who I really am. I then had major social concerns and didn't hesitate in jumping onto the poverty train to join the world at its crudest. I had to experience it, and I embraced life's struggle in every sense, with its sorrows and hopeful moments. During some of those times I was experiencing extreme poverty, there were moments of despair and also of extreme joy—a stirring sense of freedom.

Now that I'm past living on the edge, I feel fortunate to have made it through the thick of it. I've found beauty and balance in my life. For me the journey is just beginning. I do not discard the possibility of future changes, but I'm certainly better equipped for new challenges. Also, knowing where I came from is comforting. No amount of money can replace the wisdom of a life lived fully—with its good, bad, and ugly. My journey transformed me, and brought me back full circle to seeing things through the eyes of a child.

III

THE EMPRESS.

EPILOGUE: THE EMPRESS —
ONE LAST STORY

 The Empress greatly encourages compassion, beauty, and love. She is deeply connected to Mother Nature, and her influence is powerful when you absorb the energy of the natural world around you.

Today is possibly one of the most beautiful afternoons I've seen. This spectacular, peaceful scenery outside my windows is because of the COVID-19 quarantine—a well-deserved break for nature, I think! From my den, I can see bougainvillea and other flowers in full bloom outside the window while a gentle breeze rocks and rolls their top branches. I'm inspired to describe every minute; today is such a special day.

Not long after I began writing my story, I took a rare nap. When I woke up, the clock showed 5:25 PM. I assumed the clock was wrong, but I had a strange feeling that I might have missed a day. So, along with my habitual craving to make myself a cup of espresso as soon as I wake up, I also had the notion that I already had coffee earlier. But I wasn't sure. I looked at my iPhone, checking for the accurate time, and the device matched the clock's time. That could only mean one thing: the time was correct—so it was only a nap.

As I exited my room to the hallway, I saw that my daughter Mía was in her bedroom, busy with what sounded like a virtual ballet dance class, so I went straight to the piano. I've been hearing this song playing on my turntable for a few days, "Don't Talk (Put Your Head on My Shoulder)," from Brian Wilson's magnum opus, *Pet Sounds*. As beautiful as the song is, it was stalking me, constantly playing in my mind. Very profound memories attached to that song emerged: the framework, or more aptly the space-time warp, or matrix, in which a significant event occurred.

It was the mid-'60s, and we were the Living End in every sense of the word. One lazy afternoon, we were all sitting on the floor while peaking on full doses of Owsley LSD. There was a song playing, one would say "in the background," but at that instant, there was no background —"background" at that moment was an illusory concept! Everything was simultaneously present (one could say omnipresent, but I don't want to sound religious). There was dimensionality and depth—it was all alive. Being immersed in permeating love, defying any human description, remaining silently in awe as one, is a memory that I can't and would never want to erase.

Fifty-five years later, the song is still there and still carrying traces of a faded memory of a grand event and the certainty that at that moment time and space ceased to exist—only pure love pervaded. Strangely, I never tried playing the song on the piano. After waking from a deep sleep in the middle of a beautiful quiet afternoon, the time was ideal for playing it. I tried it, and it worked fine on the piano. Not all songs work well on just a keyboard, including Beach Boys songs, but this one did.

As sublime as the moment was for me playing "Don't Talk (Put Your Head on My Shoulder)," on piano, my reverie was interrupted when I heard my dear wife quietly come into the house. She had been at her fashion boutique, Royal Vintage, only a few blocks away, doing some organizing and selling a few items—as long as she could apply social distancing. I just kept on playing the piano.

Not too long after, I heard a commotion in the hallway close to Mía's bedroom. I took a peek to see what was going on and saw my wife standing there with my daughter, who was in tears.

My wife was naked, covering her private parts with her hands, and visibly shaken. I asked what had happened, and oh dear, my daughter, in a bout of hysteria, cried, "Mom just appeared naked in my virtual ballet class!!!"

Oh, well. Embarrassing, but just another day. Eventually, after offering some consolation, we all ended the event laughing, and Kat finally took her shower.

ACKNOWLEDGMENTS

Now it is my turn to get back (in kindness) at so many giving souls, past and present, who made this world a better place for me and somehow contributed, or influenced me, in writing this book. It is cathartic not only telling your story, but also getting the work published. So now that I can breathe, I can only think of all of the wonderful people who somehow have been part of the process that allowed me to complete this work. To them I express my deepest gratitude.

First of all, I'd like to thank Michel Moushabeck and Hildi for their unconditional friendship and for believing in me. Also David Klein for his knowledge and finesse on the final editing and fact checking; and everyone else at Interlink.

My deepest appreciation to Adrien Brody for his kindness and support in writing such a heartfelt quote about my book.

These people I cannot thank enough: Writer and poet Gary Moore, for encouraging me to write this book, and for helping me out of the doldrums. My editor, David Aretha, for understanding my "voice" and keeping it intact, Emily Drabek for the endless proofreadings and gentle corrections. My dear friends Robert Ford for the first manuscript reading and his valuable comments, Franky Rexach Jr., and Michelle Lavergne also for their kind assistance in the initial proofreading and feedback process.

My special appreciation to Alex Rotaru for his vision and interest in bringing my book to the "big screen."

Many thanks to Michi, Lourdes, Fausto, and the rock of the kitchen, Irving, for keeping my restaurant, Carli's, on track while I was busy writing my book; to Tamas, for your unflinching friendship and "keeping things working" even when at times I seemed too busy to pay attention;

and to Branden, for your energy, support, and for keeping the bar on fire—"You're the rock star."

Many thanks to Cheryl and Gordon, Erik Rosado, Ariana Rosado Fernandez, Vanesa Piñero, and Tom Robbins for your support and good intentions and advice in getting the book properly published; Gene Luntz, for his propitious invitation for me presenting the book at the CORE club in Manhattan; Patricia Vazques and Alexandre Marc for their support and arranging of a book presentation at Politics and Prose, in Washington, DC.

Special thanks to all the photographers: David Gasser for the cover photography, Ed Roach for sharing his wealth of photographs from when we toured together with the Beach Boys, Brenda Muñoz for some of the '70s glam pictures, and Elliott Erwitt. Big thanks to photographer James Lynn for the picture captioned "Me with dog at house on the hill." If I have failed to mention a photographer, please accept my absentmindedness. I will be happy to add it in a future edition.

These were pivotal moments for me: I would like to especially thank my dear friend film director and writer Michael Elsie, RIP, for unlocking the door for me becoming a writer. I once asked him,

"Michael, how do you become a writer?" And he answered, "Just write."

Also, I must thank my film-directing professor Ed Green, at UCLA, for teaching me about the enormous importance of Alfred Hitchcock's "McGuffin," the invisible thread that must run throughout a story.

My heartfelt thanks to Eddie Gómez, Roman Klun, Billy Drummond, and Benny Green for their kind testimonials; my soul humbly brims with gratitude for such laudatory words.

Although I didn't have the fortune of meeting them personally, my interaction with their work and their way of thinking place the following extraordinary folks high in my circle of mentors. I must express my gratitude to Albert Hofmann for the gift of his research and discovery of LSD, and Aldous Huxley for writing *The Doors of Perception*, which opened my mind to a whole new world of possibilities early in my life, while I was still a teenager. There are too many authors to mention whose pen, typewriter, or keyboard had the most profound effect on me. But among those, I must mention Douglas Hofstadter with infinite admiration for writing *Gödel, Escher, Bach: An Eternal Golden Braid*, which has been a great influence in my thinking. I must also mention Benjamin Dryer, for it was his delightfully jocular book *Dryer's English* that gave me plenty of clues, and fair warning, in approaching the task ahead.

I also thank Melissa Ayers for encouraging me to write. Also, Sofia Anzueta for bringing Benny Green back into my life, and my dog Snowy for snuggling with me on my power naps between writing sessions.

Most of all, I'd like to thank those with whom I share my roof: my dear wife, Katira, and daughter Mía, for putting up with my long moments of reclusiveness and absentmindedness, and for failing to take out the garbage.

Last, it was looking out from my den window at the beginning of the COVID lockdown and seeing the bougainvillea happily moving with the wind beneath a blue sky that inspired me to begin writing this book. Every bit of nature surrounding me then looked new and happy to be on a well-deserved break from constant and excessive human interference and pollution. It was at that moment, with lightness of being, when the muses prompted me to begin telling my story.

May we all be inspired and rejoice in God's blessings.

INDEX

THE FOOL.

THE MAGICIAN.

THE HIGH PRIESTESS

THE

THE CHARIOT.

STRENGTH.

THE HERMIT.

WHEEL

TEMPERANCE.

THE DEVIL.

THE TOWER.

THE